全球科技创新与大国博弈

［美］安德鲁·B. 肯尼迪（Andrew B. Kennedy）/ 著　卢苗苗 / 译

THE CONFLICTED
SUPERPOWER
America's Collaboration with China
and India in Global Innovation

中信出版集团 | 北京

图书在版编目（CIP）数据

全球科技创新与大国博弈 /（美）安德鲁·B. 肯尼迪
著；卢苗苗译. -- 北京：中信出版社，2021.4
书名原文：THE CONFLICTED SUPERPOWER:
America's Collaboration with China and India in
Global Innovation
ISBN 978-7-5217-2729-6

Ⅰ.①全… Ⅱ.①安…②卢… Ⅲ.①技术革新-研
究-世界②国际关系-研究 Ⅳ.①F113.2②D81

中国版本图书馆 CIP 数据核字（2021）第 032161 号

THE CONFLICTED SUPERPOWER: America's Collaboration with China and India in
Global Innovation by Andrew B. Kennedy
Copyright © 2018 by Columbia University Press
Published by arrangement with Columbia University Press, through Bardon-
Chinese Media Agency
Simplified Chinese translation copyright © 2021 by CITIC Press Corporation
ALL RIGHTS RESERVED
本书仅限中国大陆地区发行销售

全球科技创新与大国博弈

著　　者：[美]安德鲁·B. 肯尼迪
译　　者：卢苗苗
出版发行：中信出版集团股份有限公司
　　　　　（北京市朝阳区惠新东街甲 4 号富盛大厦 2 座　邮编　100029）
承　印　者：北京楠萍印刷有限公司

开　　本：880mm×1230mm　1/32　　印　张：9.25　　字　数：198 千字
版　　次：2021 年 4 月第 1 版　　　　印　次：2021 年 4 月第 1 次印刷
京权图字：01-2020-0054
书　　号：ISBN 978-7-5217-2729-6
定　　价：68.00 元

版权所有·侵权必究
如有印刷、装订问题，本公司负责调换。
服务热线：400-600-8099
投稿邮箱：author@citicpub.com

谨以此书献给我的亲人

沙姆米、萨尼亚和贾斯珀

译者序

本书作者是澳大利亚国立大学克洛弗德公共政策学院的高级讲师、外交政策专家安德鲁·B.肯尼迪。由于对美国与东亚的关系，尤其是美国与中国和印度的关系进行了长期而深入的研究，作者本人对大国之间的博弈有着自己独到的理解。

本书以创新全球化为出发点，主要解释了美国对人才和科技研发跨境流动的政策，中国和印度也参与其中并从中受益。长久以来在世界政治舞台占据主导地位的美国面对人才的跨境流动和研发活动的全球化将如何应对？中国和印度两大新兴大国如何抓住科技革命带来的新机遇？在移民与反移民的浪潮中，美国政府该如何抉择？中国和印度如何为发展本国经济吸引优秀人才？本书对这些问题一一进行了解答。

本书共有5章，第1章通过详细介绍全球创新来构建本书的背景。第2章提出了一个理论来解释为什么美国会在其全球创新政策中采取不同程度的开放性。第3章至第5章通过一系列案例研究对第2章中提出的理论进行了检验，这些案例研究的重点是从20世纪90年代中期至2016年美国的政策。第3章侧重于美

I

国对外国学者的开放性。第 4 章的重点是美国对外国学生的开放性。第 5 章探讨了美国对全球研发的开放性，尤其关注对外投资的政策。通过对以上内容的分析，总结出上述政策对国际关系的影响，特别是对未来全球创新的影响。

每个国家的政策都是为了维护本国的利益，这一点在本书中有着充分的阐释。中国政府和印度政府为了在创新全球化的浪潮中谋求自己的地位，分别出台了相应的政策，积极吸纳优秀人才。而美国政府则在签证问题上摇摆不定，针对签证问题的运动此起彼伏，相关立法乏善可陈。在时代发展中，个人命运与国家命运息息相关，没有一个人可以独善其身。而科技、经济、政治这些不同的因素交织在一起，使我们所面临的情况更加复杂。

本书的翻译历经数月，对于用词不断推敲琢磨，力图能够准确地传达出作者的本意。由于译者水平有限，书中难免有不妥之处，望读者指正。

卢苗苗

引 言

几十年来，科幻小说家一直想象着能够出现一种即时翻译软件，这种通用的翻译设备可以瞬间让人理解外语。2015年，Skype Translator 翻译软件的推出让现实世界离这样的一种技术更近了。Skype 于 2003 年在爱沙尼亚创立，此后很快便在全球范围内流行起来。2011 年，Skype 被微软收购。如果对此技术继续改进，那么增加翻译功能将会备受瞩目。但同样令人着迷的是这种设备是如何被发明出来的。微软在美国和中国的数十名研究人员在此项目上合作多年，此项机器翻译工作由一名在孟买和帕罗奥多接受过教育的印度裔科学家主导。准确地说，是跨境合作产生了这项促进国际交流的技术。[1]

美国仍然是全球技术创新的引领者，但是正如 Skype Translator 的研发等许多例子所证明的那样，美国的领导地位越来越多地涉及与其他国家的合作。这一发展反映了两大明显的趋势。第一个趋势是，从其他国家到美国的人才流动非比寻常，而人才流动是创新的终极因素。2013 年，在美国从事科学与工程工作的受过大学教育的人中，外籍人员占 27%；在拥有科学与工程领域博士学位的人中，

III

外籍人员占42%。[2]同年，在美国大学被授予科学与工程领域博士学位的人中，拥有临时签证的外籍学生占37%。[3]第二个趋势是，虽然美国一直在向内吸引高科技人才，但美国公司和大学也一直瞄准海外市场，投资海外研发中心并与外国合作伙伴合作。微软是这方面的典型代表。截至2014年，IBM（国际商业机器公司）研究院在全球六大洲拥有12个实验室，在思科（Cisco）排名前84位的工程师中有17位来自印度。[4]此外，人才的流动和跨境研发这两大发展因素也交织在一起。精通技术的人才的流动，特别是发展中国家和发达国家之间的人才流动，助力领先的公司和大学在全球拓展其研发活动。

本书介绍的就是这两大趋势背后的政治因素。具体而言，本书介绍的是世界上的老牌强国——美国，与两个最著名的新兴大国——中国和印度之间人才流动和研发活动的背后所蕴含的政治因素。通常来说，占据主导地位的国家和崛起的大国之间互不信任，因为未来可能会发生的冲突会影响它们之间的关系。[5]这种不信任虽然直到今天依然存在，但是并没有阻止这些国家之间出现显著的新型经济交换形式。在受过良好教育的劳工和学生的数量方面，中国和印度的优势无与伦比，而美国则是最受这些人群欢迎的国家之一。与此同时，美国公司在中国和印度设立研发中心，并在与中国和印度合作伙伴建立研发联盟方面处于领先地位。在某些重要的方面，创新全球化就是美国与中印两个新兴大国之间进行合作的故事。

美国与两个新兴大国之间在创新方面不断增长的合作背后究

竟蕴含怎样的力量？几十年来，虽然这些国家之间的商业贸易不断发展，但创新一直是一个特别敏感的领域，对于全世界财富和权力的分配意义重大。有人可能将企业研发全球化归因于国际上更严格的知识产权标准的传播，这使得跨国公司更容易保护其海外研究的成果。事实上，自20世纪80年代以来，美国一直致力于在全世界制定、强化和执行知识产权标准。[6] 1994年，这一运动促成了《与贸易有关的知识产权协定》（Agreement on Trade-Related Aspects of Intellectual Property Rights，TRIPS，简称《知识产权协定》）的谈判并使之成为世界贸易组织的一部分。然而，这仍然不能充分解释美国与中印两国之间不断增长的合作，因为发展中国家对知识产权保护的力度往往不够，而美国近些年来尤其重视知识产权保护，这使得美国与这些国家合作的增长更加令人费解。

技术发展是促进合作的重要因素之一。国际旅行的迅速发展以及信息和通信技术发生的革命性变化使得跨境流动和交流的规模空前壮大。中国和印度快速发展并且不断提高的教育水平也创造了前所未有的大量知识型人才储备。即便如此，没有政府的支持政策，全球创新也是不可能实现的。其中一些政策与面向人力资本跨境流动和跨国研发活动的开放性有关。

接下来将解释中国和印度如何采取宽松的全球创新政策来发展经济。在人力资本流动方面，中国和印度政府已经开始支持专业人员和学生出国，因为他们对"人才流失"的担忧逐渐消退，对"人才流动"的热情越来越高。近几年，有些人认为"人才回流"正在将部分中国和印度的留学毕业生和专业人员带回本国,中国尤其明显。[7]在研发的流动方面,中国和印度都普遍欢迎外国研发中心的进入,且鼓励与外国合作伙伴的合作,并希望这些合作能对本国经济产生积极的溢出效应。虽然中印两国的方法大有不同,但是两国都对全球创新持开放态度。

相比之下,美国的政策很矛盾。美国没有限制就读于美国大学的外国学生人数,并且继续招收比其他国家更多的外国学生。美国在很大程度上也对海外研发持开放态度,只是在某些情况下会限制服务业岗位的"离岸外包"。与此同时,美国对受过良好教育的外国劳工则不太开放,其在这方面的开放程度随着时间的推移发生了很大的变化。虽然自1990年以来,EB(基于就业的)移民签证的年度限制没有发生变化,但通过H-1B签证计划(其中许多人为高科技公司工作)的"专业劳工"上限已经大幅下降。这造成永久居住申请大量积压,许多希望留在美国的优秀人才对此非常沮丧,于是一些人只能返回祖国。从某些方面来讲,美国的政策并未有利于美国。

美国的政策和其与中印两国政治关系的发展趋势相背离,这更加令人费解。在整个"冷战"后期,美国和中国的关系都在波动。2003年,时任美国国务卿科林·鲍威尔(Colin Powell)表示,当时的中美关系是"自尼克松总统首次访问中国以来最好的"。[8]相比之下,在过去的20年里,美国与印度之间的关系已经有了非常大的缓和,目前评论员对这两个国家是否能成为"盟友"争论不休。尽管存在这些不同的趋势,美国对中国的开放模式明显优于印度。在中国最为重要的领域——高等教育——美国的开放程度是最大的。相比之下,在印度占据主导地位的领域——通过 H-1B 签证计划提供技术劳工——美国的开放程度是最小的。

简而言之,美国在全球创新方面存在很大的矛盾,其开放模式也令人费解。在此领域推动美国开放的政治力量是什么?为什么美国在某些领域比其他领域更开放?为什么随着时间的推移,对技术劳工的开放程度如此摇摆不定?美国这些政策有着怎样更广泛的意义?接下来的章节将对这些问题一一进行解答。

本书的核心观点

本书中提到的一些政策领域,学者几乎已经充分探讨过了,但是到目前为止所有的研究都还是无法回答我所提出的问题。最近的研究已经阐明了包括美国在内的发达国家如何处理高技能移民问题,但是这些研究没有考虑学生的流动,也没有探索跨国公司研发的全球化。[9]也有新的关于离岸外包政策的研究,但没有涉及本书所关注的移民政策。[10]学者也探讨国家追求创新的方式背后的政治因素,但是这类研究并没有关注美国针对移民或离岸外包的政策。[11]总之,我们仍然缺乏一个全面的框架来解释美国针对人才和研发跨境流动的政策,而这些政策支撑着全球创新。

本书旨在填补这一空白。本书首先解释了近几十年创新的全球化是如何产生的以及中国和印度是如何从中获益的,其余章节介绍了美国是如何参与其中的。这里的论点首先强调了ICT(信息和通信技术)的重要性,因为它是全球的"主导行业",在经济和军事力量方面发挥着独一无二的作用。通过引领ICT革命,美国经济和军事近几十年来一直保持着主导地位。然而,美国也诞生了一系列令人印象深刻的高科技参与者,它们非常在乎自身的利益。这些参与者包括世界顶级ICT公司和研究型大学,我称之为HTC(High-Tech Community,高科技界)。[12] 面对全球化的世界,这些利益迫使美国政府维持或制定允许HTC利用这一发展的政策。在移民方面,HTC秉持自由主义政策,使得它们能够吸引来自世界各地的优秀人才——无论是雇员还是毕业生。在研发方面,高科技公司一直寻求保持在国外进行研发的自由,即使这意味着以前在国内完成的工作要进行离岸外包。简单地讲,在美国面向全球创新的开放性方面,HTC构成了一种强大而持久的力量。

然而,HTC并非无所不能,在开放上,它有时会面临有组织的抵制。在本书中,我认为高科技利益集团所面临的有组织的抵制有力地影响了国家政策的开放程度。有三种可能的情况。第一种情况是可能没有任何抵制,在这种情况下,国家政策通常是开放的。这种变化阐明了美国对国际学生流入的政策,这种政策仍然没有上限,并且还在不断增加。第二种情况是HTC可能会面临劳工的抵制。在这种情况下,国家政策更具有争议性,开放的限制更加严格,但是劳工的相对弱势意味着其对HTC的影响仍然有限。从20世纪90年代中期到2004年，这种变化揭示了美国对于技术劳工移民的政策。美国针对研发和其他商业服务的离岸外包政策也可以用这些说法来解释。第三种情况是HTC可能会面临能够动员大量选民的公民团体的抵制。在这种情况下，HTC很难实现其目标，国家政策可能不如前两种情况开放。这种变化解释了自2005年以来美国针对技术移民的政策的变化趋势。

总之，本书认为美国的开放通常反映了HTC的力量和利益，而开放程度则反映了其他有组织的团体对HTC的抵制程度。

本书聚焦美国的原因

本书的大部分内容涉及一系列特定的支持全球创新的美国政策。其中包括外国学者的准入，外国学生的录取，以及服务（特别是研发服务）的离岸外包。这些政策通常是面对全球，而不是只针对中国或印度。但是，由于中国和印度是美国重要的合作伙伴，所以这些政策对美国与中印两国的关系具有重要意义。事实上，美国的全球创新政策在许多方面也是美国针对中印两国的政策。美国限制科学与工程领域的外国毕业生流入的政策对中国的影响将超过其他国家，美国修改有关学者流入的政策对印度的影响超过其他国家。

如前所述，美国的全球创新政策着实令人费解。因此本书的大部分内容都集中在美国。然而，关注美国的政策制定还有其他几个原因。首先，尽管创新全球化是一种全世界的现象，但美国是一个重要的焦点。自 20 世纪中叶以来，美国一直引领世界创新。近几十年来，美国通过引领世界进入 ICT 时代，进一步巩固了其地位。在人才和研发活动的流动方面，美国也深入其中。尽管美国对全球创新具有深远的影响，但是我们对美国如何应对这一现象的洞察少之又少。

其次，从研究设计的角度来讲，比较美国在不同领域的政策是有道理的。在本书所考虑的每个政策领域中，HTC 都面临着不同类型的反对，这使得利益这一自变量有足够的差异性。然而，由于每一领域都处于美国背景之下，因此它们具有广泛的可比性：这些政策都是在单一政治体系内和单一时期内制定的。在这种程度上，这项研究类似于"对照比较"。[13] 可以肯定的是，在比较对外投资政策与合法移民政策的时候存在一些固有的困难，特别是前者本身就比后者更难以监管。然而，正如接下来所要讨论的，这些困难并非不可克服。并且随着时间的推移，特别是美国针对受过良好教育的劳工流动的政策方面，HTC 面临着各种各样的反对，这使得我们能够在单一政策领域内进行"前后"比较。当然，其他变量也可以解释本研究观察到的结果，我们将在第 2 章回顾这一点。

最后，许多信息来源可用于研究美国对全球创新政策的制定。本书研究的政策都是近几十年来争议的来源。美国对于受过良好教育的劳工的准入已经在近期的立法斗争中有所体现；"9·11"恐怖袭击事件后，详细审查外国学生流入；自 21 世纪初以来，离岸外包现象引发了白领的焦虑。本书对于媒体报道进行了广泛的研究,报道中涵盖了每个案例中所涉及的游说和立法。此外,本书采访了决策过程中的许多关键参与者。本书的访谈时间跨度为2013—2017年,在美国、中国和印度共采访了72名人士,其中包括这些国家的现任和前任政府官员,以及高科技公司、商业协会、有组织的劳工、公民团体等相关组织的代表。[14] 最后,本书从大量公开和私人数据库中借鉴了定量证据,包括美国商务部、美国国务院、美国国家科学基金会、响应政治中心和汤森路透的数据库。

本书的重要性

缺少关于全球创新方面的政治的研究可以理解,因为这种现象非常新。即便如此,出于多种原因,我们在理解国际政治方面仍有重大缺失。从更大的角度来讲,全球创新很重要,因为技术创造力是人类发展的基本动力。新技术改变了人们沟通、旅行、工作和生活中几乎所有事物的方式。基于这些原因,技术创新成为推动经济增长的关键因素。特别是近几十年,经济学家一直把创新作为国民经济发展的重要推动力。[15] 虽然不断增加的资本和劳动力投入收益递减,但创新提高了这种投入的使用率,因此成为可持续发展的源泉。全球化为创新提供了新的机会,特别是通过启用新的人力资源并创造新的研发区域。然而,创新也带来了新的挑战,其中便包括政治挑战,因为创新依赖世界各国政府对经济的开放。

全球创新对国际政治意义重大。全球创新使经济更加紧密地结合在一起，并且增加它们之间相互依赖的程度。在信息时代，知识产权与新型知识的产生是最有价值的经济活动形式。从美国与中印在创造有价值的知识上的合作程度来讲，要想打破美国与这些国家的经济关系越来越不容易。然而，这种日益增长的合作并不意味着这些关系可以摆脱越来越紧张的政治关系：最近的学术研究表明，商业和政治关系的力量可以彼此独立地变化。[16] 然而，更深层次的经济依赖会降低美国与其他大国之间发生大规模武装冲突的可能。[17] 事实上，生产全球化（包括创新）的研究坚持认为这种全球化在最强大的国家中具有安抚作用。[18] 其他学者认为，对未来商业的期望可以促进各国之间的和平相处。[19] 与其他形式的经济合作相比，创新合作似乎特别有可能滋养商业贸易继续存在这样的信念，因为在创新方面的投资在本质上往往是长期性的。

创新全球化也影响权力的分配。国际关系学者很早就意识到，技术创新的实力可以巩固国家力量。例如，罗伯特·吉尔平（Robert Gilpin）强调，技术上的重大进步促使新兴国家崛起为政治强国，尽管随着时间的推移，技术知识和"创造性"会传导到其他国家。[20] "长周期"理论反而认为，由于新兴国家在新的商业和工业领域或"主导产业"中发展创新，这些创新巩固了国家的经济活力和军事实力，因此这些新兴国家开始占据主导地位。[21] 从某种程度上来讲，美国对全球创新的开放性加速了"创造性"的传导，正如吉尔平所说，这种创造性应该强调中国和印度等新兴大国的崛起。不难想象，美国公司和大学之间以及中国和印度的工人和学生之间的密切合作创造了前所未有的可能性,特别是当后者返回本国或者受雇于本国公司时。此外,虽然美国政府一直在控制敏感军用技术的扩散,但"民用"和"军用"之间的界限越来越模糊,许多军民两用的技术是不受管控的。[22]

创新全球化还有可能巩固美国的经济领导地位。特别是,可以将它理解为一种手段,美国通过该手段吸引包括中国和印度在内的全世界的人力资本。美国大学发迹于众多优秀学生的流入,许多学生毕业后仍然留在美国。美国公司有机会雇用最优秀的人才——要么是在美国境内,要么是在它们进行海外研发的地方。因此,全球创新可以通过多种方式发挥美国的优势,而不是损害美国的利益。

本书框架

引言之后有5个章节和一个总结。第1章通过详细描述全球创新来构建本书的背景。首先解释了人力资本和研发活动的跨境流动在全球创新中所起的作用,介绍了这些趋势所取得的进展。其次介绍了中国和印度在过去几十年里是如何接受全球创新的。第1章的讨论表明,中印两国都把全球创新作为促进自身发展的契机,但是也强调了两国进行创新在方式上的差别。

第2章提出了一个理论来解释为什么世界上的主导国家美

国,在其全球创新政策中开放程度会有所不同。首先,解释了美国为什么一直都是世界创新的领导者,强调了主导产业的重要性,并且指出美国在全球主导产业——ICT 中占据主导地位。接着,提出了 HTC 的概念,并解释了在过去几十年里,这些利益集团为何在 ICT 革命中如此突出。然后,提出了一种理论来解释美国对全球创新的开放程度的变化,并且重点关注 HTC 的偏好及其对手的相对力量,概述了其政策的一些可选解释。最后,介绍了各种理论阐释将如何在其余章节中得到检验。

第 3 章至第 5 章通过一系列案例研究对第 2 章中提出的理论进行了检验,这些案例研究的重点是从 20 世纪 90 年代中期至 2016 年的美国政策。第 3 章侧重于美国对外国学者的开放性。首先概述了美国的政策,特别是针对 EB 签证和 H-1B 签证的政策,指出了 1998 年、2000 年和 2004 年的 H-1B 签证年度上限是如何提高的,以及随后提高上限的尝试为何没有达到预期。为了解释这种变化,第 3 章深入研究了 20 世纪 90 年代中期以来推动美国技术移民政策的政治斗争。例如,1998—2004 年,HTC 主要面临来自有组织劳工的反对,这是一场不平衡的竞赛,因为 HTC 在很大程度上占据优势地位。然而,自 2005 年以来,HTC 也面临着来自大型公民团体的抵抗,因为高技能移民能够参与更广泛的移民立法。由于这些反对群体的势力更加强大,十多年来 HTC 均未能成功增加高技能移民数量。

第 4 章的重点是美国对外国学生的开放性。首先解释了美国在针对外国学生的政策方面比针对外国学者的政策更加开放:与 EB

签证和 H-1B 签证不同，学生签证不受年度上限的限制。第 4 章还指出了中国和印度在通过 F-1 签证计划向美国大学提供学生（尤其是科学和工程领域的研究生）方面发挥突出作用。然后探讨了美国政策背后的政治因素，重点关注了 HTC 成员（尤其是大学）为保持针对外国学生的开放政策所做的努力。该分析关注"9·11"恐怖袭击事件后美国的政策，当时安全受到的威胁阻碍了外国学生的流入。这一章展现了在几乎完全没有组织反对的情况下，HTC 如何在维持美国对外国学生开放方面发挥了重要作用。

第 5 章探讨了美国对全球研发的开放性，尤其关注对外投资的政策，因为全球研发在该领域面临的挑战最为严峻。首先解释了为何美国传统上对外投资的开放程度很高，但是也提到了近年来出现的一系列问题，特别是离岸外包对美国就业和技术主导地位的影响。然后探讨了美国政策背后的政治因素。分析表明，虽然美国联邦和各州的立法者都有机会限制外包，但他们做出的限制相对较少。为了解释这一结果，第 5 章介绍了 HTC 成员（尤其是高科技公司）如何与其他商业团体合作阻止反离岸外包立法。在这种情况下，HTC 面临的阻力仅仅来自有组织的劳工，因此在很大程度上都取得了成功。

本书总结部分首先对全书各章进行总结，然后考虑了全球创新对美国、中国、印度的影响。接下来探讨了书中所研究的利益集团斗争是否代表了一种政治衰退的形式，这种斗争是否加速缩小了中印两国与美国的差距，以及是否有其他解释。最后总结了 2016 年美国联邦选举结果的影响以及美国政策未来的走向。

目 录

译者序 ⋯⋯⋯⋯⋯⋯⋯⋯⋯⋯⋯⋯⋯⋯⋯⋯⋯⋯⋯⋯⋯⋯ I
引 言 ⋯⋯⋯⋯⋯⋯⋯⋯⋯⋯⋯⋯⋯⋯⋯⋯⋯⋯⋯⋯⋯⋯ III

第 1 章　全球创新的崛起 ⋯⋯⋯⋯⋯⋯⋯⋯⋯⋯⋯ 1
　　全球创新概览 ⋯⋯⋯⋯⋯⋯⋯⋯⋯⋯⋯⋯⋯⋯⋯⋯ 4
　　全球创新浪潮中的中国和印度 ⋯⋯⋯⋯⋯⋯⋯⋯ 17
　　结论 ⋯⋯⋯⋯⋯⋯⋯⋯⋯⋯⋯⋯⋯⋯⋯⋯⋯⋯⋯ 36

第 2 章　创新领导力与争议中的开放 ⋯⋯⋯⋯⋯ 39
　　创新与霸权 ⋯⋯⋯⋯⋯⋯⋯⋯⋯⋯⋯⋯⋯⋯⋯⋯ 42
　　"高科技界"的出现 ⋯⋯⋯⋯⋯⋯⋯⋯⋯⋯⋯⋯⋯ 45
　　"高科技界"与争议中的开放 ⋯⋯⋯⋯⋯⋯⋯⋯⋯ 55
　　理论检验 ⋯⋯⋯⋯⋯⋯⋯⋯⋯⋯⋯⋯⋯⋯⋯⋯⋯ 67
　　结论 ⋯⋯⋯⋯⋯⋯⋯⋯⋯⋯⋯⋯⋯⋯⋯⋯⋯⋯⋯ 69

第 3 章　旋转门：高技能劳动力 ⋯⋯⋯⋯⋯⋯⋯ 71
　　功能失调的系统 ⋯⋯⋯⋯⋯⋯⋯⋯⋯⋯⋯⋯⋯⋯ 74

　　　　"高科技界"的巨大胜利：1998—2004年 ………… 78
　　　　难以对付的对手：2005—2016年 ……………… 90
　　　　结论 ……………………………………………… 114

第4章　开放的大门：外国留学生 ………………… 119
　　　　大量外国学生进入美国学习 …………………… 122
　　　　"9·11"事件后为开放而进行的抗争 ………… 125
　　　　结论 ……………………………………………… 136

第5章　基本开放：全球研发活动 ………………… 141
　　　　开放对外直接投资的三大支柱 ………………… 145
　　　　针对离岸外包的斗争 …………………………… 149
　　　　结论 ……………………………………………… 166

总　结　创新全球化 ………………………………… 171
　　　　对国际关系的影响 ……………………………… 177
　　　　对美国、中国和印度造成的影响 ……………… 181
　　　　观往知来 ………………………………………… 185

注　释 ………………………………………………… 189
参考文献 ……………………………………………… 236
致　谢 ………………………………………………… 270

第 1 章
全球创新的崛起

第 1 章 全球创新的崛起

如果技术创造力经常聚集在特定的一些国家，那么加强创新的过程就会越来越超越地域的限制。全球最具创新性的一些机构，尤其是美国的企业和大学，通过海外投资和建立联盟，积极招聘外国雇员，并且大规模招收外国学生，它们在这一转变中发挥了引领作用。与此同时，世界上两个最著名的崛起大国——中国和印度，一直在寻求利用这些趋势，以凭借自身实力成为创新领导者。这并不意味着中国和印度一定会成功：全球创新对两国构成了重大挑战，它们必须继续在国内进行改革。[1] 然而，这的确意味着美国帮助创造了一个绝无仅有的国际环境。

本章将探究近几十年来出现的全球创新图景。第一部分介绍何为"创新"和"全球创新"，并强调了全球创新的两个不同方面：人才流动全球化和研发活动全球化。我特别关注美国在此过程中所起的引领作用以及信息和通信技术行业的发展。

本章后半部分将探讨中国和印度如何拥抱全球创新，并在此过程中试图利用全球创新。我还研究了中印两国拥抱全球创新的不同方式，中国政府更为积极地参与全球创新，而印度则更加依赖侨民。

3

全球创新概览

创新可以通过多种方式来定义。在约瑟夫·熊彼特（Joseph Schumpeter）的研究之后，学者经常将创新过程中的许多阶段区分开来，这些阶段包括：新产品或流程的发明、将发明商业化或以其他方式付诸实践的艰难尝试、发明的传播，以及其他人对创新的效仿。[2] 本书将重点放在支持企业和大学参与第一项任务的跨国过程中：创造一种"对世界来讲很新颖的"产品或技术。[3] 当然，这种对世界来讲很新颖的技术可以通过多种方式来呈现，通常分为"激进性"创新和"渐进性"创新。[4] 每次提及创新一词，我们经常想到激进性创新——这是指全新技术（例如飞机）或组织生产方式（例如流水线）的创新。渐进性创新不那么引人关注，但仍然具有非常重要的意义。在使新技术变得有用的时候通常需要渐进性创新，并且随着时间的推移，一系列渐进性创新的累积效应可能是深远的。[5]

支持创新的跨国过程究竟是怎样的？在过去，学者经常关注企业的"全球创新网络"。[6] 这些可能是企业内部网络，跨国公司将某些研发任务分配给离岸子公司，也可能是与多家公司合作的企业网络。本书采取了更广泛的方法，具体而言，我不仅对跨国研发活动感兴趣，而且对高科技劳动力的跨境流动感兴趣。[7] 正如接下来所要阐述的，高科技劳动力的跨境流动既重要又广泛，并且与研发活动的全球化密切相关。因此,本书中"全球创新"指的是创新过程中投入的多种跨国活动,涉及资本和劳动力。[8]

人才流动全球化

从本质上来讲,人才是创新的核心。创新需要合适的人才,他们聪明、有创造力、受过良好教育且勤奋。或者用社会科学术语来说,创新需要相应的人力资本:具有技能的劳动力、教育和能够推动前沿技术的品质。多年来,创新派学者已经意识到这一点。保罗·罗默(Paul Romer)撰写的一篇经典论文认为,新知识产生的过程是一个函数,这个函数只有两个输入值:现有知识存量和人力资本。[9]当然,人力资本涉及一系列属性,从受过教育的人口比例到在科学领域中有博士学位的人口比例均有涉及。因为这项研究的重点对世界来讲是新颖的创新,所以我对该领域受教育程度较高的一方感兴趣。正是这种人力资本使各国能够发挥技术引领作用。

受过高等教育的人群分为两类。第一类受过高等教育的人群为专业人员,他们完成学业并受雇于企业从事研发工作。在某些行业,例如生物技术,其从业者通常具有研究生学位。在其他行业,例如信息技术,本科学位就可以提供必要的专业知识。在美国,私营企业是这类人群的最大雇主。2013年,美国科学与工程行业的科学家和工程师共有570万人,营利性企业雇用了62%,高等教育机构雇用了18%,公共部门雇用了12%,非营利组织雇用了5%。[10]最倾向于在企业工作的是工程师(76%)和计算机科学家（73%）。[11]

　　第二类受过高等教育的人群为学术人员，特别是研究生和博士后。虽然科学和技术领域的学术研究由资深科学家领导，但大部分劳动力由研究生和博士后等研究人员组成。例如，2013年，美国学术界聘用了144 400名全职科技和工程领域的教师，他们的工作都与研究有关。[12] 相比之下，美国2013年有457 000名全日制研究生和大约43 000名博士后研究人员。[13] 科学研究的合作性质意味着这些研究生和博士后对重要实验室研究的执行来说往往至关重要。2013年，研究助理工作的收入是美国近115 000名科技和工程领域研究生的主要收入来源。[14] 同时，学术研究可以在更广泛的国家创新活动中发挥重要作用。[15] 举一个著名的例子，20世纪50年代末，伦纳德·克兰罗克（Leonard Kleinrock）在麻省理工学院发表的论文中解决了让计算机相互通信的难题。1969年，克兰罗克在加州大学洛杉矶分校的实验室发送了美国高级研究计划署网络（Advanced Research Projects Agency Network，ARPANet）上的第一条消息，这就是互联网的前身。顶尖大学也可以帮助创建"区域集群"，成为创新公司选址的关键位置。在经典案例中，斯坦福大学和加州大学伯克利分校帮助硅谷快速成长，而麻省理工学院和哈佛大学则帮助了波士顿外的128公路（Route 128）。

　　无论是受过良好教育的员工还是学生，人才的跨境流动都有悠久的历史。19世纪和20世纪的大规模人口流动中，大多数移民都没有受过良好的教育，但也有例外。[16] 19世纪末期，英国公司经常会聘请德国化学家，所以英国化学界中最成功的企业家都是德国人。[17] 20世纪30年代和40年代，犹太科学家从纳粹德国逃往美国。第二次世界大战后，大量纳粹科学家秘密逃往美国。这些都促进了美国战后科技领袖地位的形成。[18] 20世纪60年代，人才迁移更加明显，尤其是随着美国、英国、加拿大和澳大利亚等国的移民法中种族政策的松动。随之而来的是从发展中国家到发达国家的大量人力资本流动，"人才外流"成为一个问题。[19]

自1990年以来，人力资本的跨境流动达到了前所未有的高度。据估计，1990—2000年，OECD（Organisation for Economic Cooperation and Development，经济合作与发展组织）成员国中的技术移民——即那些接受高等教育的移民——增长了64%，发展中国家技术移民的数量增加了93%。[20] 2000年1月到2010年11月，OECD国家中的高等教育移民人数增长了70%，达到3 500万人。[21] 这些移民的最大来源国是印度（220万人）、菲律宾（150万人）和中国（150万人）。美国是这些移民最大的目的国，约占移民总人数的1/3。[22]

这些人力资本流动不再仅仅是从发展中国家到发达国家的单向流动，受过良好教育的移民现在经常访问或返回本国，在某些情况下，"人才外流"变成了"人才回流"。[23] 即便如此，仍然有许多受过良好教育的人留在国外，并在OECD国家中成为科学与工程领域的重要力量。即使在美国这样大的国家也是如此。截至2013年，在美国科学与工程领域，外籍人口在受过大学教育、拥有硕士学位、拥有博士学位的人口中所占的比例分别是17%、34%和42%（如图1.1）。外籍人口在ICT行业尤为突出。2013年，美国科学与工程行业里，在计算机和数学领域获得博士学位的人中，外籍人口占 50% 以上。[24] 对这类人才来讲，硅谷特别有吸引力。根据一项估计，2015 年，在硅谷从事计算机和数学工作的 25~44 岁的员工中，外籍人口占 67%。[25]

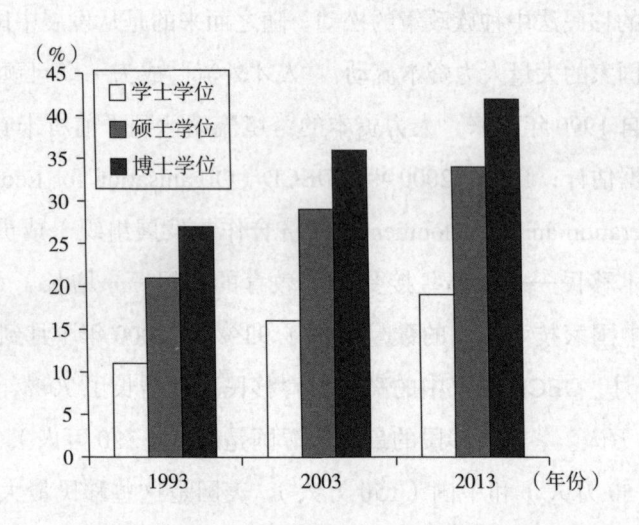

图 1.1 美国科学与工程领域外籍员工的比例

按教育程度划分：1993 年、2003 年、2013 年。

资料来源：美国国家科学基金会，2016 年科学与工程指标（阿灵顿，弗吉尼亚州：美国国家科学基金会，2016 年），第 3 章，第 101 页。

国际学生人数也在飙升。1975—1990 年，全球的外国学生人数从 80 万增加到 130 万。[26] 然而，在接下来的 15 年里，这一数字增长了一倍多，达到 300 万。2005—2012 年，这一数字跃升至 450 万。亚洲学生数量的增加占据了很大部分：2012 年，53% 的国际学生来自亚洲国家。[27] 中国成为这些学生的主要来源国，占 OECD 国家中外国学生人数的22%。印度是第二大来源国，占OECD国家中外国学生人数的6%。最受两国学生欢迎的目的国是美国。[28]

科学与工程领域的外国研究生人数也急剧增加。截至2010年，这一点在国际学生的三大目的国——美国、英国和澳大利亚——中表现得非常明显。[29] 2002—2014年，澳大利亚研究生课程中的外国学生人数几乎增加了四倍。到2014年，自然和物理专业中外国研究生的比例在38%以上，工程和信息技术专业中外国研究生的比例在50%以上。[30] 与此同时，在英国，科学与工程项目中外国研究生的比例从20世纪90年代中期的29%上升到2013年和2014年的48%。[31]

然而，考虑到美国高等教育部门的规模，外国科学与工程类学生的重要性日益增加。1977年，拥有临时签证的外国学生在美国大学获得科学与工程领域博士学位的比例为17%，但到2013年，这一比例为37%。[32] 中国和印度再次成为主要来源国。[33] 与此同时，在科学与工程和医学领域，外籍博士后的比例从1983年的18%增加到2013年的48%。[34] 获得临时签证的外籍博士毕业生在ICT行业尤为突出，例如，在计算机科学领域，他们占53%的份额。[35] 这些毕业生反过来成为该国学术研究的重要力量。2013年，在美国计算机科学领域的学术人员中，拥有美国博士学位的外籍学者占50%，占该领域全职教师的52%。[36] 当然，在科学与工程领域拥有学位的外国毕业生也越来越多地受雇于美国企业。2013年，有460万名受过大学教育的外籍科学家和工程师在美国就业，其中240万人在美国的大学获得了他们的第一个学士学位。在其他国家获得第一学位的220万人中,有近70万人获得了美国大学的研究生学位。[37]

受过良好教育的人才是创新的关键,而这种劳动力的供给流动异于以往。无论是企业研发人员还是知名研究型大学的研究生候选人,大部分相关人力资源都来自国外,这比以往任何时候都要多。

研发全球化

研发已成为现代创新的核心。在19世纪及以前,像托马斯·爱迪生这样的天才在发明中发挥了关键作用。到了20世纪初,工业研究工作已成为化学和电气工业发展的关键基地,并且越来越重要。[38] 简单地将其称为"研发"具有欺骗性,因为它掩盖了各种各样的创造性活动。实际上,要想确定哪些活动有资格作为研发、哪些活动不能作为研发并不容易。在参考了通用的国际惯例之后,美国国家科学基金会对研发的三个部分进行了如下区分。

- 基础研究:基础研究的目标是在没有特定应用的情况下获得更全面的知识或对研究对象的理解。虽然基础研究可能没有特定的应用作为目标,但它可以针对目前或潜在的兴趣领域开展研究。通常由行业或任务驱动的联邦机构进行的基础研究就是这种情况。
- 应用研究:应用研究的目标是获得知识或理解,以满足特定公认的需求。工业领域的应用研究包括调查以发现在产品、流程或服务方面具有特定商业目标的新科学知识。
- 开发：开发是对知识的系统运用和理解，这些知识包括一些直接面向可用的产品、装置、系统和方法的研究，包括原型和工艺的设计和开发。[39]

与人力资本供应一样，研发正在走向全球化。过去几十年来，通信和运输技术的进步以及越来越多的现代跨国企业的出现促进了这一发展。与人力资本流动一样，全球研发也采取不同的形式。其中包括跨国公司对跨国研发中心的投资以及各种组织间的跨国研发合作。[40] 下面依次进行阐述。

随着越来越多的一流跨国公司在全球多地建立研究中心，海外研发投资越来越普遍。这一发展引发了人们的担忧，即发展中国家的创新能力正在被"挖空"，因为跨国公司正在利用发展中国家廉价且受过良好教育的劳动力。[41] 现实并非如此戏剧性。事实上，对美国而言，全球创新并没有像人才的跨国流动那样迅速发展。例如，2000—2010年，美国企业在境内的研发份额从88%下降到84%。[42] 这种渐进性转变反映了一些限制因素：跨国公司在本国的嵌入性、跨国公司内部凝聚力的需求、管理全球研发网络的挑战，以及研发所需的当地基础设施和知识产权保护。[43]

跨国公司正在努力克服这些挑战，它们在国外研发中心投入的资金比以往任何时候都要多。[44] 2013年，主要来自其他发达国家的外国企业在美国的研发投入达540亿美元。[45] 同年，美国公司在海外研发上花费了490亿美元。[46]大部分支出（61%）发生在欧洲，特别是德国和英国（见表1.1）。值得注意的是，美国在发展中国家投入的费用正在增加。20世纪90年代，美国公司在中国和印度投入的研发费用甚至不足一提，但到了2013年，这两个国家在美国海外研发支出中的占比接近10%。[47]

美国的ICT公司一直是全球研发的领导者。1956年，IBM在瑞士建立了第一个海外研究实验室，另外两个实验室则相继在以色列（1972年）和日本（1982年）建立。英特尔于1974年在以色列建立了第一个海外研发中心。微软亚洲研究院于1998年在北京成立，并已成为微软第二大研究机构。截至2013年，由ICT公司主导的工业企业在美国所有企业的海外研发中占据相当大的份额。研发领域包括计算机和电子产品（75亿美元）、计算机系统设计（24亿美元）和信息（40亿美元）。[48]

从传统上来看，两种不同类型的海外研发之间存在重要区别。第一种形式是资产利用式（或基于母国的利用）研发。[49]这种方式的重点是开发，但只是一种有限的开发，目的是使现有产品适应国外市场。这种适应是必要的，以使产品在新环境中更具竞争力或适应性。第二种形式是资产增强式（或基于母国的互补性扩大）研发。这种方式的重点是利用可能具有全球相关性的当地知识或能力。在资产增强式研发中，有可能进行实际研究和更复杂的开发，目的是改善现有资产、获取或创造新资产。[50]

表 1.1　2013 年美国企业海外研发投入

国家	总额（10 亿美元）
德国	8.2
英国	5.4
瑞士	3.7
加拿大	3.2
比利时	2.6
印度	2.6
法国	2.4
日本	2.4
中国	2.2
以色列	2.1

资料来源：美国经济分析局，"2013 年美国国外直接投资，所有拥有其多数股权的外国子公司的研发支出"，《国际数据：直接投资和跨国企业》，2016 年，www.bea.gov / iTable / index_MNC.cfm。

第二种形式的全球研发涉及不同国家的组织汇集资源以参与跨境合作。这种合作的主要形式是研发联盟，公司、大学甚至政府会与其他国家的合作伙伴共同合作进行项目研究。研发联盟在 20 世纪 70 年代极为罕见，在 20 世纪 80 年代普及开来，然后在 20 世纪 90 年代初呈现爆发式增长，这显然是对互联网的出现所带来的"技术冲击"的回应。[51] 研发联盟对公司非常重要，特别是作为一种手段来获取互补专业知识、分担风险和成本以及应对加速而来的技术变革。[52]

研发联盟活动的全球化速度比企业研发支出的全球化速度还要快。汤森路透 SDC 白金数据库是关于此类联盟的最全面的数据库。

该数据库显示，1990—2014 年，全球共创建了 12 686 个研发联盟（包括合资企业），其中 6 448 个是国际性的（即不止一个国家参与）。就联盟活动总数和国际性联盟活动而言，美国在这方面一直非常积极（见表 1.2）。西欧国家和日本一直是美国研发联盟中主要的外国合作伙伴。然而，近些年来，中印两国与美国的合作比过去要多得多。2010—2014 年，中国所占的比例几乎与日本相当。[53]

还有其他形式的跨国研发合作。无论是风险投资公司还是企业风险投资部门，跨境风险投资已经非常普遍。虽然欧洲风险投资公司长期从事跨境投资，但在 21 世纪，美国风险投资公司在这方面更加活跃。例如，2011 年对美国风险投资公司的调查显示，49%的美国投资者已经在海外进行投资。该调查还发现，在被调查者中，有 72%的人计划在未来增加或维持其海外投资。[54] 在美国，外国风险投资也在增加。例如，2016 年第一季度，在美国所有风险投资中，有 27%的公司总部设在国外，[55] 主要来源是英国、中国和以色列。在全世界，风险投资仍然与 ICT 行业密切相关。例如，2015 年和 2016 年第一季度，全球风险投资支持的交易中，76%~79%属于 ICT 行业。[56]

表 1.2　美国研发联盟

时间	总数	国际性	西欧	日本	中国	印度
1990—2014 年	9 894	4 741	2 184	1 272	177	89
2010—2014 年	376	210	107	24	23	9

资料来源：汤森路透 SDC 白金数据库。2015 年 4 月提取的数据。

学术方面还有更多形式的合作。虽然研发联盟往往相对集中，但一些大学已经建立了更广泛的研究伙伴关系。例如，2007年，麻省理工学院和新加坡国家研究基金会建立了新加坡—麻省理工学院研究与技术联盟（Singapore-MIT Alliance for Research and Technology），这是麻省理工学院第一次在海外建立研究中心。[57]一个由两所美国高等教育协会编制的数据库显示，截至2009年，其成员一共确定了369个国际研究伙伴关系。[58]这种伙伴关系有助于研究人员与外国同事建立长期合作关系，有时还可以获得外国研究经费。[59]不同国家的实验室之间也有大量的小规模合作，国际合作作者的数据便表明了这一点。从世界范围来看，由一个以上国家的作者发表的科学和工程类文章的比例从2000年的13%跃升到2013年的19%。美国又一次走在了前面：包括所有外国合著文章在内，美国科学和工程类文章所占的份额从2000年的19%跃升至2013年的33%。[60]

总之，研发活动的很多方面都呈现出全球化趋势，尽管这种发展趋势并不总像近几十年来的人才流动全球化一样迅速。此外，研发全球化和人才流动全球化密切相关。例如，在中国和印度，美国的ICT公司经常依赖有美国工作经验的中国和印度员工，这些人在当地的研发中发挥重要作用。[61]微软亚洲研究院的创始董事李开复，出生于中国台湾，分别在哥伦比亚大学和卡内基梅隆大学获得了计算机学士学位和博士学位。加入微软之前，李开复在苹果公司的研发部门工作了六年。[62]后来李开复成为谷歌中国的首任董事。同样，IBM位于印度班加罗尔的研究实验室的首任主任是古鲁都·班阿瓦尔（Guruduth Banavar）。班阿瓦尔在班加罗尔大学获得本科学位，之后在犹他大学获得计算机博士学位。他在 IBM 纽约研究院工作了 10 年，然后承担了班加罗尔的工作。[63] 2004 年，雅虎印度任命帕萨德·瑞姆（Prasad Ram）为首席技术官。瑞姆在位于孟买的印度理工学院获得本科学位，之后在加州大学洛杉矶分校获得了计算机博士学位。之后，瑞姆在美国施乐公司（Xerox）从事了六年科学研究。离开雅虎印度之后，2006—2011 年，瑞姆担任谷歌印度的研发负责人。[64]

在学术方面，移民和全球研发互相交织。这从美国与中国的关系中已经可以看出来。美国给予来自中国的学生和学术访问签证比其他任何国家都多。[65] 虽然许多人留在了美国，但有越来越多的人返回中国。2015 年，38 928 名获得美国 J-1 签证的中国人往往会被要求在其计划结束后两年内返回中国。中国科学家的回归推动了美国和中国科学机构之间的合作迅速发展。2013 年，中国与美国的科学家和工程师合著发表了近 31 000 篇文章，而 1999 年，这个数量还不到 2 500 篇。[66] 因此，中国已成为美国科学论文合著者的主要来源。2013 年，中美科学家合著文章的数量是美英科学家合著文章数量的 1.5 倍，是美日科学家合著文章数量的 3 倍，是美印科学家合著文章数量的 6 倍。

人力资本的流动和研发全球化紧密相连，共同开创了全球创新的新时代。美国在推动二者的发展进程方面发挥了主导作用，世界上人口最多的两个国家也在全球创新中发挥着关键作用。中印两国已经成为向其他地区输出人才的重要来源国，并且开始在全球研发中发挥更重要的作用。

全球创新浪潮中的中国和印度

中印两国长期以来一直渴望通过对核心技术的投资实现技术现代化，试图将各自的国家转变为先进的经济大国。[67]近几十年来，中印两国一直在进行经济改革和开放计划，并且越来越多地参与全球创新，特别是在ICT领域。在此过程中，中国和印度非常清楚地意识到其中的风险。有才能的学生和劳动力可能并不归国，这是非常可怕的人才流失，会加剧中印两国与发达国家之间的差距。建立研发中心的外国公司可能会垄断国内最优秀的人才，而且这些研发中心与当地经济的联系微乎其微。[68]尽管如此，中印两国还是将全球创新视为机遇。两国都将有才能的学生和劳动力外流视为提升本国经济发展中人力资本的实力和参与全球经济的契机。中印两国都积极参与全球研发，希望能够对自己的创新能力产生积极的溢出效应。尽管方法各异，但中印两国都将创新全球化视为不容错过的机会。

中国

中国已经向全球创新开放，并且雄心勃勃。2006年，中国政府发布了《国家中长期科学和技术发展规划纲要（2006—2020年）》（下文简称《科技发展纲要》），以迅速推进"自主创新"，使中国成为世界级的"科技力量"（科技强国战略）。[69]尽管在追求目标的过程中，产业信息活动的作用备受关注，但这种活动只是中国在成为创新领导者过程中的一个尝试。[70]自20世纪70年代以来，这些尝试包括参与西方国家的国际人力资本流动。近来，中国也开始尝试开放全球研发。

1. 人才流动

将学生送到西方国家学习是中国经济改革和开放计划开始之初的重要部分。20世纪70年代初，中国开始向澳大利亚、加拿大、法国和英国等西方国家派遣少数学生。[71]20世纪70年代末，随着经济改革的开始，中国呼吁更多的学生走出国门，了解更多的先进技术。1977—1983年，已有26 000名官方资助的学生和访问学者走出国门，另外还有7 000名自费留学生主动到国外学习。这是1950—1977年中国留学生人数的两倍，其中一半以上的学生去了美国。[72]

然而，20世纪80年代，中国开始重新考虑将这么多学生送到国外的事情，很多中国学生在完成学业后并不归国。针对这种情况，中国1987年和1988年上半年出台了新政策，开始限制海外学习的机会和研究的持续时间。正如当时的资深评论员所说，这些政策反映了"一定程度上对潜在人才流失的担心"。[73]

在接下来的几年里，中国政府的态度发生了巨大的改变。1988年中期，中国官员和官方媒体开始展示出更多的自信，认为中国有能力应对海外留学带来的挑战。[74]1988年末，一位中国记者说道:"解决这个问题的关键在于发展经济,而不是改变面向海外学生的政策。"[75]

1993年11月,中共十四届三中全会正式采用新口号:"支持留学,鼓励回国,来去自由"。[76]值得注意的是,有关部门还赞同"采取各种措施鼓励海外人才为祖国服务",这反映出人们越来越认识到并非所有学生都会回国。

在21世纪,越来越多的中国学生出国留学。联合国教科文组织(UNESCO)估计,2003—2013年,中国接受过海外高等教育的学生人数从31.3万人跃增到71.2万人。[77]中国也加大了吸引学生回国的力度。早在2004年,中国就已在海外学生最集中的38个国家建立了52个教育机构,这些教育机构帮助组建了2 000多个海外学生协会。[78]这些海外学生协会帮助中国政府向中国学生介绍国内的发展情况。

中国很多部门也已经直接参与到从国外招聘人才的努力中。2003年,中共中央政治局成立了中央人才工作协调小组(以下简称"小组"),由中央组织部领导,并有十几个部委参与。[79]2008年,"小组"公布了"千人计划",计划在未来5~10年中吸引2 000名高素质人才归国。[80]该计划对于能够"在关键技术方面取得突破"或在新兴科学领域的领军人才特别感兴趣。随后的举措包括2010年的"青年千人计划",2011年的"千人外聘专家计划",2011年的"人才特区计划",以及2012年的"万人计划"。[81]国内不断增多的高科技园区也吸引了一部分高科技人才回国,这些园区能帮助归国人员获得资金等资源,以及减税等奖励措施。[82]最近,中国努力改革科研经费筹措制度，制订新计划和推进改革，赋予科学家更多的权力。[83]

中国在鼓励移民回归的工作方面取得了成功。虽然在过去10年中，出国的学生人数显著增加，但归国的人数增长更快，如图1.2所示。因此，归国人员与出国留学人员的比例都在上升。2007年，归国的学生人数占出国人数的31%。2013年，这一数字已跃升至85%。从那时起，这个数字稳定在78%~80%。

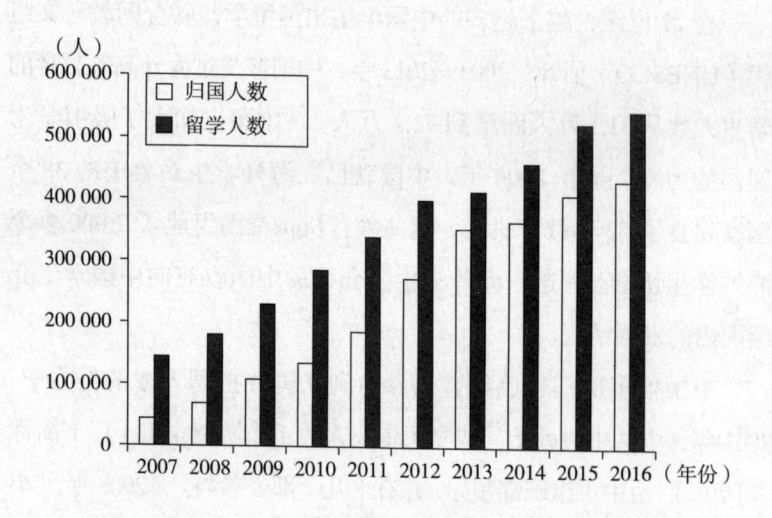

图1.2 2007—2016年中国留学人数与归国人数

资料来源：中华人民共和国教育部"留学人员归国统计"，中华人民共和国教育部官网，访问于2017年3月1日，www.moe.edu.cn。

中国专注于吸引科技和工程领域人才的计划也取得了一些成功。截至2012年，已有2 263名人才通过"千人计划"归国，这个数量超过了最初的目标。[84]针对40岁以下人才的"青年千人计划"也取得了成功。2011年宣布了首批143名归国青年人才名单。[85] 2015年、2016年和2017年，分别有661人、558人和590人回国。[86] 美国的数据也表明科学人才回归中国的趋势。2001年，在美国的大学获得科学与工程领域博士学位的中国学生在毕业后前五年留在美国的比例是98%，到2011年，这一数字已降至85%。[87]

然而，中国仍有很长的路要走。中国正在努力吸引非中国籍人才：截至2017年，已有381人被选为"千人外聘专家计划"。[88] 此外，"千人计划"一直在努力吸引最顶尖的人才，尤其是学术界人才。

中国也像其他发展中国家一样接受了"侨民模式"。[89] 在这种观点中，不归国的侨民成员仍然可以通过学术交流、业务往来和其他类型的合作参与国家发展。20世纪90年代，中国政府通过"春光项目"对该方法进行实践，海外人员能够通过该项目进行短期访问。2001年，中国政府接受了由五个部委共同撰写的文件中所介绍的侨民模式，即使这些侨民没有返回中国，也鼓励他们"为国服务"。[90] 具体来说，鼓励海外华人进行以下活动：

1. 充分利用其专业优势；
2. 在中国和海外兼职；
3. 在国内外从事合作研究；
4. 返回中国教学和进行学术与技术交流；
5. 在中国设立企业；
6. 进行检查和磋商；

7. 从事中介服务，如开展会议、引进技术或外国资金，或助中国公司寻找海外市场。[91]

尽管如此，中国对侨民模式的热情有限。事实上，中国对于在国外学习和工作的学生和专业人士提供更多机会的态度存在不确定性。中国媒体有时会将美国的工作签证描述为对中国的挑战。2013 年，由于美国总统巴拉克·奥巴马及其在国会的盟友正在敦促全面放开美国移民政策，中央人才工作协调小组的高级官员告诉《人民日报》，中国必须通过付出双倍的努力来面对这种由其他国家移民政策带来的挑战。这位官员说："我们必须保持这种势头，利用更加灵活的政策和机制参与国际人才竞争。"[92] 强调人才竞争是中国的一个重要主题。事实上，中国专家王辉耀写过一篇关于全球人才争夺战的文章，其中提到中国正在与美国和其他国家竞争，以吸引世界上最优秀和最聪明的人，但这种言论并非中国所独有。[93]

展望未来，中国希望通过政策的改变达到想要的结果。在此背景下，中国国家留学基金委员会——一个直属于中国教育部的非营利机构——近年来加大了对中国留学生的资金支持力度。2012—2017 年，中国国家留学基金委员会计划的奖学金数量从 16 000 个增加到 32 500 个。[94] 奖学金资助通常要求学生学成后归国。2014 年，中国国家留学基金委员会的报告称，自 1996 年以来，其所资助的 98% 的学生已经学成归国。[95]

近年来，中国对学生和受过良好教育的专业人员的移民采取了自由主义的政策，但也加大了将这些人带回中国的难度。这些努力卓有成效，但中国目前的领导层显然希望在未来能取得更大的成果。

2. 全球研发

中国以各种方式参与全球研发。长期以来，拥抱对外投资都是中国改革开放进程的关键因素，开放外国研发已经成为中国改革开放进程的重要组成部分。即便如此，当跨国公司首次表示它们对设立海外研发中心感兴趣时，它们仍然对于在中国设立研发中心存在担忧。

近年来，这种担忧已经消退。现在，许多中国一流企业在研发方面投入了大量资金，国内公司的机会和工资变得更具吸引力。[96]此外，中国出现了越来越多的创业公司，它们也在争夺人才。[97]中国已经清楚地意识到国家必须深化与外部世界的融合才能取得进步。这一理念在重要的国家文件中有很明显的体现。2006年发布的《科技发展纲要》认为，中国应加强与世界其他地区的科技合作。[98]中国的大学和研究机构与外国机构建立联合实验室，并邀请跨国公司在中国设立更多的研发中心。2010年，一份概述新工作的通告《国务院关于加快培育和发展战略性新兴产业的决定》也强调了继续开展国际合作的必要性。[99]与《科技发展纲要》一样，该决定也呼吁外国公司在中国设立研发中心，并呼吁更多的外资投资重要产业。2011年，"十二五"规划鼓励"外国企业在中国建立研发中心"，使国家"积极融入全球创新体系"。[100] 各种激励机制鼓励国内外企业在中国发展。[101]

可以肯定的是，近年来有关美国海外网络监控的披露引起了中国的怀疑，这破坏了位于中国的美国科技公司与中国政府之间的关系，并对其在中国的业务产生了影响。[102] 即便如此，中国政府吸引外国研发公司（包括美国公司）的兴趣仍然浓厚。[103] 2014年1月，《人民日报》提到中国对"吸引跨国公司的重要研发活动"表示欢迎。[104]

在中国的外国研发在本质上有很大差异。过去，资产利用式研发，也就是使现有的产品适应中国市场，一直占据主导地位。[105] 在某些情况下，为了适应过时的本地流程或在价格上取得竞争优势，这种研发模式会使产品不那么先进。[106] 例如，一家著名的国际风力发电公司在中国重新设计了变速箱以降低成本，但在此过程中，该公司将产品的耐用性降低了一半。[107] 然而，在其他情况下，重新设计适用于中国市场的产品产生了很多适用于全球的技术。[108] 换句话说，资产利用式研发与资产增强式研发之间的界限日渐模糊。

资产增强式研发在中国也有所发展。2008年的一项调查确定了51家进行"创新"研发的跨国公司（即与公司的全球研发业务相关），[109] 其中一家便是微软在北京设立的重要的研究中心，截至2014年，该研究中心已有230名终身研究员，并且每年有数百名访问学者。[110] 通用电气位于上海的中国技术中心是该公司在海外经营的四个跨学科研发中心之一，该研发中心在制造技术和材料科学等领域开展了先进的研究。[111] 英特尔中国研究中心与位于美国、印度、韩国和俄罗斯的研发团队密切合作,尽管全球产品开发也在其他地方进行。[112]

与此同时,中国企业正在扩大海外研发投资。例如,2007—2013年,中国企业在美国的研发投入从几乎为零增长到4.49亿美元。[113] 这种增长得到了中国政府的支持。例如,《科技发展纲要》呼吁"鼓励和帮助(中国公司)在海外建立研发中心或工业化基地"。[114] 同时,中国公司在投资外国科技公司方面也更加活跃。2005—2016年,中国企业花费近580亿美元在外国科技公司增加股权或收购外国科技公司,其中大部分活动发生在近几年。[115] 中国政府也经常在此方面提供支持。有人认为中国政府支持中国企业进行海外收购,尤其是半导体收购,已经引起了美国的关注。[116] 截至2017年,中国政府对于审查海外投资更加谨慎。

中国也开始接受跨境研发合作。美国科学家和中国科学家之间的合作和共同著述迅速增加,例如,《科技发展纲要》鼓励"研究机构和大学与海外研究机构建立联合实验室或研发中心"。[117]《国务院关于加快培育和发展战略性新兴产业的决定》的发布反而能够呼吁产生更多的"由企业领导,有研究机构和高校加入的技术创新联盟",虽然这个目标并非专门针对外部世界。[118] 中国政府也在其他官方文件中支持国际研发合作。[119] 这种开放性反过来又使中国成为跨国研发联盟中更重要的合作伙伴,如表1.2所示。在某些情况下,此类合作旨在促进外国产品在中国的本土化。例如,高通已为此与许多中国合作伙伴达成了协议。在其他情况下,跨境研发合作发展得更加迅速。例如,位于广州中山大学的达安基因与圣迭戈生命技术公司于 2012 年创建了一家合资企业,开发分子技术,以帮助诊断早期癌症、传染病和遗传性疾病。[120]

中国也对外国风险投资开放,尽管这需要进行很多工作。1992 年,随着 IDG 公司的进入,外国风险投资公司开始进入中国。但是直到 2001 年,这些公司才获得中国法律的认可。[121] 尽管此后进行了各种改革,但国内监管环境依然充满挑战。例如,在 ICT 领域内,对互联网公司的外国投资者的限制给外国风险投资人带来了很多影响。通俗地讲,中国政府对首次公开募股和股票市场的管理使得风险投资公司难以退出在中国境内的投资。[122] 中国政府对国内风险投资基金的支持也对市场造成了一些混乱。即便如此,包括红杉资本和 KPCB 在内的知名外国风险投资公司在中国仍然很活跃,它们在很多方面发挥了重要作用,包括使中国创业公司走向国际化,帮助其海外上市,并将它们引荐给外国银行家、会计师和律师。[123]

过去的几十年,中国政府已经对全球研发的许多方面进行了开放。打消了初步的疑虑后,中国政府热情地欢迎外国研发中心进入中国,同时欢迎与外国合作伙伴的合作。近年来,中国在这方面越来越开放。

印度

与中国一样,印度也在寻求利用全球创新来实现发展目标。这些目标看起来非常有野心。2013 年,印度政府公布了其科学、技术和创新政策,目标是到 2020 年印度进入"全球五大科学强国之列"。[124] 2017年初，印度总理纳伦德拉·莫迪（Narendra Modi）立下誓言，到2030年之前，印度将会名列"科技三大强国之一"。[125] 然而，在进行全球创新的方式方面，印度与中国有很大不同。印度并没有像中国一样鼓励逆向移民或吸引外商投资。即便如此，在领导人与公司对这种移民模式的接受度上，印度的表现很突出。

1. 人才流动

印度在将受过良好教育的人输送到海外方面有悠久的历史。19世纪30年代，英国殖民地终止奴隶制之后，劳动者的大规模迁移开始了，其中大多数移民前往南亚或东南亚。虽然这批移民大多数都不具备专业技能，但在20世纪上半叶，以职员、官僚和商人为主的专业技工引发了第二次移民浪潮。[126] 然而，在印度独立之后，印度政府最初认为其公民没有权利出国。事实上，在20世纪60年代中期之前，政府认为签发护照是其在外交事务中的自由裁量权问题。直到1966年，印度最高法院才将"旅行权"确立为印度宪法规定的基本权利，这促使印度议会于1967年颁布了《护照法》。[127] 即便如此，旅行权仍然受到监管：如果政府认为这样做不符合"公共利益"，该法案允许政府拒绝签发护照。[128] 1983年颁布的《移民法》规定，如果阻止移民出境符合"大众"的利益，则政府可以阻止"任何等级的人"出境。[129]

至少在理论上讲，印度政府对遏制移民有一些法律权力。它还可以通过各种方式阻止移民，比如，从税收到大众舆论，都可以使出国更加困难。[130] 在实践中，印度政府并没有这样做，但其背后的原因已经随着时间的推移而改变。[131] 从 20 世纪 60 年代中期开始，印度移民到美国的速度加快，尤其是受过更多教育的公民开始移民，同时印度对人才流失的担忧也在加剧。20 世纪 70 年代，高科技领域的人才外流具有特别重要的意义，因为有越来越多的印度理工学院的精英毕业生赴美深造，然后留在美国继续工作。[132] 印度政府并没有试图阻止人力资本流出，部分原因是保守派政治领导人不希望剥夺印度社会精英成员离开印度的机会，特别是在国内经济疲软、机会有限的时候。与此同时，新派政治领导人很高兴看到保守派群体的成员离开印度。换句话说，人才流失在当时是印度的"安全阀"。[133]

随着时间的推移，印度允许受过良好教育的公民出国的理由变得更加积极。20 世纪 80 年代，时任印度总理拉吉夫·甘地（Rajiv Gandhi）将印度侨民形容为"人才库"，是印度发展的资产。20 世纪 90 年代初，这种思维方式开始流行。[134] 从那时起，来自印度人民党和国大党的总理都强调增加与海外受过高等教育的印度人的互动，而不是试图限制人才流出。[135] 正是在这种背景下，受过良好教育的印度工人以惊人的速度流入其他国家，特别是在 20 世纪 90 年代后半期互联网热潮开始之后。这对受过高等教育的印度人的移民产生了影响，印度高等教育人群的移民率从 1990 年的 2.6% 跃升至 2000 年的 4.2%。[136] 到 2010 年，OECD 国家中，印度已有 220 万受过高等教育的侨民。移居美国的印度人被称为"IT 一代"，因为这些人中有很多人从事 ICT 行业。事实上，到2012年，美国国内有四分之一的印度人从事与计算机相关的职业。这一群体的数量仍在继续增长。到2014年，印度已成为美国最大的移民来源国，仅次于墨西哥。[137]

印度学生也遍及全球。根据联合国教科文组织的统计，1999年，有55 770名印度人在海外学习。10年后，这个数据已经上升至203 497，而印度政府估计当时有超过250 000印度人在国外。[138] 最受印度学生欢迎的目的地是美国，2014—2015年，共有132 888名印度人在美国高等教育机构学习。[139] 2001年2月至2008年9月，在美国的印度学生人数超过其他任何国家。有相当一部分印度学生攻读美国的科学与工程研究生课程。例如，截至2014年11月，超过72 000名印度学生在美国学习科学与工程研究生课程，其中绝大多数学生学习工程和计算机科学课程。[140] 印度还派遣了大量学生到其他英语国家学习。2012年，近30 000名印度学生在英国学习，2013年有超过40 000名印度学生在澳大利亚注册。不过，近年来这些数字波动很大。[141]

与中国政府一样，印度政府一直希望其海外专业人士和学生回国。正如拉吉夫·甘地在1985年提出的："我们必须创造良好的环境和基础设施以使归国人员能在工业上有所发展，在研究上有所成就，在学术上有所建树。"[142] 为此，印度政府制订了鼓励侨民归国的计划，有些计划已经产生了一定的成果。[143] 尽管如此，印度政府吸引侨民回归的努力在规模和强度上都不如中国政府。印度并没有类似于中国的国家留学基金委这样的机构，中国国家留学基金委资助学生在海外学习并要求学生学成后归国。[144] 印度也没有中国的"千人计划",这是一项备受瞩目且要耗费大量资金的工作,旨在将有突出才能的侨民吸引回国。这是可以理解的,印度政府没有中国政府所拥有的资源,而这些资源基于更大的经济体。此外,印度公司在研发方面的投资只相当于中国公司支出的一小部分,印度的大学并不像中国的大学那样满怀壮志。因此,印度国内对高端人才的需求并不像中国那样迫切。[145]

到目前为止,印度移民的回归率尚不明确。与中国政府不同的是,印度政府从未公布过从国外返回的学生人数的数据。然而,来自美国的数据显示,许多印度人留在海外的意向十分强烈。21世纪初期,有临时签证的印度人在美国成为永久居民的比率非常高,可能超过90%。[146]虽然这一比率可能在近几年有所下降,但有传闻称,印度籍人口成为美国长期居民的人数仍然以每年超过10万的数量增长。[147]与中国一样,印度继续努力将其最有才能的学生召唤回来。2001年,在科学与工程领域获得博士学位的印度学生在毕业后的头五年仍留在美国的比例是86%。[148]到2011年,这个数字已下降到82%。[149]随着时间的推移,这个数字不断下降,但比例仍然相当高,并且下降的速度要比中国慢得多。最近的研究还表明,印度学生归国的意愿与其能力、移民后的教育和收入呈负相关。[150]

如果印度不像中国那样专注于移民回流,那么印度对侨民模式的热情将岌岌可危。虽然印度与其侨民的关系在独立后数十年间一直不甚亲近,但这种关系却在世纪之交经历了重大转变。1999年,印度总理阿塔尔·比哈里·瓦杰帕伊(Atal

Bihari Vajpayee）政府成立了印度侨民高级委员会（High Level Committee on the Indian Diaspora）。委员会的大量报告引发了印度与其侨民团体关系的"范式转变"。[151] 报告提供了一系列建议，并且得出结论："如果印度政府执行正确的政策框架和倡议，那么可以牢牢巩固并且深入挖掘印度侨民之间的善意储备。"[152]

随后，印度政府采取了各种举措。2002年，瓦杰帕伊政府修改了PIO（印度血统）计划，降低了一些印度血统的外国人访问的费用。2004年，政府成立了印度海外侨民事务部，以增加与海外侨民的接触。2006年，总理曼莫汉·辛格（Manmohan Singh）政府正式启动了扩大的OCI（印度海外公民）计划，该计划针对的是从印度移民并在另一个国家获得公民身份的个人。2009年，辛格政府成立了总理全球咨询委员会，以促进印度政府与重要海外侨民之间的沟通。[153]

过去，观察印度政府工作的评论员指责印度政府专注于狭隘的激励计划，却忽略了更广泛的经济改革，而这些改革可以吸引更多的海外侨民归国，事实证明正是如此。[154] 在纳伦德拉·莫迪政府的领导下，这已经发生了变化。莫迪巩固了以前的努力，特别是将印度海外侨民事务部并入外交部，并将PIO和OCI计划合并，这些举措促进形成了已有的工作成果，放松了印度经济对侨民的限制。

2015年9月，莫迪在硅谷向印度侨民发表讲话。莫迪说，受过良好教育的印度人留在国外并不是人才流失，而是"人才储备"，"无论机会什么时候来临"，这些"储备的人才"都可以通过各种方式为其国家服务。[155] 为了标榜他的改革主义记录和相关证明，莫迪声称为"印度母亲"服务的机会已然来临。

印度对包括其海外 IT 工作者在内的海外侨民的积极态度，反映了印度政府多方面的考虑。首先，印度官员一直试图吸引海外印度劳工的资金流入，近几十年来这种流入量大幅增加，尤其是汇款形式。[156] 虽然并非所有资金都来自职业人士，但这类人群显然有助于提高全国资金总额。2014 年，世界银行估计印度的汇款收入超过 700 亿美元，比任何国家都要多。[157] 这一数字相当于印度国内生产总值的 3.7% 和外汇储备的 23.5%。

与之相关的是，印度一流的科技公司已经开始依赖一种商业模式，这种模式的基础是拥有大量受过良好教育的劳工。这种模式在美国尤其明显，印度公司依靠 H-1B 签证计划向美国客户出口服务。20 世纪 90 年代以来，这些公司已将这一计划（以及在较小程度上，用于公司内部转移的 L-1 计划）用于将印度计算机程序员和软件工程师派往美国各地，并且已成为公司战略的重要部分。[158] 事实上，2014 年，由塔塔集团、印孚瑟斯和威普罗领头的七家印度公司收到了分配的 85 000 个私营部门 H-1B 签证中的 16 573 个。[159] 这些海外员工使得印度公司能够为北美的客户提供高科技劳动力，这是他们迄今为止最大的市场。

由于这些变化，印度政府对美国移民政策的看法与中国政府差异很大。中国担心美国制度更加开放，但印度更担心的是相反的情况。事实上，自 20 世纪 90 年代末以来，印度一直敦促美国增加其提供的 H-1B 签证数量，并使印度人更容易在美国工作。[160] 此外，当美国政府为这一流动造成了障碍时，印度在世界贸易组织提出抗议，甚至威胁要对美国采取行动。[161] 2015 年，时任美国总统巴拉克·奥巴马访问印度时，印度总理莫迪就表达了印度政府对 H-1B 签证计划限制的担忧。[162] 印度政府对就业签证的关注度较低，因为印度公司很少为美国雇员寻求绿卡。[163] 当然，一些印度评论员担心美国就业签证激增，特别是面向科学与工程领域的外国毕业生的就业签证的增加，可能会吸引更多的印度学生出国，这使印度成为科学强国的工作变得更加复杂。[164] 至少到 2014 年，当提及美国提供更多的就业签证所带来的前景变化时，印度政府的高层官员一般都漠不关心。[165]

印度传统上采取了自由主义的政策来应对人才的跨境流动，几十年来，印度学生和海外专业人士的数量创了新高。然而，与中国不同的是，印度没有投入大量资金来吸引其海外人才，印度更依赖海外侨民模式。

2. 全球研发

与中国一样，印度已经接受了全球研发，但这个过程是渐进式的。20 世纪 70 年代早期，德州仪器的主席帕特里克·哈格蒂（Patrick Haggerty）访问印度，并提议建立一个集成电路的制造和研究设施。虽然印度总理英迪拉·甘地（Indira Gandhi）对这个想法持开放态度，但她怀疑这会影响政治体系。[166] 1985 年，德州仪器再次尝试，这次它成功地在班加罗尔设立了一个设计中心。从那时起，德州仪器与许多在印度建立研发中心的知名跨国公司合作，特别是班加罗尔已经成为此类业务的重要枢纽。例如，位于班加罗尔的通用电气约翰·韦尔奇技术中心拥有 5 300 多名技术专家，这使得该中心成为通用电气在美国以外最大的实验室。[167] 虽然从整体上来讲，印度对外商直接投资（FDI）的开放程度不如中国，但是印度在信息科学领域相对开放，包括软件开发和研发，这都要归功于印度侨民提供的与外部世界的联系。[168] 一份官方研究确定，2003—2009 年，印度共有 964 个研发领域的外商投资项目，总价值超过 290 亿美元，占当时印度总体外商投资的 8%，大多数项目都集中在 ICT 领域。[169] 咨询公司 Zinnov 的数据显示，截至 2016 年，已经有来自 943 个跨国企业的 1 208 个外国研发中心落户印度。[170] 印度的外国研发的本质多种多样，包括资产利用式和资产增强式。过去的研究认为，与中国相比，外国公司更倾向于在印度进行资产增强式研发，特别是跨国公司将其研发活动外包给班加罗尔和印度其他地区。[171] IBM 在北京和班加罗尔设立研究实验室很好地体现了这种趋势：北京实验室更专注于开发适合中国市场的产品，而班加罗尔实验室则更多地参与 IBM 的全球研发工作。[172] 近些年来，随着越来越多的外国公司开始在中国开展面向全球的研发，这种趋势可能并不如以往一样普遍。无论如何，印度的资产利用式和资产增强式研发之间的界限会比在中国更加模糊不清，为印度市场开发的产品也可能在全球销售，特别是当跨国公司依靠"节俭工程"在印度开发了更便宜的发达世界产品版本，并随后在全球推广这些产品时。[173]

印度还展开了国际合作。印度公布的《2013 科学、技术和创新政策》（2013 Science, Technology and Innovation policy）表明，印度将通过双边和多边合作实现"战略伙伴关系和联盟"。[174] 此外，该政策还关注"全球研发基础设施"的高成本，鼓励印度企业参与"国际合作"，这将使印度工业在一些高科技领域获得全球经验和竞争力。"印度许多著名的公司和组织已经与外国企业建立技术联盟进行合作，这证明了印度政府对技术联盟这种形式的兴趣。"[175] 这里的印度公司包括 Reddy 博士实验室、格伦马克制药公司、印度空间研究组织、印孚瑟斯、鲁宾、马恒达、信实和塔塔公司。如果算上软件开发和计算机编程联盟，那么印度公司的名单还包括 HCL、塔塔咨询和威普罗等。

在印度总理纳伦德拉·莫迪的领导下，印度特别热衷于与跨国公司在研发方面合作。可以肯定的是，印度政府的首要任务是吸引外国的制造业投资，印度不断增长的人口意味着需要创造更多的就业岗位，制造业投资为增加就业带来了潜力，"印度制造"运动便证明了这一点。[176] 即便如此，印度的领导人也确实希望扩大该国在全球研发中的作用。2015 年 1 月，莫迪指出："在研发方面有越来越多的国际合作趋势，我们应该充分利用这种趋势。"[177] 莫迪当年 9 月在硅谷的讲话赞扬了当地印度人在高科技创新中的作用，并鼓励大家在印度的发展中发挥更大的作用。[178] 如果发展制造业是印度的首要任务，那么印度领导人更渴望提高印度在全球研发方面的知名度。

过去的几十年，印度在向外国风险投资开放方面也取得了很大进展。1993 年，美国投资者维诺德·科斯拉（Vinod Khosla）开始了在硅谷和印度之间的奔波,他希望在印度发展风险投资业务。但三年后,他放弃了。[179] 截至 1999 年,许多外国风险投资公司在印度开展业务,并且印度约有 80% 的风险投资来自外国公司。尽管如此,创业公司和风险投资仍面临各种监管和法律障碍。近年来,这种情况得到了很大改善。在 Flipkart 和 Ola 等成功案例的启发下,在过去 10 年里,印度创业公司更加活跃。与此同时,自 2014 年阿里巴巴首次公开募股 250 亿美元以来,外国风险投资公司对印度产生了更大的兴趣,它们希望在此找到"下一个风口"。[180] 莫迪政府致力于鼓励这样的趋势。莫迪的"创业印度"倡议为新公司创造了激励机制并增加了资金投入,截至 2017 年中期,这项工作仍在进行。[181] 印度政府也更加欢迎外国风险投资公司,允许它们在没有经过中央银行事先许可的情况下,投资任何行业的创业公司。[182]

过去几十年来,印度在全球研发方面取得了相当大的进展。虽然印度政府没有像中国那样力求快速发展,但在印度的外国研发数量已经大大增加。印度还通过研发联盟和风险投资寻求更多的国际合作。

结 论

近几十年的创新全球化正在经历前所未有的发展。技术人员和学生流动越来越活跃,跨国公司和研究型大学进行跨境研发投资和合作比以往更多。与此同时,世界上最著名的崛起大国,已经欣然接受了这些发展,致力于凭自身实力成为创新领袖。

然而,这种开放并不意味着无视风险。相反,中国和印度都逐渐提升了对全球创新的热情,并且偶尔会反思这种开放。中国和印度在不同程度上担忧派往海外的人才是否会回归,而且也一直担心外国研发中心吸引国内顶尖人才。在这两种情况下,潜在的风险都是可以理解的,但主流观点认为,开放的潜在好处超过了潜在的风险。

中国和印度以不同的方式接触全球创新。中国政府更具有目的性也更加积极主动,其鼓励海外人才回归并努力吸引外商在研发方面的投资。相比之下,印度的做法似乎更有针对性。虽然印度对"逆向移民"感兴趣,但印度更加适应并且更加依赖"侨民模式"。在这两种情况下,该国都有信心和希望从全球创新中获益。

这些发展为许多国家提出了重要问题,尤其是对世界主导国家和技术领袖而言。在接下来的章节,我将阐述其他影响美国参与全球创新的力量。

第 2 章
创新领导力与争议中的开放

第 2 章 创新领导力与争议中的开放

如果说对外经济政策很重要，那么这个世界上最强大的国家的对外经济政策尤其重要。因此，在过去的几十年里，主导国家对外经济政策背后的力量吸引了如此多的关注，也就不足为奇了。[1] 专注于研究全球霸权的理论家将其描述为一种世界经济中开放与秩序的力量，要么是公共产品的提供者，要么是利己的最大化福利者。[2] 更加以国家为中心的理论家重点关注国家政策制定者的利益和权威或国家机构的持久影响力。[3] 其他理论家强调经济思想的作用，包括在相关国家占据主导地位之前就已经根深蒂固的经济思想。[4] 还有大量的理论学说是关于社会利益在塑造美国对外经济政策中所起作用的。[5] 有些学说则将两种或更多种因素结合在一起。[6]

本章提出的理论将聚焦全球创新的政策，对几个不同的学术领域进行综合。基于其他学者的工作，第一部分强调了主导国家在国际体系中的创新领袖地位。这里主要关注主导国家在"主导产业"中的优势地位，并且阐述了这种优势如何支持霸权国的首要地位。第二部分，记录了过去两个世纪工业创新在主导国家的演变，尤其是近几十年来美国 HTC 的出现。第三部分关注 HTC 的发展对于主导国家的全球创新政策意味着什么。具体来说，我提出了一个专注于 HTC 内部共同利益以及 HTC 与不同类型对手之间的政治竞争的理论，并且概述了主导国家对全球创新政策的其他几种解释。第四部分解释这个理论是如何在后面的章节中得到验证的。

创新与霸权

正如约瑟夫·熊彼特在几十年前提到的，创新在时间和空间上不是随机分布的，而是有聚集趋势的。[7] 在研究国际关系的学者中，罗伯特·吉尔平是首批将这种理解付诸实践的人，他指出了"技术革命"在英国和美国崛起成为超级大国的过程中所起的关键作用。[8] 吉尔平还认为，随着时间推移，技术知识和"创造性"的重要性会传播到其他国家，这会导致主导力量衰落并扰乱既定秩序。[9] 最近，"长周期"理论探讨了以下三者之间的关系：创新领导力、经济活力以及全球主导地位。[10] 这些理论认为，新兴国家已经占据了主导地位，因为它们在"主导产业"中开展了一系列创新。这些是相对较新、增长很快的产业，它们产生了积极的溢出效应，并推动了国家和世界经济实现更为广泛的变革。[11] 近几年来，其他国际关系学者也强调了主导产业的创新如何支撑霸权主义。[12] 虽然"主导产业"一词在其他学科中不经常使用，但这一概念经常出现在其他各种名称之下。[13]

在过去的两个世纪，主导产业的创新轨迹已经从英国转移到美国。在工业革命早期，英国在蒸汽和铁路技术方面处于领先地位。工业革命后期，英国将钢铁、化工产品和电力的主导权交给了美国和德国。20世纪中叶，美国在汽车、航空和电子领域占据主导地位。20世纪后期和21世纪初期，美国在信息和通信技术方面处于领先地位。[14]

如今，美国主导产业创新的集群效应凸显。虽然ICT革命已经不局限于北美，但是任何国家都无法复制美国在一流ICT公司和相关学术领域的集聚效果。[15] 近些年来，美国的人口占比不足世界总人口的5%，占OECD成员国人口的1/4。[16] 然而，根据研发支出来衡量，在2016年全球百强软件公司中，美国的公司占65家，[17] 其他发达国家均不超过5个。也是在2016年，在全球百强ICT硬件公司中，美国的公司占56家。相比之下，中国台湾地区有13个，日本有10个。2013年，ICT公司占美国所有商业研发的41%，在OECD的36个成员国中，仅有4个国家或地区超过了该份额。[18] 相关的顶级大学也聚集在美国。在《泰晤士高等教育》发布的2014—2015年度排行榜上排名前20位的工程与技术类大学中，美国的大学占了14所。[19] 简而言之，美国在ICT领域发挥着无与伦比的领导作用。

如果主导产业创新集中在主导国家，那么它是如何形成并保持首要地位的呢？第一点并且也是最基础的一点就是，创新是经济增长的关键来源。特别是自20世纪90年代以来，经济学家一直把创新视为国家繁荣的根本动力。[20] 资本和劳动力投入的增长会造成收益递减的问题，而创新则提高了这些投入的使用效率，从而成为长期增长的可持续来源。

主导产业的创新对增长有很大的影响。例如，虽然英国在

18世纪已经非常强大,但将其推向全球领先地位的是19世纪的工业革命。这不是因为英国是世界上最大的经济体——它并不是——而是因为蒸汽和铁路技术使其一跃成为世界上拥有最先进生产力的国家。[21] 1860年,英国仅占全球人口的2%,占欧洲人口的10%,却占全球现代工业产能的40%~45%。[22] 如今,ICT革命仍在不断发展,但其已经促使美国的生产力比欧洲更具有优势。[23] 同样显著的是,ICT对美国的工业创新越来越重要,因为非ICT公司正越来越多地将其研发支出用于将软件和高科技服务纳入其产品。[24]

创新占据首要地位的第二点因素是新技术通常具有军事和情报应用。汽车、飞机和信息技术是几个近期主导行业的典型例子。虽然新技术,特别是军用技术,通常遍及整个国际体系,但这些技术的传播速度有很大差别。有些新技术价格不菲,有些新技术难以被军事组织应用,有些新技术则同时面临这些问题。[25] 在这种情况下,新技术扩散的速度可能会非常缓慢。当然,这样也无法保证发明新技术的国家将率先挖掘其在军事领域的潜力。尽管如此,发明并主导新技术生产的国家相比其竞争对手还是具有相当大的优势。这些优势包括规模经济、更低的生产成本,以及更多进一步开发和生产的专业知识。[26] 这表明美国作为ICT行业的领袖已经引领世界将这些技术应用于军事。

简而言之,主导国家的经济力量非比寻常。这些国家是创新的领导者,它们在一些主导产业占据主导地位,这些主导产业将熊彼特的"创造性破坏理论"运用到国家和世界经济中,而这种领导力巩固了它们的国家实力。

"高科技界"的出现

如果主导国家传统上一直专注于主导部门的创新，那么在过去两个世纪里，负责产出这些创新的行动者已经发生了巨大的变化。在 18 世纪的英国，创新通常由个体发明者主导，他们经常需要借鉴前人的工作成果。19 世纪后期，特别是在德国和美国，系统性的工业研究越来越普遍。如今，一流的产业创新主要由 ICT 公司主导，它们在美国的研发机构和研究型大学投入巨资。

工业发明简史

第一次工业革命时，英国的领导地位源于个体发明者的天赋。早期工业革命的典型技术——蒸汽机，是由 18 世纪和 19 世纪的一系列发明者发明的，其中包括杰出发明家詹姆斯·瓦特（James Watt），我们可以把他在电力技术中的成就比作物理学中的牛顿。其他发明家，如亨利·贝塞麦（Henry Bessemer）在钢铁发明中尤为突出。英国两位业余发明家设计了一种用欧洲广泛存在的富磷铁制造钢铁的方法。同样，化学工业诞生的关键突破之一来自英国化学家威廉·珀金（William Perkin），他于 1856 年偶然发现了一种人造染料，使得许多人跟随其脚步。[27]

19 世纪下半叶，特别是德国化学工业领域，形成了更具有组织性、更系统的研究。[28] 19世纪60年代，包括拜耳和巴斯夫在内的几家德国化学公司成立。这些公司的创始人通常都是受过教育的化学家，而那些没有专业人才的公司会迅速与专业公司合作。1877—1886年，德国七大化学染料公司建立了专门的实验室。到1890年，德国最大的三家公司雇用了350名受过学术训练的化学家。这种趋势很快就在其他地区流行起来。1902年，杜邦在新泽西州建立了东部实验室，其使命是通过科学研究改进公司的烈性炸药产品。[29] 大学又一次成为化工企业人力资本的重要来源。[30]

19世纪，电力成为系统性研究的另一个主题。1876年，托马斯·爱迪生在新泽西州门洛帕克的"发明工厂"竣工，爱迪生很快组成了一支由其本人负责的发明家团队。[31] 1878年，爱迪生成立了爱迪生电灯公司。14年后，他帮助创建了通用电气。1900年，通用电气在一个谷仓建立了通用电气研究实验室。这是美国第一个工业研究机构。[32]

第二次世界大战爆发前的几十年，工业研发在美国更加成熟。[33] 化工产品是工业研发中的主要内容。1899—1946年，化工产品和与化学相关的产业（如石油）占据了美国工业实验室研究内容的40%（美国制造业雇用的研究科学家和工程师也占相同的比例）。随着时间的推移，电气机械和仪器工业也成为雇用研究科学家和工程师的重要行业。在这样的情况下，大学在支持工业发展方面发挥了关键作用，虽然当时的美国还没有引领全球学术研究，但是州立大学密切关注当地经济需求。第一次世界大战期间，美国军方已经主导了出于战争目的的研发和生产，只有弹药需要依赖杜邦公司。然而，第二次世界大战期间，美国政府提供了更广泛的军事研发和生产，成立了一个新机构——科学研究和发展办公室，该机构建立的目的是监督这种更多样化的活动，包括政府与私企和大学的合作。

第二次世界大战后，工业研究在美国经济中更加突出和广泛。1946年，工业产业中雇用的科学家和工程师不到5万人，到1962年，已经雇用了约30万人。[34] 在此期间，新兴主导产业开始形成，包括汽车、电子和航空等产业。事实上，第二次世界大战结束后，包括汽车和航空在内的运输设备业成为五大研究密集型产业之一。[35] 因此，尽管杜邦公司在20世纪初的研发能力还保持着领先地位，但此时新公司已经开始涌现。例如，1955年，通用汽车推出了雪佛兰小型V8发动机，这是一项革命性的创新，兼具强大的动力、轻巧的尺寸、耐用性和简洁性。[36] 同年，通用汽车成为历史上第一家报告盈利超过10亿美元的公司，在《财富》杂志世界500强排名中独占鳌头，通用电气首席执行官也被《时代》杂志评为"年度人物"。[37] 1957年，波音公司开始生产波音707，这是第一架成功适用于商用的民用运输喷气式飞机，此举巩固了波音在航空业的领导地位。[38]

然而，从重要性的角度来讲，我们目前所知道的HTC行业在当时还没有出现。首先，美国研发支出的主要来源是美国政府。从20世纪50年代至20世纪70年代，由于战后的繁荣，联邦政府在研发方面的支出超过了当时的商业支出。在1964年的高峰时期，联邦政府在研发方面的支出占据美国研发总额的67%。[39] 在此期间，联邦政府投资的研发往往具有显著的衍生潜力，特别是军事技术（如喷气发动机和微电子产品）之后都转为商用。[40] 在这一时期，企业和大学是研发领域的主要执行者，但不是主要的投资者。其次，高科技公司也严重依赖政府采购。直到20世纪60年代后期，美国政府往往是航空、半导体和计算机硬件领域最先进技术的主要客户，也许是唯一的客户。[41] 简而言之，这是一种伙伴关系，工业界和学术界表现出色并推动了技术创新，政府则是重要的投资者和客户。

20世纪的最后25年，美国的高科技公司更加独立。推动这一趋势的是新兴主导产业——ICT的到来。到目前为止，ICT公司已经发展多年，一些"旧经济"公司，如IBM和AT&T（美国电话电报公司），都诞生于19世纪和20世纪初。然而，从20世纪40年代后期到20世纪70年代初，晶体管、集成电路和微处理器的发明为新技术的发展奠定了基础。尽管IBM开创了个人计算机的革命，并于1981年宣布了个人计算机的诞生，但这家标志性公司最终被苹果、思科、英特尔和微软等当时的"新经济"领导者超越。从20世纪80年代末开始，新公司还主导信息和通信技术的融合，特别是在创建互联网的同时，ICT成为这一新领域的标签。[42]

ICT的独立性反映了两个重要变化。第一个重要变化是工业界以美国研发的主要投资者身份出现。20世纪80年代，工业界一直为美国研发提供近一半的资金。20世纪末，政府投资所占的比例下降到 40%。[43] 20 世纪 90 年代，随着 ICT 行业的蓬勃发展，工业界投资份额迅速提升，到了 2000 年，工业界在美国的投资份额已经达到近 70%，而政府的份额则下降到 25%。包括英特尔和微软在内的研发密集型 ICT 公司推动了这一转变。[44] 截至 2016 年，美国七家 ICT 公司跻身全球二十家研发支出最高的公司行列，包括：亚马逊、阿尔法特、英特尔、微软、苹果、思科和甲骨文。[45] 大学在这方面发挥了重要的支持作用，它们提供了人力资本，巩固了硅谷和其他地方的创新集群，并在为基础研究进行资金资助方面承担了更多的重担。从一定程度上讲是由于大学的转变，联邦政府在基础研究经费中的份额从 1964 年的 71% 下降到 2013 年的 47%。[46]

第二个重要变化是美国政府作为高科技产品市场的衰落。尽管在最初，美国政府，尤其美国国防部是先进 ICT 产品的主要客户。但是，商业市场很快就占据了主导地位。例如，20 世纪 60 年代中期，国防相关机构是美国集成电路的主要客户，它们的购买额约占总销售额的 70%。然而，到了 1980 年，它们所占的份额已下降到 10%。[47] 反之，ICT 行业向商用市场的转变也影响了军事采购。20 世纪 90 年代中期，为了避免增加购买政府特定系统的成本，国防部开始更多地购买"商业现货"。因此，为商业用户开发的 ICT 技术在美国军队中变得越来越普遍，为商业市场设计的创新成为军事创新更重要的组成部分。[48] 这种转变导致公共和私人之间的新变化。虽然政府曾经是不可忽略的客户，但是如今，是美国国防部长前往硅谷，期望能够说服高科技公司与美国军方合作。[49]

这里的重点并不是说美国联邦政府在高科技创新方面已经不重要，而是说美国政府已经适应了不断变化的创新格局，为政府与行业的合作创造了新的模式。[50]美国联邦政府仍然是基础研究的最大单一投资者，是高风险种子项目的重要支持者，也是最大的信息技术购买者。[51]然而，特别是对著名的ICT公司而言，合作规则已经发生了变化。例如，谷歌已经缩减了与国防部关于机器人技术的工作，进而专注于商业用途，而苹果则拒绝为美国联邦调查局解锁iPhone。[52]通俗地讲，一些高科技公司减少与美国军方的合作，以免失去其他国家的市场。[53]总之，ICT领域的高科技创新仍然维持着政府、工业界和学术界之间的合作关系，但是这种合作关系已悄然发生变化，非政府部门的重要性和自主权已经极大地提升了。

华盛顿地区的HTC

虽然ICT领域HTC的出现成为20世纪末美国重要的经济和技术现象，但是HTC在华盛顿地区的表现大有不同。一般来讲，我们可以认为HTC由两部分组成——企业界和学术界，它们都在华盛顿开展了自己的业务。

在企业界方面，一流的ICT公司经常在华盛顿地区设立自己的代表处。[54]1975年，IBM成立了公共政策办公室，此后该公司的领导人亲自维系IBM与华盛顿的关系。[55]英特尔于1986年效仿了这一方式。苹果公司20世纪80年代初在弗吉尼亚州设立了一个小办公室，于1989年搬到华盛顿，在20世纪90年代短暂关闭了该办公室，1999年重新启用。[56] 微软的动作相当迟缓，1995年才在华盛顿设立办事处，而且该办事处最初是在1991年的反托拉斯调查中设立的。1998年，思科在华盛顿设立办事处。亚马逊、谷歌和脸书等新涌现的公司分别于2000年、2005年和2009年在华盛顿设立了办事处。此外，许多ICT公司聘请专业说客或律师事务所在华盛顿当地代表公司处理事务，来代替他们自己的办公室或作为补充，而其他人则在其总部负责管理与联邦政府的关系。

随着越来越多的ICT公司在华盛顿设立办事机构，它们也大大增加了游说预算。20世纪90年代后期，IBM、英特尔、微软和甲骨文等知名公司已经投入了大量资金（见表2.1）。近几年来，这些公司中涌现了许多互联网公司，特别是亚马逊、脸书和谷歌。事实上，在2012年，美国公司中谷歌投入的游说费用最多，总共花费了1 800万美元。

表2.1　1998年与2016年美国主要ICT公司的游说费用

公司	游说费用（百万美元）	
	1998	2016
亚马逊	0	11.4
谷歌	0	15.4
英特尔	1.1	4.2
微软	3.9	8.7
苹果	0.2	4.7

续表

公司	游说费用（百万美元）	
	1998	2016
思科	0.6	2.0
甲骨文	1.9	8.6
高通	0.4	5.6
IBM	5.6	4.0
脸书	n/a	8.7

注：研发支出数据是基于 2016 年 7 月 1 日之前报告的最新全年数据。参见 Barry Jaruzelski，Volker Staack 和 Aritomo Shinozaki，《2016 全球创新 1 000 研究》，普华永道，2017，www.strategyand.pwc.com/innovation1000；高通，《2016 高通年度报告》（加利福尼亚州圣迭戈市：Qualcomm，2016 年），15，http://investor.qualcomm.com/annuals-proxies.cfm。

资料来源：响应政治中心，《游说数据库》，OpenSecrets.org，2017 年 3 月 3 日，www.opensecrets.org/lobby/。

在推动政治运动方面，ICT 行业也变得更加积极。事实上，如表 2.2 所示，特别是在 21 世纪，电子制造商、计算机软件公司和互联网公司政治募捐更加活跃。这些捐赠中相对较小的份额来自 PACs（政治行动委员会）和联邦候选人。相比之下，大部分捐款来自行业中受雇于联邦候选人的个人，还有些捐赠采取"软资金"或"外部费用"的形式。[57] 例如，2016 年，由电子制造商捐赠的 8 630 万美元中，有 4 100 万美元是以个人的形式捐赠给候选人的，有 3 800 万美元是外部费用。电子制造业的捐赠通常备受青睐。

共和党人在 20 世纪 90 年代开始受到支持，但从 2004 年开始，民主党人开始受到支持。软件和互联网行业通常受到民主党人的青睐，直到 2008 年，这一差距才开始变大。ICT 行业对民主党人的明显偏好反映了个人捐赠而不是 PACs 捐赠的重要性；ICT 行业的企业 PACs 往往偏爱共和党人。[58]

最后，ICT 公司还建立了各种商会和其他组织来代表它们。[59] 其中有一些起源于早期的工业团体。1916 年，美国办公设备制造商协会成立。1994 年，该协会成为信息技术产业委员会。为了确保国防合同的权利，西海岸电子制造商协会于 1943 年成立，1978 年，该协会更名为 AEA（美国电子协会）。成立于 1960 年的数据处理服务组织协会，于 1991 年更名为 ITAA（美国信息技术协会）。2009 年，ITAA 和 AEA 与其他团体合并成为 TechAmerica，并于 2014 年被另一个行业团体合并。

表 2.2　ICT 行业的政治募捐（百万美元）

年份	电子制造业	计算机软件	互联网
1990	2.9	0.3	0
1992	7.5	1.5	0
1994	6.3	0.8	0
1996	12.5	2.0	0.2
1998	11.7	3.8	0.1
2000	34.5	14.4	6.6
2002	27.8	14.3	2.1
2004	31.4	12.9	3.6
2006	22.4	9.2	2.5
2008	43.6	17.5	8.2
2010	26.0	10.6	4.3
2012	57.6	25.9	17.4

续表

年份	电子制造业	计算机软件	互联网
2014	28.1	12.9	11.9
2016	86.3	46.3	30.7

注：根据上报到联邦选举委员会的数据，这些数据基于 200 美元及以上的捐款，包括由 PACs 和个人向联邦候选人的捐赠和由 PACs、软资金（包括直接来自公司和工会的资金）和个人捐助者向政党以及外部支出团体的捐赠。请注意，一些公司已被分配到表中三个类别中的多个类别，因此不应合并总计。

资料来源：响应政治中心，"利益集团"，OpenSecrets.org，访问于 2017 年 3 月 3 日，www.opensecrets.org/industries/。

其他 ICT 团体成立的时间较晚。半导体行业协会成立于 1977 年，总部最初设在硅谷。微软于 1988 年创建了商业软件协会，旨在打击盗版软件。该协会后来成为商业软件联盟，然后成为"BSA | 软件联盟"。计算机系统政策项目成立于 1989 年，后来转变为技术 CEO 委员会。顾名思义，它由知名 ICT 公司的首席执行官组成，通常由其中一位担任主席。TechNet 成立于 1997 年，是一个由高科技公司和风险投资公司组成的团体。

在学术界方面，HTC 有一系列的协会。最突出的是 ACE（美国教育委员会）。这是一个伞式组织，不仅包括大学，还包括其他高等教育协会的成员。更通俗地讲，ACE 是华盛顿高等教育集团"六巨头"（Big Six）之一。其他五个分别是 AAU（美国大学协会）、APLU（公共和土地赠款大学协会）、美国州立大学协会、美国社区学院协会和全国独立学院与大学协会。[60] ACE 还组织了华盛顿高等教育秘书处的会议，其中包括大约50个与教育有关的高等教育团体。[61] 还有一些专门面向国际学生的游说团体。全美外国学生事务协会代表国际教育专业人员，一直积极地支持外国学生的流入。美国国际教育研究所开展一系列活动，包括宣传、研究和培训，以促进国际教育发展。

代表研究型大学的方式有多种。在上文列出的"六巨头"中，AAU和APLU以代表研究型大学而闻名。截至2017年，AAU包括62所一流的公立和私立研究型大学，而APLU包括235所公立研究型大学和其他机构。虽然它们的游说预算相对较少，但APLU通常每年在联邦游说支出方面投入40万~60万美元。此外，政府关系委员会每年会为研究型大学、医疗中心和研究机构提供建议，联邦政府至少会提供1 500万美元以资助其进行研究。主要的研究型大学一般在华盛顿设有办事处，并进行大量的游说活动。例如，哈佛大学和耶鲁大学在2016年分别花费了55万美元和50万美元用于联邦游说，普林斯顿大学花费了28万美元，斯坦福大学则花费了25万美元。[62] 最后，研究型大学还与大型ICT公司进行正式或非正式的合作，一起进行游说，这在接下来的章节中将会提到。

"高科技界"与争议中的开放

世界主导国家HTC的崛起意味着它如何应对全球创新呢？

要回答这个问题，我们必须转向理论维度。第一，我们必须理解HTC在多大程度上拥有一套关于全球创新的共同利益，且这些利益可以构成集体行动的基础。第二，在存在这种共同利益的情况下，HTC何时能够成功地争取到这些共同的利益？前提假设是有关国家拥有多元化、自由的民主政治制度。第三，必须考虑可替代的理论方法来解释全球创新政策。

HTC 的共同利益

在全球创新政策方面，HTC的共同利益是什么？正如其他学者所指出的，商界内部存在着广泛的共同利益，即使在特定行业内也是如此，更不用说包括ICT公司和大学在内的高科技密集区。[63] ICT行业本身并不是单一的：该行业一流的公司有时会放弃共同利益，追求相互冲突的议程。[64] 有必要解释在全球创新政策方面，为什么ICT公司和研究型大学会拥有一系列共同利益，并且还要记录下它们的共同利益是什么。在研发方面投入巨资的大型ICT公司最有可能对资本和劳动力的跨国流动有浓厚的兴趣，以推动其全球运作以及游说联邦政府。较小的ICT公司可能有类似的利益，但它们的偏好可能不那么强烈，或者它们可能不太适合追求共同的利益。说到这一点，需要特别考虑三个关键领域：外国技术劳工、外国留学生和全球研发。

首先，讨论面向专业技术劳工的政策。以前的研究强调了"高技能资本"对自由民主政体中技术移民政策的偏好。[65] 可以预见的是，在研发方面进行投资的大型ICT公司将成为特别强大的倡导者。技术娴熟的移民增加了整体劳动力,从而增加了可用于研发的人才供应,提升了多样性。这可以使它们更容易获得最有才能和创造力的劳工,增加满足特定需求的机会,实现增加就业竞争力并抑制工资增长的承诺。这一点非常重要,因为ICT公司的研发工作特别耗费人力。2013年,劳务成本分别占美国ICT公司服务和制造业领域国内研发成本的76%和67%。[66] 相比之下,制药和航空航天业的数字均低于40%。反过来,研究型大学的需求也会促进ICT公司对技术移民的需求。这些大学也是人力资本密集型的机构,它们也希望为外国毕业生提供留在美国国内就业的机会——这样的机会可以帮助它们吸引外国学生。ICT公司对开放的偏好可能会随着时间的推移而变化,当然,这取决于行业发展的命运。经济增长期可能会增加对劳动力的需求和对开放的兴趣,而经济衰退期可能会产生相反的效果。然而,随着时间的推移,HTC的企业和学术机构很可能成为对技术移民开放的坚定支持者。

其次,讨论针对外国学生的政策。大学对获得更多这类学生的兴趣最为浓厚。我们经常会注意到,这样的人才获取有利于大学的发展,要么是因为外国学生扩大了学生群体,要么是因为对外国学生收取更高的学费从而增加了大学的收入。[67] 研究型大学对此的兴趣特别明显。在这样的情况下,外国学生的录取不仅扩大了本科学生的申请人数,而且还使大学能够在研究生阶段招收更多的人才,提高了学校学术环境的整体质量和生产力。招收有天赋的外国研究生也提高了大学作为全球精英机构的声誉。与此同时，ICT 公司也与对外国学生的自由政策有着密切的关系，因为这些公司与公立大学的成功息息相关，技术领域的外国毕业生代表了公司在未来可以获得的优质劳动力。虽然公司可以从国外聘请外国毕业生，但国内大学的外国毕业生非常受国内雇主的欢迎。公司在当地找毕业生更加容易，因为他们拥有更优质的资历，并且比没有类似经验的外国毕业生更适应当地文化。[68]

最后，让我们讨论 HTC 在全球研发政策中的利害关系。正如第 1 章所提到的，大型 ICT 公司和研究型大学都参与跨国研发合作。因此，这些公司和大学自然会对这方面的宽松政策感兴趣，因为这种开放性增加了合作的可能性。考虑到海外研发投资，大型 ICT 公司可能是最感兴趣的一方。[69]这种兴趣是多方面的。第一，最简单的原因是，外国研发劳动力可能比国内劳动力廉价。尽管这种潜在动机是最简单和最具争议性的，但在大多数情况下，这种原因似乎并不是主要的考虑因素，大多数海外研发仍由发达国家在其他发达国家公司进行。[70]第二，外国研发中心允许公司参与资产增强式研发——获取与国内可用技术或知识相辅相成的特定技能或知识。随着近年来创新的增长速度和复杂性增加了对来自多个地区的专业知识的需求，这种动机显然更加重要。[71]第三，由于这些研发中心位于国外市场，它们完全有能力了解这些国家的消费市场并使产品适应当地的偏好和要求。也就是说，它们非常适合进行资产利用式研发。后两个因素对于激励与外国合作伙伴组建研发联盟也很重要，因为这些合作伙伴也可能具备专业知识或更了解国外市场。

虽然 HTC 的多元化是很显而易见的，但可以预测，HTC 会对面向全球创新的自由政策产生浓厚的兴趣，包括人力资本的迁移和全球研发。当然，需要注意的是，尽管公司机构也与这些政策有利害关系，但是学术机构对面向外国学生的政策更感兴趣。虽然双方都对全球研发合作感兴趣，但企业界（特别是大型跨国公司）与面向海外投资的政策利益攸关，而学术界则没有。基于此，下面转向下一个问题：HTC 何时能成功地争取到这些利益？

争议中的开放

以前，学者们往往把注意力集中在商业利益上，因为它们在影响国家对外经济政策中国家偏好方面起决定性的作用。[72] HTC 不仅包括一流的 ICT 公司，还包括著名的研究型大学。很显然，HTC 很有可能成为这一领域的巨头。最明显的是，高科技公司的利润很高。截至 2015 年，《财富》500 强中最赚钱的 25 家公司包括美国顶级 ICT 公司：苹果、微软、谷歌、IBM、英特尔、甲骨文、高通和思科。[73] 这样的利益关联为政治运动的游说和募捐提供了充足的资源。此外，高科技创新的积极溢出效应是巨大的，没有政策制定者希望被指责为"杀死下金蛋的鹅"①。[74] 事实上，随着美国军方开始依赖商业产品，一些政府官员现在将 ICT 公司的利润视为一种国家安全的问题：ICT 公司需要推动研发，这将有助于创造下一代军事技术。[75]

---

① 来源于《伊索寓言》，寓意为人们应该满足于现有的东西，切不可贪得无厌。——译者注

尽管研究型大学无法与一流 ICT 公司的财务资源相媲美，但作为一个群体，其拥有巨大的声望、与知名官员的私交，以及令人印象深刻的地域多样性。高科技利益团体具有潜在的强大作用，因为它们能够向政策制定者通报拟议的政策变化所带来的影响。[76] 鉴于高科技研究的高度技术性以及政策制定中固有的不确定性，政策制定者很难对政策变化将如何影响高科技行业有先见之明。ICT 公司和研究型大学在解决此类问题方面具有独特的优势。

当 HTC 迫切地需要开放全球创新时，人们很容易想象它会有自己的一套方式。然而，正如过去 20 年来针对利益集团的学术研究所表明的那样，强有力的商业利益并不总能成功地塑造国家政策。[77] 虽然企业往往掌握相当多的资金，但是这些资源几乎无法保证它们能参与政策的制定。[78] 事实上，即使商业利益统一，商界也很难实现其政治目标。[79] 这里的重点是，虽然金钱很重要，但是它不是决定游说成败的唯一因素。[80] HTC 追求其利益的环境相当重要。

在这方面，有组织的反对派可能是一个关键变量。几十年来，学者们一直认为，反对派在塑造特定利益集团是否能够成功实现其目标方面发挥着重要作用。[81] 即便如此，反对团体的潜在重要性并不总能受重视：游说影响力的定量研究有时会忽略竞争对手的活动。[82] 反过来，这种反对最可能的来源是其他有组织的利益集团。虽然政府官员（无论是来自立法部门还是行政部门）可以成为强有力的反对者，但是相对全面的研究表明，利益集团更常见的反对来自其他利益集团。[83] 实际上,最近的一项研究表明,游说者认为其他有组织的利益集团是其实现目标的主要障碍。[84]

在这项研究中,我不仅仅对是否存在相冲突的利益感兴趣,而且对三种不同类型的有组织的反对感兴趣。第一种可能性是HTC可能几乎不会遇到有组织的抵抗,在这种情况下,它通常能够成功实现目标。例如,其他相关群体并未将特定政策领域的开放视为威胁。实际上,全球化通常会使劳工面对复杂的问题,使得感知利益的具体方式成为一个重要变量。[85] 例如,移民对薪资的影响是一个复杂的主题,此外,国外劳动力的涌入对就业和薪资的影响仍不明晰。[86] 调查显示,高技能移民比低技能移民更受美国人的欢迎。[87] 在外商投资方面,劳工的利益也可能不明确。如果仅将外商投资视为主导国家的工作岗位流出,高科技劳工很可能会反对这一观点。或者说,国外的工作岗位可能被看作是对主导国家工作的补充——事实上可能就是这样。[88] 例如,海外研发首先需要适应当地的情况来促进销售。在这种情况下,提高主导国家在海外的产品质量可能被视为至关重要的,这也非常符合劳工的利益。

第二种可能性是HTC将面临劳工的抵抗。最可能的反对来源是高科技劳工,或者说是主导产业的高技能劳动力。例如,最近关于技术移民的政治研究表明,同一产业的本地工人将技术移民视为威胁。[89] 当高技能的工作受到许可证的要求并且技术娴熟的本地人增加对获得地方级许可程序的控制时,外国劳工的流入会受到阻碍。[90] 技术娴熟的当地人可能会试图通过国家专业协会或与国家劳工运动合作来影响国家政策。

如果是这样的话，问题就变成了 HTC 及其劳工对手的相对政治力量。一般而言，高科技劳工很可能难以与 HTC 争夺影响力。虽然财务资源并不能决定游说结果，但是当双方的资源不平衡时，财务资源可能很重要，因为这很有可能是决定性因素。[91] 问题就在于高科技劳工是否可以通过采用"外部"或"基层"策略，例如，通过大规模动员向政策制定者或雇主施压。[92] 这可能很难。劳工在特定产业中动员的能力在很大程度上受该产业工人工会成员的影响。[93] 高技能劳工的工会化率往往较低，特别是在软件领域，这些人往往将自己定义为独立的专业人员而不是集体。[94] 尽管高科技专业协会可能会与国家劳工运动建立联盟，但这种合作面临着一些制约因素。大规模动员是一项复杂而昂贵的工作，高技术专业人员（特别是当许多人不是工会成员时）很难说服更广泛的劳工运动将其全部能力投入他们的事业。[95] 此外，国家劳工运动可能会在一些利益问题上出现冲突。具体而言，工会面临移民政治的两难境地：是倡导限制性政策，关闭劳动力市场，还是支持开放以便将移民纳入劳工运动并对所有人执行统一的标准。[96] 因此，HTC 在面对劳工的反抗时很可能会相对成功，当然，如果没有遇到有组织的抵抗的话，HTC 可能会更成功。

第三种可能性是 HTC 将面临大型公民团体的抵抗。这些团体包括：能够动员群众的游说团体、捐赠者或围绕其职业或专业以外问题的活动家，如塞拉俱乐部或全国步枪协会。[97] 这些团体可能是很难对付的反对者。事实上，近期的研究表明，在反对商业利益方面，公民团体比工会更容易成功。[98]这项研究显示，在能够用大规模动员能力来抵抗HTC的财富、声望和专业知识的情况下，他们很容易发挥作用。这种动员可以采取多种形式，从省力的策略（例如，向当选的代表办公室打电话或发送电子邮件）到高效的策略（例如，亲自与立法者会面），公民团体往往擅长使用低成本的方式。特别是最近的研究表明，加入美国的公民团体大大增加了个人与国会联系的可能性，而加入贸易或专业团体则没有这样的影响。[99]从大的角度来看，这些接触很重要。它们不仅告知政策制定者选民对特定问题的情绪，而且还告知这种情绪的强度。如果没有这种接触，信息决策者在获取这些信息上比较困难。[100]一个协调良好的动员活动可以证明特定群体在选举日动员选民的能力。[101]因此，相比没有抵抗或面临劳工抵抗的情况，当HTC面临来自大规模公民群体的反对时，HTC更有可能实现其目标。

以前文的讨论为例，我们可以提出以下三个关于主导国家对合作开放程度的提议。首先，当HTC在推动开放方面面临的阻力很小或没有阻力时，实现其目标的难度相对较小，而主导国家将采取相对开放的方法。其次，当HTC面临来自有组织的劳工的阻力时，政策制定会更具争议性，政策的开放程度将小于第一种情况。然而，正如论证的那样，劳工与HTC竞争的能力有限，因此对开放性的限制也是有限的。最后，当HTC面临来自一个或多个擅长基层动员的大型公民群体有组织的抵制时，它在推动开放方面将面临更大的困难，而主导国家的政策的开放程度将弱于前两个情况。

在进行下一部分的内容之前，我先提出一个词——有序。前面的提议集中在主导国家内部社会利益竞争的相对影响。通过赋权 HTC 及其在影响国家偏好方面的潜在反对者，我采用了一种自由主义的理论方法，特别是一种能将商业观念和自由主义结合起来的方法。[102] 然而，当主要的政治动态涉及 HTC 与国家行政部门之间的博弈时，该理论并未被应用于预测政策结果。正如本研究所做的，出于易处理性和简约性，关注政治进程在对外经济政策研究中很常见。[103] 然而，在某些情况下，特别是当 HTC 对于开放性的追求，与政府部门为确保国家安全的首选方式冲突时，国家与社会的博弈将成为主要动力。在这种情况下，可能会产生一系列结果。HTC 必然不能就国家安全问题向行政机构规定条款。但是，政府部门必须关注重要的国有企业和大学的发展。当主要内容技术性很强且政府信息有限的时候，政府部门还需要确保对商业的限制不会产生意想不到的后果。结论部分将对此进行讨论。

可考虑的解释

这里概述的理论侧重于高科技行业的人所扮演的角色和其他能够推动主导国家迈向全球创新的国内利益。然而，对于主导国家的政策还有其他解释。现在探讨几种具体的替代方案，从更具战略性的方法开始，然后转向其他相关的国内政治的解释。

第一种解释认为主导国家的方法是国家驱动的蓄意行为,而不是社会驱动的随意的行为。具体来说,主导国家的政策可能反映出围绕全球创新收益分配的担忧。著名的现实主义学者认为,在与新兴国家进行商业贸易时,主导国家应该对其相对收益高度敏感,因为这些国家的发展有可能动摇其首要地位。[104] 从这方面来看,鉴于技术领先在历史上产生并维持主导国家地位的方式,创新方面的合作似乎是一个特别敏感的问题。[105] 尽管如此,安全问题并不意味着全面禁止主导国家和新兴国家之间的合作。相反,主导国家可能在只有限制合作才能有望改善相对地位的情况下,才会这样做。其他学者认为,当两个条件都满足时有可能出现这种情况。[106] 首先,有效限制合作必须是可行的。如果主导国家不对相关资源或机会拥有垄断权,则单方限制可能无效,反过来,多边措施可能难以安排。其他国家可能不会主动分担主导国家的担忧,也可能寻求搭便车。[107] 其次,对于占据主导地位的国家而言,对商业的限制成本必须要低于相关竞争对手。简而言之,我们应该期待主导国家的开放性能反映出其相对于新兴国家的相对收益计算方法。我称其为"战略性霸权假设"。

还有一些关于国内政治的解释,它们有不同的关注点。第一个侧重于广大公众更广泛的信念和态度。一些学者认为,商业利益共有的问题往往是"具有意识形态的,附有党派的,并且在公众中非常突出"。[108] 在这种情况下,除非得到公众舆论的大力支持,否则商业利益难以普及。那么,当公众舆论有利于其目标时,

HTC 将是最成功的。我称其为"舆论假设"。

第二种解释关注政党及其与关键利益集团的关系。鉴于后者的财富、突出性和在国家中的重要性，高科技利益群体可以期望与进步党和保守党都建立关系。然而，这些政党很可能与 HTC 的潜在对手形成鲜明对比。与保守派同行相比，工党运动通常与进步党派的联系更紧密。与此同时，根据其使命的性质和成员资格，公民团体通常可以划分为更接近进步或保守的政党。因此，随着时间的推移，这些潜在对手的力量可能是依情况而定，而不是一致的。具体地说，我们可以预测，当进步党占主导地位时，有组织的劳工将具有更大的力量来抵抗 HTC。还可以预测，特定公民群体抵抗 HTC 的能力将根据其优先党派的政治命运而变化。简而言之，我们观察到劳工和公民群体应对 HTC 议程的能力存在广泛差异，而不是像之前的理论所讲的那样，始终如一地提高公民团体的能力。我称其为"优先党派假设"。

第三种解释关注国内政治问题，主要是关于 HTC 是否在努力捍卫或改变现状。改变现状通常比捍卫现状更困难：政策变化需要克服政治体系中所有相关的否决点，而捍卫现状只需要在一个否决点上取得成功。盲目支持、政策制定者的短见、对意外后果的恐惧，以及威胁性变化即将来临时动员的特殊利益，都会强化现状偏见。[109] 因此，通过关注 HTC 挑战的性质，我们可以解释政策结果的变化。简而言之，在捍卫现状的时候，HTC 应该会相对容易成功；在试图改变现状的时候，HTC 会面临更多的困难。我称其为"现状假设"。

第四种解释关注联盟的力量。尽管利益集团的结盟非常普遍，但研究往往未能发现这些联盟在制定政策方面能起到有效的作用。然而，近期的研究表明，在其他条件相同的情况下，更大和更有凝聚力的联盟对政策有更大的影响。[110]这意味着，相较于公司与学术机构其中一方非常不活跃的情况，要么是出于搭便车，要么是因为在相关问题上的利益不大，只有当双方都积极参与特定问题时，HTC 才能取得最大的成功。此外，研究发现，一般的商会并不特别强大，但商业团体往往占上风，因为它们的数量相对较多，而且当它们结盟时，力量得到聚合。[111]这一发现意味着，在追求共同目标的情况下，当企业与其他商业团体进行联盟时，HTC 最有可能成功。因此，我们可以根据联盟的力量做出两个预测。首先，当 HTC 的双方都积极参与特定情况时，HTC 将取得最大的成功。其次，当 HTC 的企业与其他商业利益结盟时，HTC 将取得最大的成功。我称其为"联盟力量假设"。

理论检验

本书通过一系列案例研究来检验本章提出的命题，这些案例研究侧重于美国的全球创新政策。第一方面关注技术娴熟的高科技人群流向美国。第二方面侧重于学术人员的流动，特别是学生流向美国大学。第三方面侧重于美国对全球研发的政策，特别是对外投资领域。这三方面涉及不同的政治格局，使我们能够评估不同程度的有组织的抗议对HTC所带来的影响。此外，第一个案例研究包括随着时间推移对HTC有不同的抵制，这使得我们能够在控制政策领域的同时对该变量所造成的影响进行推断。

接下来的三章首先概述了相关领域美国的政策。然后，每一章都深入研究美国政策制定过程背后的政治因素，尤其关注利益集团在影响美国政策中的作用。这些深入的案例研究执行三个关键的分析任务，它们记录了HTC面临的反对的性质。第一，我设想了三种有组织的反对派：没有抵抗、有组织的劳工的抵抗和公民团体的抵抗。第二，每一个案例研究记录了HTC在开放性方面的利益，并且评估相关案例中追求这种利益时成功的程度。这部分分析相对较长，并涉及详细的过程追踪，使得我们能够确定针对HTC的反对在影响结果方面的相对重要性。[112]第三，每章的结论部分都讨论了在特定情况下，相互冲突的解释如何能够解释观察到的结果。

在继续接下来的内容之前，我们需要讨论衡量标准的问题。在之前的部分，我注意到每个案例研究都会评估HTC在追求开放性利益方面的成功程度。因此，我们需要一种有效的方法来比较案例研究的结果。通过移民政策来比较开放性是相对直接的：关键变量是跨国人员流动是否受到年度上限的限制，如果受到限制，最高限额是什么。[113]然而，应该如何比较移民政策与全球研发政策之间的开放水平还不清楚。从本质上来讲，全球研发比跨境人员流动更难以监管，这两个领域也涉及不同的指标。尽管如此，正如以下章节所阐述的那样，美国政策制定者已经有机会限制本书所关注的每个政策领域的开放性。在这种情况下，通过开放是否实现来关注进程是非常有用的。也就是说，询问 HTC 在相关的案例中成功实现其具体目标的程度是有用的。它是完全成功、部分成功还是不成功？通过关注 HTC 的成功水平，我们可以比较不同经济活动类型的案例的结果。

在本书的结论部分，每个章节中的案例分析都得到了更广泛的比较案例分析的补充。本次讨论还阐述了本章提到的可考虑的解释在三个案例研究中的应用。

结 论

本章提出了一种理论来解释主导国家的全球创新方法。这一理论的出发点是主导国家的经济和其中的社会利益。从历史角度来看，占主导地位的国家拥有极具创新性的经济，这在产生和维持其在国际体系中的地位方面发挥了重要作用。近几十年来，HTC 在全球创新开放性中具有集体利益，其主导国家创新的角色已经成为一股强大的政治力量。反过来，HTC 在追求这一目标方面的成功取决于有组织团体的抵制程度。接下来的章节将对这一理论进行检验。

第 3 章
旋转门：高技能劳动力

第 3 章 旋转门：高技能劳动力

尽管美国在创新方面领先世界，但美国的许多创新者都出生在国外。事实上，近几十年来，外籍创新者的数量显著增加。例如，1993 年美国科技和工程领域获得博士学位的劳动力中有 27% 为外籍人口。到了 2013 年，这一数字已跃升至 42%。[1] 中国和印度继而成为高技能劳动力的主要输出国。2013 年，在美国科技和工程领域获得博士学位的劳动力中，中印两国占 36% 以上，[2] 但美国对技术移民的开放程度在过去几十年中变化显著。美国在 20 世纪 90 年代末和 21 世纪初明显更加开放，但此后开放程度较低。

本章将分析美国政策的奇妙演变。该分析同时考虑了 EB 签证（也称为基于就业的绿卡）和临时签证（特别是 H-1B 签证计划）。首要的关注点是 H-1B 签证计划，因为该计划随着时间的推移发生了很大的变化。本章的第一部分概述了美国针对技术移民的政策及其自 1990 年以来的演变。第二部分记录并阐述了 1998—2004 年技术移民的扩展。在此期间，HTC 主要面临有组织的劳动力的阻挠。这是一场双边竞赛，HTC 在此过程中通过一系列立法获得了胜利。第三部分重点关注 2005—2016 年，HTC 为提高 H-1B 上限所做的努力与更广泛的美国移民政策自由化的努力交织在一起。由于这一变化，HTC 还不得不应对大型公民团体组织的激烈抵抗。自 2004 年以来，这些团体有效地阻碍了扩大技术移民政策的实施。

功能失调的系统

尽管美国经常被描述为"移民国家",但是随着时间的推移,美国对受过良好教育的海外劳动力的开放程度发生了很大的变化。在过去的 25 年,《1990 年移民法》在很多方面定义了美国的政策。该法案将 EB 签证的数量从每年 54 000 个增加到每年 140 000 个,并分配到五个就业类别,还提高了高技能劳动力及其家属所占的份额。[3] 该法案还修订了临时招收技术劳动力进入美国的计划。从 20 世纪 50 年代开始,H-1 签证计划已经承认"具有显著优点和能力"的劳动力"暂时来美国提供服务",并且没有对这种签证设定上限。[4] 1989 年,H-1 计划分为 H-1A 和 H-1B 签证计划。H-1A 计划是为护士设计的,H-1B 计划是为 H-1 类别的其他技术劳动力设计的。《1990 年移民法》修改了 H-1B 签证计划,并为在科学、艺术、教育、商业或体育等方面具有"非凡能力"的个人创建了 O 签证。

1990 年 H-1B 签证计划的变化影响深远。该法案删除了"杰出的功绩和能力"的表述,并在"专业职业"中引入了工人概念。这些职业需要具备以下要求:高度专业化的知识;获得专业(或同等学历)学士学位或更高学位。[5] 雇主必须提交劳动条件申请,以雇用获得 H-1B 签证的工人,但不需要检测国内劳动力市场。新的 H-1B 签证有效期为 3 年,可以延长 3 年。该计划的上限为每年签发 65 000 个签证。[6]

总之,《1990 年移民法》中关于技术移民的规定反映了一项蓄意的计划。在众议院中,这些条款的主要设计者——移民小组委员会主席布鲁斯·莫里森（Bruce Morrison）试图限制这些外籍工人的角色，并强调通过绿卡系统进行移民。正如莫里森后来所说："我们的目标是通过运用我们与其他国家相较而言的最大的经济和公民优势来提升美国的经济竞争力，这在世界各国中几乎是独一无二的。美国不仅仅承认外国人是工人……我们还欢迎来自世界各地的高技能人才成为新美国人。"[7]因此，H-1B计划受到限制，EB签证数量大幅增加，H-1B工作人员也有望能够迅速拥有移民身份。[8]

然而，该计划在法案通过之前就开始瓦解了。为了促进EB签证的使用，莫里森试图用收费以及一项较为有限的劳动力短缺评估取代该计划中的劳动力认证要求，即一个国内劳动力市场测试。理由是认证要求在很大程度上是毫无意义的，因为这涉及法律而不是对劳动力市场的认真分析，并且每年认证更多的EB签证会造成扰乱性的处理延迟。相比之下，以收费为基础的制度可以更快地处理申请，并确保雇主只在出现迫切需要时才雇用外籍工人。最后，国会众议院筹款委员会的领导层将这些费用视为"税收"，这并不在莫里森小组委员会的职权范围内。[9]1990年以后，EB签证计划保留了劳动力认证要求。

20世纪90年代，美国技术移民系统进一步偏离了《1990年移民法》背后的愿景。缓慢发展的EB签证系统对雇主没有吸引力，并且在20世纪90年代后5年从未达到140 000的上限。相比之下，备受欢迎的H-1B签证计划在1998年、2000年和2004年得到了扩展。这些扩展包括对某些类别的申请人的豁免和年度上限的临时增加，2001—2003年，这一数字上升至195 000（如图3.1）。美国H-1B签证劳动力数量大幅增加。事实上，近年来，有些人认为H-1B签证人口已经超650 000。[10]其带来的间接结果是EB签证计划的恶化。随着越来越多的H-1B劳动力寻求绿卡，经历耗时的认证过程，以及可以为各个国家发行的绿卡数量达到上限，出现了大量积压的绿卡申请。在某些情况下，这种等待的时间超过10年。1990年以来，外籍工人的范围已经扩大，从外籍工人到移民身份的过渡已成为一个有很大问题的过程。

在过去的20年里，H-1B签证计划的主要用户是ICT公司，而大学和其他研究机构则代表了较小但更稳定的需求来源。[11]硅谷雇主对签证的需求特别强烈。情况并非总是这样：1995年，超过一半的H-1B签证用于物理治疗师，只有1/4用于计算机专家。[12]然而，到了2000年，58%的H-1B接受者都集中在计算机相关领域，12%分布在"建筑、工程和测量领域"（包括电气工程师）。[13]随着该计划的发展，印度成为这些劳动力的主要来源，中国位居第二。这也是一个巨大的变化。1989年，获得H-1B签证的劳动力主要来自菲律宾（24%）和英国（10%）。[14]中国和印度总共仅占这类劳动力的3%。然而，到了2000年，49%的H-1B劳动力来自印度，9%来自中国，3%来自加拿大。[15]截至2015年，印度的份额已跃升至71%，中国的份额为10%。[16]

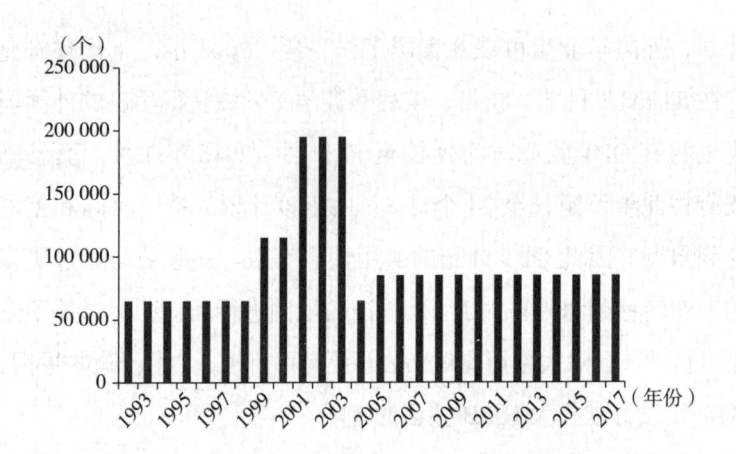

图 3.1　1992—2017 年 H-1B 签证数量年度上限

资料来源：美国公民及移民服务局（U.S. Citizenship and Immigration Services），H-1B 签证职位专业性工人的特征：2015 财年（*Characteristics of H-1B Specialty Occupation Workers: Fiscal Year 2015*，华盛顿特区：美国国土安全部，2016 年），3~4 页。

2004 年后，H-1B 签证计划在免税方面和上限增长方面都有所停止，这令许多高科技企业感到非常沮丧并促使它们寻找变通方法。例如，这些公司可以通过 L-1A 签证和 L-1B 签证计划将外籍劳动力从海外吸引到美国，这些计划没有年度限制。因此，当 H-1B 签证出现问题时，一些公司已经在海外聘请了高技能外籍劳动力，然后将他们转移到美国。然而，这种解决方法并非十分奏效。L-1 签证的申请人必须在申请前为公司工作至少一年，并且他们的申请受到不同标准的约束，可能面临相当严格的审查。另一个变通的方法是聘请从美国大学科学和工程专业毕业的外国学生。一般而言，根据 F-1 签证的 OPT（选择性实践培训）

计划，外国毕业生可以在美国工作一年。2008 年，布什政府允许在 STEM（科学、技术、工程和数学）领域获得学位的外国毕业生将其 OPT 就业时间延长至 17 个月。2016 年 3 月，奥巴马政府将此项目延长至 24 个月。[17] 由于该计划的持续时间和范围受到限制，因此 OPT 计划的实用性也有限。一些公司通过更多的工作转移到海外来对 H-1B 签证的限制进行回应，但这并不总是可行的，且对大公司比对小公司更有可行性。[18] 由于这些原因，HTC 继续寻求扩大 H-1B 签证的上限。

为什么美国在 1998 年、2000 年和 2004 年扩大 H-1B 签证计划呢？为什么美国从那时起不提高技术移民签证的上限呢？本章其余部分回答了这些问题。

"高科技界"的巨大胜利：1998—2004 年

20 世纪 90 年代前半期，对于高科技公司和整个商业环境来讲，技术移民的法定限制并不是一个严重的问题。《1990 年移民法》将 EB 签证限额增加到 140 000，这实际上超出了商界的要求。[19] 当然，有人担心 H-1B 签证计划的限制，但就像一位杰出的商业倡导者所说的那样，这些都是"理论上的"性质。[20]《1990 年移民法》通过后，65 000 个 H-1B 签证的上限超过了商界的要求，并且在 20 世纪 90 年代的头五年从未达到上限。[21] 就 HTC 而言，它在《1990 年移民法》中关于限制的谈判中并没有发挥突出作用。1990年商业联盟游说中支持技术移民的"主要推动者"是美国商会、全国制造商协会和美国移民律师协会。虽然技术公司对此表示了一些兴趣，但"并不像今后几年那样有组织，也没有那么集中"。[22]

随着ICT产业在20世纪最后五年中蓬勃发展，HTC对技术移民的限制，特别是H-1B签证计划，产生越来越大的兴趣。由于没有复杂的认证程序，H-1B签证计划成为向美国科技公司汇集外国劳动力的首选工具。H-1B签证计划的具体用户各不相同。目前使用该计划的美国ICT公司包括思科、英特尔、微软、摩托罗拉和甲骨文等。[23]该计划也受到印度公司的高度欢迎，包括印孚瑟斯、塔塔咨询服务公司和威普罗。这些公司开发了一项业务，为美国公司提供H-1B劳动力作为合同工——这种模式也被包括埃森哲、德勤和IBM在内的一些美国公司采用。20世纪90年代末，大学在该计划中的表现并不突出，每年获得的签证数量为6 000~10 000个。[24]部分原因是大学的招聘相对缓慢，它们很难与私营部门竞争有限的签证池。正如哈佛大学联邦关系高级主管凯文·凯西（Kevin Casey）2000年10月所提出的："在过去的两年，随着H-1B签证的加速使用，企业正在把签证名额都用光，所以当我们开始进行招聘时，企业已经把名额都用完了。"[25]

随着签证的上限成为制约因素，知名科技公司开始游说美国政府维持和扩大该计划。1995年，ITAA聘请美国国会前工作人员和移民问题游说专家哈里斯·米勒（Harris Miller）为主席。[26]在思科、英特尔、微软等ICT公司的资金支持下，一个新的游说团体，ABLI（商业移民律师联盟）成立了，专注于 H-1B 签证问题。[27] 这种转变成为许多高科技公司走向更广泛的"成熟时期"的一部分，这些公司早先拒绝了政治的参与，特别是华盛顿。[28] 正如米勒在 2000 年回忆的那样："五年前，几乎没有人（游说过）……他们没有参与政治进程……他们有一个基本的信念，即如果他们忽视了华盛顿，它就会消失。"[29] 提高 H-1B 签证上限的运动将成为高科技公司可以共同发挥多大影响力的例子。

高科技利益群体具有一系列使其获得成功的优势。首先，20 世纪 90 年代中期，立法者发现高科技公司可能是竞选资金的有利来源。美国总统比尔·克林顿在 1996 年的连任竞选活动中走进硅谷，这甚至改变了他在证券欺诈诉讼中的立场，民主党全国委员会也从中获益。[30] 虽然克林顿不再参选，副总统艾伯特·戈尔正在为自己的总统竞选做准备并培养技术公司的支持。民主党人还担心，如果他们拒绝硅谷，硅谷将成为支持共和党人的基地。

事实上，共和党战略家们希望在 H-1B 签证问题上的分歧会使硅谷与民主党，尤其是与戈尔之间产生隔阂，这将为共和党创造可以利用的机会。[31] 最后，同样重要的是，科技公司有极好的信誉并且能够接触立法者。1998 年，一位知名记者撰写了一篇关于 TechNet 的文章——这是一个由硅谷高管组成的团体："TechNet 能够与最高级别官员建立亲密关系的能力确实令人印象深刻。TechNet 在其成员和各种政治家之间已经举办了 70 多场'简报发布会'——经常被比作'新经济毕业研讨会',参与人员包括纽特·金里奇(Newt Gingrich)议长和副总统戈尔。"[32]

增加 H-1B 签证上限的主要反对意见来自劳工。一般来说,高科技劳动力倾向于避开工会。事实上,根据美国劳工部的数据,截至 20 世纪 90 年代末,只有不到 2% 的北美高科技劳动力是工会成员。[33] 即便如此,一些劳动力属于政治上活跃的专业协会。其中,IEEE-USA(美国电气和电子工程师协会)在反对 H-1B 签证扩张方面最为突出。1998 年 3 月,IEEE-USA 主席约翰·赖纳特(John Reinert)告诉美国国会:"高科技公司劳动力短缺的说法被夸大了,可用的国内劳动力供应被低估了,高科技公司高估了移民的智慧。"[34] 赖纳特敦促美国国会让劳动力市场纠正任何现有的不平衡现象,而不是将移民作为"快速的解决办法"。

截至 1998 年,IEEE-USA 大约有 22 万名成员,但由于多种原因,它在政治舞台上与高科技公司的竞争中处于下风。[35] 首先,有限的资金限制了它可以花费在说客或竞选捐款上的金额。其次,该组织在组织基层抗议活动方面处于不利地位,因为其成员往往远离政治,并且在观念上持自由主义态度。该组织还存在内部分歧,学术成员往往对工业界人士所关注的事情毫不在意。IEEE-USA 也受到其上级 IEEE 保持其地位的压力。作为一个成员遍布全球的组织,IEEE 担心对 H-1B 签证计划的批评将诋毁其中一些非美国成员。IEEE-USA 也难以与另一方的"明星力量"和公众信誉相媲美,例如微软首席执行官比尔·盖茨。可以肯定的是,IEEE-USA 可以依赖其他劳工组织的支持,特别是 AFL-

CIO（美国劳工联合会和工业组织大会），他们认为 H-1B 签证计划容易被滥用。然而，AFL-CIO 的影响因技术工人的工会密度低而受到限制。AFL-CIO 前移民政策主管表示，缺乏"宣传层面的工人声音"，使得针对 H-1B 签证问题的游说和基层行动变得困难。[36]

目前，一些反移民团体也反对 H-1B 签证的扩张，但这些团体几乎没有基层动员的能力。最成熟的团体 FAIR（美国移民改革联合会）成立于 1979 年。但是，FAIR 的公平竞争规模较小。1998 年 3 月，该组织声称拥有约 70 000 名成员，其他人则认为其成员数可能大幅下降。[37] 1996 年，一家名为 NumbersUSA（数字美国）的新组织成立，其任务是减少移民。NumbersUSA 最终将超过其他反移民群体，并通过互联网更有效地动员活动人员。然而，20 世纪 90 年代末期，NumbersUSA 刚刚站稳脚跟。那时它在华盛顿没有全职的游说办公室，截至 2000 年 1 月，它只有不到 4 000 名"电子邮件活动人员"。[38] 简而言之，在 20 世纪 90 年代末，在 H-1B 签证问题上，反移民运动几乎没有能力与 HTC 竞争。

正是在这种背景下，1998—2004 年，高科技利益集团取得了多项立法上的胜利。第一场胜利涉及防守。在共和党议员拉马尔·史密斯（Lamar Smith）和艾伦·辛普森（Alan Simpson）分别在众议院和参议院提出的限制合法和非法移民的法案中，提出了对 H-1B 签证计划的限制。企业和其他支持移民的团体成功地剥夺了对合法移民的限制，这确保了与 H-1B 签证相关的条款不会在其他反移民浪潮中通过。[39]即便如此，在1998年早期，提高H-1B签证上限的运动仍然面临不确定的前景。1998年1月，美国商务部部长威廉·戴利（William Daley）表示克林顿政府不支持增加上限，他称之为"在政治上不可行"。[40]相反，他敦促技术公司的高管去关注以前被忽视的群体，例如，妇女、少数民族和残疾人。他还呼吁他们与学校更紧密地合作。"与学校交谈，就像你与供应商交谈那样，"他告诉商界领袖，"学校为你们提供了最重要的人才资源。"[41]1998年3月，当美国审计总署（现为政府问责办公室）发布了一项针对IT工作人员供应的报告时，美国的政治局势变得更加复杂。1997年，美国商务部和ITAA各自发布了一份报告，称美国存在IT劳动力短缺的问题。作为回应，美国审计总署发布的报告指出，美国商务部和ITAA的报告分别存在"严重的"和"重大的"方法上的缺陷，需要有更多的研究来证明是否确实存在这种短缺。[42]这一结论似乎支持了IEEE-USA这样抵制H-1B签证扩张的群体，它们认为短缺的呼声"言过其实"。[43]

如果高科技公司努力证明存在劳动力短缺问题，那么未来几个月华盛顿将继续存在这种情况。第一次胜利来自参议院。参议员斯宾塞·亚伯拉罕（Spencer Abraham）1997年聘请ITAA报告的作者为他的移民政策主任，亚伯拉罕赞成在3月初的立法上提高上限。5月18日，参议院以相对较少的反对意见，即78：20的票数比，通过并批准了这项法案。然而，提高上限的努力将面临众议院和白宫的更大阻力。在众议院，作为司法委员会主席，拉马尔·史密斯（Lamar Smith）是关键人物，他显然对提高上限缺乏热情。克林顿总统继而威胁称,如果提高上限没有对美国工人提供实质性保护,就要否决立法。具体而言,政府希望立法为培训计划提供资金,包括对美国工人的保障。反对派开展了一轮针对高科技企业的游说。政府部门首席谈判代表,副总统艾伯特·戈尔接受了惠普和英特尔等公司高管的电话,而一些CEO则致函白宫。[44]

最终出现了一个解决方案。克林顿和史密斯同意大幅度提高H-1B签证的上限:在1999和2000财年允许发放115 000个签证,在2001财年允许发放107 500个签证。作为交换,通过在签证申请上征收新费用为工人培训和教育提供资金。然而,工人保障措施仅限于"依赖H-1B签证"的公司。[45]对员工人数超过50人的公司来说,只有当获得H-1B签证的工人至少占其员工总数的15%时才适用。这项规定确保了保障措施不适用于英特尔和微软这些知名的美国公司,因为这些公司足够大,可以雇用许多获得H-1B签证的工人而无须达到门槛。在白宫表示会接受这些条款之后,1997年9月24日,众议院通过了从288条修订为133条的立法。由于参议员汤姆·哈金(Tom Harkin)的反对,新议案在参议院重新提出时几乎停滞不前,但高科技公司一直坚持不懈地努力。正如一份报告所说,ITAA和TechNet在幕后"紧张忙乱地"设计解决方案。[46]最后,该法案纳入《1999财年综合紧急拨款法》,由总统于10月21日签署生效。[47]

结果是HTC取得了巨大的胜利。尽管1998年1月克林顿政府对提高签证上限仍然持反对态度,但到了7月,他们开始寻求协商。10月，克林顿总统签署了一项法案，其中的保障措施不适用于大型雇主。由于签证法案和其他立法的胜利，《华盛顿邮报》报道称"高科技是国会山之王"。[48]英特尔的政府事务经理总结道："对于我们来说，忧虑和厄运兼具。"[49]ITAA副主席乔纳森·恩格兰德（Jonathan Englund）称之为"一个标志性的日子"，标志着"技术在华盛顿发挥影响力的时代已然来临"。[50]克林顿总统在法案通过方面并没有浪费时间，他在9月众议院通过该方案后立即前往加利福尼亚进行了为期一周的筹款活动。[51]

意料之中的是反对该法案的劳工感到非常愤怒。"白宫向工业集团投降，"IEEE-USA主席约翰·赖纳特说，"结果是促成了一项让成千上万美国工人处于危险之中的法案。"[52]AFL-CIO专业雇员部门主席杰克·戈罗德纳（Jack Golodner）认为该法案中的保障措施"只是表面的"，因为它不适用于绝大多数使用签证计划的公司。[53]众议院的一名民主党员工抱怨道，政府已经让国会中那些寻求更强有力的工人保护的人受到了谴责。可以肯定的是，劳工在一方面确实占上风：增长只是暂时的，2001年之后上限将恢复到65 000。然而，除了劳工对民主党的影响，其中还有更多的故事。正如一位前行业代表后来指出的，随着时间的推移，立法者有强烈的动机将这种临时提高作为一种将竞选捐款最大化的手段。[54]与持续增长相比，临时提高的方式确保技术公司将继续征求关键立法者的支持。

情况确实如此。2000年，高科技公司再次推动提高签证的上限。这一次，为了扩大支持，他们努力与研究型大学结盟。高等教育说客最初不愿意参与其中，因为大多数额外的 H-1B 签证名额将被工业界占用，大学竞争稀缺签证的难度很大。作为回应，高科技公司提出修改其拟议立法。根据新提案，来自大学和非营利组织的申请人申请的 H-1B 签证不再计入年度上限，这使学术和企业雇主都更加轻松。高等教育机构签署并同意支持该法案。[55]

增加 H-1B 签证上限的主要抵制又一次来自劳工。2月，AFL-CIO 发布了一项有里程碑意义的声明，要求将无证外国劳动力和其他移民措施合法化，但该组织仍然反对像 H-1B 签证计划这样的客工计划。[56] 主要民主党人士赞成提高签证上限，并随后与 AFL-CIO 主席约翰·斯威尼（John Sweeney）会面，以减轻他对 H-1B 扩张的反对，但斯威尼仍然持反对意见。[57] 硅谷的公平就业联盟（the Coalition for Fair Employment）代表了许多高科技领域的黑人劳动力，该组织对歧视表示担忧，并且反对提高上限。[58] 就其本身而言，IEEE-USA 调整了立场。该组织认为，问题在于 H-1B 工人就像"契约仆人"，因为如果他们想要获得绿卡，他们就不能离开最初赞助他们的雇主。[59] 因此 IEEE-USA 认为 H-1B 工人应该获得加急的 EB 签证，这将使工人获得更大的自由，而不是简单地反对提高上限。这项提议源于一种真正的信念，即这种改变会改善问题，但它也反映了一种认识，即单纯反对 H-1B 计划不太可能成功。[60]

反对派的弱点很快就显现出来。5月，克林顿政府表示支持硅谷，提议在未来三年内将 H-1B 上限提高到每年 20 万。[61] 随后在国会西班牙裔核心小组中的民主党人寻求通过名为《拉丁裔公平性提案》的修正案来扩大该法案后，立法很快就失去了推动力。[62]这些将为政治难民扩大现有的合法化计划，同时也允许在1986年之前进入美国的无证移民申请公民身份。最后，民主党领导人决定通过其他方式推行这些提案，并允许将以H-1B计划为重点的法案搬上台面。[63]

该法案很容易地通过了。10月3日，参议院以96票赞成1票反对的结果通过了该法案，众议院在几个小时之后以口头表决的方式通过了该法案。新法案将在2000年、2001年和2003年将H-1B签证上限提高到195 000。它还提供给研究型大学名额，为高等教育、政府研究部门和非营利机构工作的外国人将不再计入签证上限。在过去六年内被H-1B签证拒绝的工人也获得了豁免。新法案还删除了在其他就业类别中有额外签证的EB签证申请中对每个国家的限制——主要受影响的是来自印度的申请人。该法案还制订了新计划，以改善美国工人在科学和技术领域的教育和培训，并鼓励美国移民及归化局加速处理所有与移民有关的申请。[64]

新法案的通过是HTC的一大胜利，科技公司在新法案的制定中所起的作用得到了广泛关注。据一位立法者所说，事实上，许多立法者只是害怕对抗如此强大的利益集团。

犹他州参议员罗伯特·贝内特（Robert Bennett）说："一旦明确签证法案即将通过，所有人都会报名参加，因此没有人能够被指责反对高科技。"事实上，有很多人反对这个法案，但因为他们正在利用HTC进行竞选筹款，所以他们不想在公开场合承认这一点。[65]在美国全国公共电台的节目中，乔治城大学的一位教授林赛·洛威尔（Lindsay Lowell）将 ICT 产业称为"一个巨人"。[66]反对派的弱点同样明显。IEEE-USA 主席保罗·克斯特克（Paul Kostek）表示："工业界愿意花钱来投票……无论如何雄辩地提出（反对提高上限的）情况，都没关系。"[67]或者正如记者胡安·威廉姆斯（Juan Williams）对一个反对者所说："在这场斗争中，你们没有政治权力的支持。所有人都与高科技人才为伍。"[68]一边是强大的支持者，另一边是弱势的反对者，这场争论的结果很容易预测。

21 世纪初期，H-1B 签证问题的紧张局势一度消退。部分原因是签证供应增加，但这也反映了在该法案通过后不久互联网泡沫破裂，因此减少了对签证的需求。事实上，当 2003 年 10 月 H-1B 上限恢复到 65 000 时，《华尔街日报》就曾报道，随着科技公司命运的起伏，它们对签证的需求下降，因此上限的削减只引起了硅谷"相对较小的不安"。[69]然而，2004 年，H-1B 签证的竞争再次加剧，该计划成为美国国会另一场争议的焦点。

争议的焦点是美国国会议员拉马尔·史密斯（Lamar Smith）的提议。从 21 世纪初开始，史密斯对移民的立场已经开始改变，并开始讨好高科技公司。这一转变伴随着其选举区的重新划分，划分后的选举区内包括几家科技公司的办公室。[70]2004 年 4 月，史密斯提出了一项迎合这些公司利益的法案，该法案没有提高 H-1B 签证的上限，却将从美国大学获得硕士及以上学位的外国学生中不受上限限制的人数从 20 000 提高到了 85 000。

高科技公司和研究型大学将再次联合支持该提案。这一次联合开始正式化：2004 年初，ABLI 更名为"Compete America"（竞争美国），新团体不仅包括美国著名的高科技公司和行业协会，还包括高等教育组织。[71] 后者包括两大能够代表研究型大学的重要团体——AAU 和 APLU，同时还有全国外国学生事务协会。[72] Compete America 首任主席桑德拉·博伊德（Sandra Boyd）后来回忆说，他们刻意努力创建一个"由雇主驱动的联盟"，这个联盟包括商业和高等教育团体，"因为我们有共同的话题"。[73] 为了形成统一战线，31 位杰出的企业和学术领袖——包括微软首席执行官史蒂夫·鲍尔默（Steve Ballmer）、甲骨文总裁萨弗拉·卡茨（Safra Catz）、麻省理工学院院长查尔斯·韦斯特（Charles Vest）在 2004 年向国会联合致信以支持史密斯提出的新的豁免提案。[74]

该提案又一次遭到 AFL-CIO 和 IEEE-USA 的抵制。[75] 此外，还有更多反移民运动的抵制。[76] 其中的关键团体是 NumbersUSA，该团体发起基层电话运动以抵制该法案。[77] 即便如此，NumbersUSA 的势力仍然相对较小，2004 年初约有 16 000 名电子邮件活动人员。[78] NumbersUSA 的规模很小，加上其成员反对该法案的时间有限，所以其能够对国会施加的压力很有限。[79] 于是，HTC 仍然占据上风。2004 年 12 月，在国会的"跛脚鸭"（lame-duck session）会议期间，史密斯的提案作为一项修正案纳入《2005 年综合拨款法案》。拨款法案的通过是两党的优先事项，并在两党的支持下通过。[80]

1998—2004 年，HTC 在 H-1B 问题上取得了一系列对抗有组织的劳工的胜利。就其本身而言，劳工组织已经不敌 HTC 在政治上的"主宰"力量。但是，截至 2004 年，显而易见的是，高科技利益集团开始面临来自新型对手的阻力：专门从事基层动员的反移民组织。来自这些和其他公民团体的越来越大的阻力将阻碍 HTC 在 2004 年之后提高 H-1B 上限的努力。

难以对付的对手：2005—2016 年

2004 年之后，围绕着扩大 H-1B 签证计划的政治环境发生了戏剧性的变化。美国总统乔治·W. 布什和巴拉克·奥巴马将进行持续不懈的努力，他们将放宽美国的移民政策，这不仅针对技术移民，而且针对美国数百万无证移民。在这一背景下，HTC 必须面对比以往更大的阻力。使无证移民合法化的综合法案遭遇了来自公民团体的共同抵制，特别是 NumbersUSA，以及来自茶党（Tea Party）运动的保守思想团体。与此同时，扩大技术移民的针对性法案将受到全面改革倡导者的抵制。拉丁裔团体特别能够理解，单独处理技术移民的法案将会削弱对综合性改革的商业支持，使其无法实现无证移民的合法化。面对这些强大的对手，HTC 又一次未能实现其目标。

2006 年和 2007 年的抗争

在 2004 年 11 月连任后，美国总统布什致力于全面放宽美国的移民政策，这一政策可以赋予美国众多的无证移民以合法地位。布什总统 2004 年 1 月宣布了他的愿景后，遭到了本党派成员的抵制，政府当年没有做出任何努力来推动该倡议的实施。[81]事实上，直到2005年1月，合法化的拥护者对于布什政府对此事不守承诺而感到失望。[82]但是，在2005年，政府开始以更大的热情推行其计划。尽管共和党内部仍有一些争议，但是共和党战略家希望这一倡议能够扩大该党在美国快速增长的拉丁裔人口中的吸引力。[83]民主党也不甘示弱，其领导人将民主党视为全面改革真正的支持者，并且出台"有助于保障所有拉丁裔家庭和所有美国人的明智政策"，正如参议员约翰·克里（John Kerry）所说。[84]因此，展望未来，重点是将扩大技术移民作为更广泛的自由化一揽子计划中的一部分。

就其本身而言，HTC仍然对开放政策感兴趣。尽管在2000年和2004年获得了豁免，但是在2005年8月，H-1B签证的数量就已经达到了2006财年的上限。两个月后，Compete America在致立法者的信中写道，需要进一步提高上限才能确保美国的"竞争力"。[85]该组织还呼吁放宽EB签证制度，该制度下的签证申请现在已经积压。Compete America警告称，EB系统中的功能越来越失调，使中国和印度的技术工人"几乎不可能"获得永久居留权。[86]其他团体同样致力于放宽政策。移民改革的商业团体不仅来自美国商会，也来自在移民劳工身上有特殊利益的团体，如全美餐馆同业会和全美农业雇主委员会。[87]对无证移民合法化的展望得到拉丁裔团体的大力支持，这有助于2006年在美国各地组织大规模的改革示威活动。[88]罗马天主教会在拉丁裔群体中有深厚的基础，也很受支持。全民移民论坛等支持移民的伞式组织对全面自由化也提供了支持。

支持改革的努力也得益于有组织的劳工内部的分歧。虽然劳动力普遍支持无证移民合法化，但现在对于客工计划存在分歧。2005 年，SEIU（服务雇员国际联盟）等几个团体脱离了 AFL-CIO，形成了名为"变以求胜"（Change to Win）的劳工联盟。分歧原因部分是对移民的不同意见：AFL-CIO 反对客工计划，包括 H-1B 签证计划，而 SEIU 对这些计划持开放态度，并将其作为改革的一部分，这将提高其组织工人的能力。[89]

尽管在劳工方面存在分歧，但是由于反移民运动越来越激烈，HTC 面对的反对派比以往任何时候都更加强大。尤其是 NumbersUSA 利用互联网扩大其会员基础并动员积极分子。自 2004 年以后，移民改革逐渐成为热门话题，其集团成员迅速扩充。虽然该组织在 2004 年 1 月仅有 16 000 名活动人员，但这一数字在 2006 年 1 月上升至 126 000，在 2007 年 1 月上升至 236 000，在 2008 年 1 月上升至 529 000。[90] 该组织的电子邮件分发名单要大得多。事实上，截至 2007 年，其邮件列表已经收到了约 150 万份邮件。[91] 随着会员数量的增加，NumbersUSA 成为移民政治中的一股强大力量。该组织向其订阅人群提供了新法案的摘要，并提前通知他们重要的立法行动。这将为大量反移民选民提供机会，使他们能够以及时和果断的方式权衡立法。NumbersUSA 还开发了一个记分卡系统，显示每位国会议员每次就移民相关问题进行的投票，并为每位成员分配一个字母等级。对于共和党人来说，低级别是主要挑战者的素材。该组织的成员也非常有组织性，并且通过针对性的办公室访问将其影响力发挥到最大。

例如，如果某个特定成员有某种宗教信仰，NumbersUSA 会将该教派的成员派到办公室为自己站台。[92] 简而言之，反移民运动已成为"难啃的硬骨头"。

1. 2006 年的抗争

首轮检验在 2006 年如期而至。尽管反移民团体获得了新的力量，但是他们在参议院中仍然面临许多困难。共和党多数党领袖，田纳西州的比尔·弗里斯特（Bill Frist）宣布，他将从参议院退休，并且要参加 2008 年的总统选举。"弗里斯特在参议院还有最后八个月的时间，"弗吉尼亚大学的拉里·萨巴托（Larry Sabato）说道，"在这时候，相对于当一名多数党的领袖，他对成为总统候选人的兴趣更大。"[93] 因此，在参议院的初选中，弗里斯特不会受到挑战。此外，他已经清楚地计算出通过一项全面的移民法案将有助于他的总统竞选。因此，弗里斯特支持布什政府推动全面改革。虽然大多数共和党人不愿意支持他，但弗里斯特可以指望民主党参议员支持一项能够吸引拉丁裔团体和高科技公司的法案。对于他们来说，反移民团体明白阻止参议院通过法案将会很困难。"任何事情都有可能发生在参议院，" NumbersUSA 的卡罗琳·埃斯皮诺萨（Caroline Espinosa）说道，"最后它真的会影响会议中发生的事情。"[94]

3 月中旬，弗里斯特推出了《确保美国边境法案》，旨在减少非法移民并增加合法移民。然而，弗里斯特没能获得阻止相关辩论的支持。因此，4 月 7 日一项新法案被引入，该法案包括一系列旨在吸引不同群体的措施。[95]该法案致力于建立基金以提升边境安全，同时也为无证移民成为公民创造了条件。它还大大扩展了 EB 和 H-1B 签证计划，为减少前者的积压，该法案在 2016 年将 EB 签证的上限提高至 450 000，然后在 2017 年将其设定为 290 000，并附有一些措施。该法案将 H-1B 签证的上限从 65 000 增加到 115 000，并且只要达到上一年的限制，就可以再增加 20%。它还豁免了对所有从美国大学获得 STEM 学位的外国学生的限制。现有的 20 000 个豁免名额适用于从外国来的大学毕业生。在弗里斯特的支持下，5 月 25 日，参议院以 62：36 的比例通过该法案。大多数选票（38 票）来自民主党人和一名独立选票，其中 23 票来自共和党人。弗里斯特将该法案的通过称赞为"美国人民的胜利"。[96]

现在将注意力转向众议院。众议院于 2005 年 12 月通过了移民法案，但其重点是加强边境安全并惩罚那些协助无证移民入境的人。该法案还致力于将美国的无证件存在从轻罪变为重罪。关键问题是，众议院领导层现在是否会试图将这项法案与参议院通过的全面改革协调。新闻发言人丹尼斯·哈斯特尔特（Dennis Hastert）是一位核心人物。2005 年 4 月，哈斯特尔特表示愿意在与参议院的会谈中扩大众议院的法案。[97]5 月初，白宫官员乐观地认为，他们可以依靠发言人来召集足够多的共和党人支持改革工作。[98]

白宫对此很失望。NumbersUSA 发起针对哈斯特尔特的有目的的游说活动，强调如果他在没有大多数共和党领导团体支持的情况下通过移民改革，其领导能力将大受损害。[99]哈斯特尔特对此类威胁非常敏感。2003年底，他阐述了"哈斯特尔特规则"（又称多数中的多数规则），该规则坚持认为"发言人的工作不是加快违反大多数人的意愿的立法"。[100]哈斯特尔特当时已经严重依赖民主党成员来通过有关移民和竞选经费的立法，这引起了他所属领导层的不满。虽然他此后并不总是遵循这一规则，但由于反移民运动日益增多，他在2006年5月面临了特别严重的移民抵制。IRC（国会移民改革核心小组）由国会议员汤姆·坦克雷多（Tom Tancredo）于1999年发起，已经从刚成立时的16名成员扩展到2006年中期的97名成员，几乎所有成员都是共和党人。[101]这种增长反映了坦克雷多和NumbersUSA的共同努力。[102]NumbersUSA已经要求其成员联系他们的代表，要求他们加入IRC，加入的国会议员在NumbersUSA评级系统中获得了额外的积分。该组织还针对被视为IRC潜在候选人的特定成员。例如，明尼苏达州的基尔·库特耐特（Gil Gutknecht）在受到来自与NumbersUSA工作的选民的压力下加入了IRC。该团体还与IRC的领导密切合作，使核心小组的工作更有效率。2002年初，两位NumbersUSA说客在坦克雷多的办公室里称自己为"虚拟工作人员"。[103]特别是，哈佛大学法学院毕业生罗斯玛丽·詹克斯（Rosemary Jenks）作为NumbersUSA的成员，"几乎每天"都在坦克雷多的办公室工作，为一些悬而未决的法案提供法律分析。[104]在IRC和其他合法化批评者之间，共和党立法者估计，75%的众议院共和党人甚至反对参议院法案的缓和版本。[105]

面对这种程度的抵制，哈斯特尔特寻求以他的名字命名的规则的庇佑。5月23日，哈斯特尔特的一位发言人表示，对于移民问题，发言人将援引多数中的多数规则。[106] 一位共和党参议员称这一年对移民改革来说是"致命的打击"，事实确实如此。[107] 虽然国会在选举前通过了关于边境安全的其他立法，但是哈斯特尔特已经杀死了全年的全面改革——没有任何提高 H-1B 上限的希望。

此后不久，移民的倡导者承认他们在 2006 年面临反移民运动的困扰。"限制主义者的声音非常响亮，"全国移民论坛副主任安吉拉·凯利（Angela Kelley）说："我认为他们并不强大，但是他们的动静非常大，并且能够通过拥有大量的会员联系人，以非常强大的方式集中成员，我们不会这样做。"[108]

2. 2007 年的抗争

2006 年 11 月的中期选举为通过一项全面的法案提供了新的机会。民主党控制了国会两院，布什总统仍然不遗余力地推进改革，HTC 仍然致力于这项任务。4月，Compete America 的一位新闻发言人针对提高 H-1B 上限的问题做出了评论，"现在我们专注于把全面（移民法案）作为工具"。[109] 5月9日，参议院多数党领袖哈里·里德（Harry Reid）提出了《2007 年边境安全、经济机会和移民改革法案》，改革势头开始形成。

正如 2006 年的法案所述，新法案努力增加了边境安全的内容，同时也为一些无证移民创造了获得公民身份的机会。与 2006

第3章 旋转门：高技能劳动力

年的法案一样，新立法将 H-1B 签证的上限提高到 115 000，其限额可能会根据需求而提升，并且所有从美国大学获得 STEM 学位的外国学生都可以免除限制。虽然高科技公司对后来的这些变化表示欢迎，但是这些公司对于与 H-1B 计划相关的费用增加和新的规定很不满。[110] 对 EB 签证制度的拟议修改也存在一些争议。虽然该法案旨在减少 EB 签证积压，但它取代了现有的以雇主为基础的制度，而采用基于绩效的积分制度，以技能、教育、英语水平等因素为基础来对劳动力进行认证——此举被批评为苏联式的中央计划。[111]

虽然高科技利益集团对该法案有些许担忧，但是其他集团明显不同。AFL-CIO 特别关注创建一个新的客工计划以填补主要的低技能工作的条款，这个计划最初有 40 万个签证，在以后的几年内可能会有更多。[112] 劳工倡导者也对合法化措施感到担忧，他们认为此项任务过于繁重。与此同时，反移民组织将无证移民合法化谴责为"特赦"。[113] 他们还通过媒体宣传动员了反对该法案的意见。正如一位参与该问题的民主党员工之后所说的："NumbersUSA 和 FAIR 设法说服福克斯新闻在 24 小时的新闻频道播放反移民的观点。"[114]

6 月初，里德试图结束针对该法案的辩论。民主党参议员拜伦·多根（Byron Dorgan）在劳工的支持下，成功地为新的客工计划增加了落日条款，这一努力被打乱了。"毒丸策略"（poison pill）修正案在民主党人和四名共和党人的投票中以 49：48 的比例通过。由于"特赦"条款，四名共和党人希望抵制这项法案（或

97

者受到抵制该法案的压力）。[115] 随后，在少数共和党人的支持下，该法案的投票未能通过。在白宫游说之后，参议院在 6 月底重新处理此事。该法案经过修改后被重新引入，包括为保障边境安全提供更多资金，以吸引摇摆不定的共和党人。[116] 里德也为数量有限的修正案打开了大门。科技公司努力抓住这次机遇。正如《纽约时报》报道的那样，微软高管比尔·盖茨和史蒂夫·鲍尔默正在带领"一大批高科技高管到国会山"，试图影响不断发展的立法。[117] 一般来讲，商界希望该法案能够实施。通过这样的影响可以修改法案以解决他们在会议阶段（例如关于 EB 签证的积分系统）的问题。[118]

然而，劳工和反移民运动都抵制这最后一次行动，NumbersUSA 尤其活跃。NumbersUSA 主席罗伊·贝克（Roy Beck）声称其团队向国会提出了超过 200 万份传真，反对 5 月和 6 月的移民改革。[119] 参议院原计划在 6 月 28 日结束讨论并进行投票，反移民活动人士愤怒地打电话到国会，导致国会大厦的总机被关闭。[120] 反对派的强烈反应不仅引发了共和党参议员的担忧，还引发了一些中间派民主党人的担忧。[121] 抗议活动引发了内华达州的共和党参议员约翰·恩斯格（John Ensign）的评论："针对这项法案的紧张程度和激愤，前所未见。"[122]

NumbersUSA 也针对重要的参议员展开活动。参议院少数党领袖米奇·麦康奈尔（Mitch McConnell）和参议院少数党党鞭特伦特·洛特（Trent Lott）作为著名的拥护合法化的共和党人，成为特别的目标。事实上，麦康奈尔是将法案重新纳入参议院的关键人物。[123] 作为回应，NumbersUSA 在分别位于美国肯塔基州和密西西比州的麦康奈尔和洛特的家乡，动员了大量的基层力量来反对该法案，这两地聚集了大量的 NumbersUSA 积极分子。[124] 这场活动包括抗议、广播报道和电视广告。洛特对于其中一场运动印象深刻，他在 6 月下旬表示，"那些真正推动这项法案的人并没有像那些反对这项法案的人那样有效率"，洛特当时在美国密西比州杰克逊市的办公室被请愿者包围，并且反对者持续不断地打来电话。[125] 即便如此，洛特是一个很难搞定的目标。他显然并不打算竞选连任，他在 2006 年的连任之前已经处于退休状态了，实际上，他正式从参议院退休是在 2007 年底。[126] 因此，尽管受到来自 NumbersUSA 的压力，洛特仍然在 6 月 28 日投票支持结束辩论。

麦康奈尔是另一种情况，他寻求能在 2008 年连任。为了应对来自基层的压力，麦康奈尔在投票前几天几乎不见踪影。[127] 最后，他在 6 月 28 日投票反对该法案，对这位总统的盟友来讲，这是一次重大转变。麦康奈尔随后解释了他在参议院的决定。他赞扬了这项法案，说道"这是我们实现目标的最好机会"。然而，来自家乡的阻力不容忽略。"我从很多肯塔基人那里听说过，成千上万个聪明且消息灵通的人打电话到我的办公室谈论这个法案。他们不喜欢（这个法案）……我今天对每个人说'你的意见已经收到了'。"[128] NumbersUSA 主席罗伊·贝克后来回忆说，即使麦康奈尔投了支持票，他也希望能够停止这项法案，但是这位少数党领袖的彻底转变使得失败成为一种必然。[129] 最后，结束辩论提议获得了 46 个支持票和 53 个反对票。通过一项全面法案的努力已经连续两年失败了。

支持改革的联盟对此结果不满意也不足为奇。ITAA 主席菲尔·邦德（Phil Bond）表示他"非常失望"。[130] 然而，支持改革阵营也承认他们再次被打败，特别是被 NumbersUSA 打败。国家移民论坛执行主任弗兰克·谢里（Frank Sharry）说："NumbersUSA 发起并推动了民粹主义反抗移民改革计划。"[131] 在另外一个场合，沙里说："你必须给予他们信任，电话、传真、出现在市政厅和会议中的人们，你必须承认 NumbersUSA 动员的人数规模数量可观。"[132] 多年以后，谢里回忆道："他们对这项法案提出了很多反对意见，这是我们失败的重要因素。"[133] HTC 及其盟友很清楚地意识到谁击败了他们，以及他们是如何做到的。

奥巴马时代

2008 年 11 月巴拉克·奥巴马当选为美国总统，开启了美国移民政治的新篇章。此前，作为总统候选人，奥巴马已经为提高 H-1B 签证上限提供了支持，但他对全面改革更感兴趣。[134] 这使 HTC 陷入两难境地。虽然科技公司在公开场合支持全面的自由化，但他们似乎不愿意对那种如此不确定的提案进行投资。一名国会工作人员在 2010 年说："目前尚不清楚（科技公司说客）投资多少，我们希望看到更大的投资力度。"[135] 高科技公司的犹豫是有原因的，这些科技公司在 2006 年和 2007 年中追求全面合法化的过程中失败了，因此，它们对此时进行更大的投资是否值得持怀疑态度。正如一位高管所说："必须对现实情况中通过的概率进行计算……如果该法案不会通过，你就不会打电话给首席执行官。"[136]

然而，仅仅关注技术移民是很困难的。随着一项全面的移民法案的提出，一项针对技术移民的法案现在面临其他支持自由化群体的反对。正如信息技术产业委员会主席迪安·加菲尔德（Dean Garfield）2010年4月所说的："如果高科技部门试图通过一项针对技术移民的法案，那么（支持移民的联盟中）会有反对我们倡议的人。"[137]或者正如一名高等教育说客之后所说的："那些将被遗弃在火车后面的人不希望火车在没有他们的情况下前进，所以他们会阻止火车前进。"[138]拉美裔群体尤其会从这种高技能移民的独立立法中损失很多，因为这种立法会改变高科技公司支持一项使无证移民合法化的法案的动机。[139]拉美裔群体非常庞大。拉美裔全国委员会（the National Council of La Raza）是美国最大的由拉美裔群体构成的组织，总部设在华盛顿，呈伞式组织，在全美有近300个社区附属机构，为全美约500万拉美裔人提供服务。[140]拉美裔人的关注点对民主党立法者来讲尤为重要，民主党立法者并不急于无视在2008年选举中强烈支持该党的团体。[141]

面对这种困境，在奥巴马任职期间，HTC既追求有针对性的改革也追求全面的改革。但是这两种方法都不成功。

1. 勉强通过的法案

在 2010 年中期选举之后，共和党重新控制众议院，而不是参议院。在竞选期间，共和党立法者表示他们将优先考虑技术移民措施。[142] 最初的尝试集中在 EB 签证的积压上。2011 年 9 月，共和党众议员杰森·查菲茨（Jason Chaffetz）提出了《高技能移民公平法案》。该法案取消了 EB 签证对每个国家的限制，特别是帮助来自中国和印度的申请人，同时将每个国家家庭签证的上限提高到 15%。Compete America 和其他高科技集团非常支持该法案，而 NumbersUSA 对该法案没有采取任何立场，因为该法案并没有导致移民数量的增长。[143] 该法案于 11 月以 389 : 15 的比例在众议院通过。

在共和党方面，参议员查尔斯·格拉斯利（Charles Grassley）和杰夫·塞申斯（Jeff Sessions）都反对该法案。在增加关于预防 H-1B 签证欺诈和滥用的条款之后，格拉斯利的态度在 2012 年出现缓和，但塞申斯并没有。[144] 民主党方面也有人担心。参议员罗伯特·梅南德斯（Robert Menendez）是国会西班牙裔核心小组的重要成员，他希望采取额外的措施促进家庭团聚。[145] 但是，这些措施使该法案在共和党方面更加难以接受。因此，该法案在参议院被否决。

虽然这种情况正在发生，但第二项针对 EB 签证的举措也在进行。2011 年底，众议院司法委员会主席拉马尔·史密斯和参议院移民、边境安全与难民小组委员会主席查尔斯·舒默

（Charles Schumer）之间展开谈判。[146] 讨论的重点是为获得美国大学 STEM 学科学位的外国毕业生提供 55 000 个 EB 签证，并取消多元签证计划，该计划为在美国代表人数不足的国家的移民提供了相当数量的签证。新兴法案对大学和高科技公司具有天然的吸引力。IEEE-USA 也表示支持，因为该法案代表了从 H-1B 签证到 EB 签证的转变。[147] 如果移民没有出现净增加，由史密斯提供咨询的 NumbersUSA 表示愿意持观望态度。[148]

然而，寻求妥协的努力遇到了障碍。为了安抚拉美裔群体，舒默想要做出一些改变，这些改变会促进美国境内外国人与国外亲属的家庭团聚。根据舒默身边的工作人员的说法，史密斯同意在这方面做出微小的改变，但他不愿意做出大的调整，也无法达到舒默的预期。[149] 同年 9 月，当舒默和史密斯引入竞争法案时，他们开始在公众场合争论。史密斯的法案，即《2012 年 STEM 就业法案》，取消了支持 STEM 签证的多元签证计划。相比之下，舒默的法案为 55 000 个 STEM 签证创建了一个为期两年的试点项目，并且没有取消多样性签证计划。[150] 然而，舒默的法案没有提交表决，史密斯的法案则进行了表决。9 月 20 日，众议院根据暂停规则对该法案进行了投票，这是一项限制辩论但需要三分之二多数通过的快速程序。民主党人指责史密斯试图通过民主党投票通过这项法案，旨在向舒默施加压力，但立法未能获得所需的绝大多数人的支持。[151]

史密斯的法案在 11 月选举后被重新考虑。但是，拉丁裔团体的担忧在这一点上显得更加突出，因为他们已经帮助推动了奥巴马再次当选。11月下旬，白宫表示，它"强烈支持立法，以吸引和留住获得高级 STEM 学位的外国学生"。[152] 但是，白宫继续表明，白宫不能支持"不符合总统针对全面移民改革所制定的长期目标的提案"。该声明指出，"重要的优先事项，例如为无证个人开拓一条获得公民身份的途径"——明确认可拉美裔群体。在奥巴马发表声明后的几天，该法案在众议院获得通过，大多数共和党人和 27 名民主党人投票赞成。[153] 由于白宫不感兴趣，民主党在参议院的领导层选择不接受该法案，由此结束其成为法律的可能。2013 年 3 月，舒默向技术说客解释为什么民主党人不可能支持这样的立法："如果试图通过高端的高科技移民法案，那么猜猜谁会大发雷霆呢？答案是西班牙裔群体。"[154]

2. 推动全面改革

推动全面改革的新希望诞生于《STEM 就业法案》被否决之后。2013 年 1 月，奥巴马明确表示，全面的移民改革将成为他第二任期内的头等大事。同月，参议院两党的"八人团"（Gang of Eight）揭开了全面法案的框架。作为其中的一位成员，参议员舒默要求企业和劳工运用双方都能够支持的语言，这促成了 2 月的联合原则声明。[155] 支持者也比过去更精通媒体。在马克·卢比奥（Marco Rubio）的带领下，八位参议员向保守派媒体求助，以争取全面改革的支持。此项努力并没有赢得电台主持人拉什·林博（Rush Limbaugh）的支持，但它与福克斯新闻的合作非常成功。[156]

HTC投入巨资来争取它们支持的法案。在微软的带领下，领先的美国科技公司在2013年主导了移民说客名单（见表3.1）。微软的整体游说费用从2012年的810万美元跃升至2013年的1 050万美元，因为其在这一问题上的活动有所增加。[157]事实上，美国高科技公司在2013年上半年与立法者的接触被称为是"非比寻常的"。[158]高科技公司深入地参与起草立法，所以他们的游说者有时会在"八人团"的一些参议员之前了解新规定的细节。2013年4月，脸书首席执行官马克·扎克伯格和其他硅谷高管创立了FWD.us，这是一个旨在通过媒体宣传和其他渠道倡导移民改革的非营利组织。[159]

表3.1 2013年针对移民的主要游说者名单

当事方	提交报道的数量
1. 微软	64
2. 英特尔	22
3. 消费技术协会	20
4. 脸书	19
5. 甲骨文	18
6. 商业圆桌会议	17
7. 两党政策中心	16
8. 高通	16
9. 全国住宅建筑商协会	15
10. 美国商会	15
11. 高知特	14
12. 计算机科技集团	14
13. 娱乐软件协会	14

续表

当事方	提交报道的数量
14. 谷歌	14
15. 摩托罗拉系统公司	14

注：数据基于参议院公共档案办公室（the Senate Office of Public Records）的诸多报告。来源：响应政治中心，《移民游说当事方年度数据》（*Annual Number of Clients Lobbying on Immigration*），2017。Opensecrets.org, www.opensecrets.org/lobby/issuesum.php?id=IMM。

最终，参议院提出的法案《2013年边境安全、经济机会和移民现代化法案》成为美国对移民制度进行彻底改革的大胆尝试。该法案使得许多无证移民有可能获得合法地位并最终获得公民身份，从而确保了来自拉丁裔团体和其他进步组织的支持。与此同时，该法案在十年内投资460亿美元用于加强边境安全。该法案还为低技能劳工制定了新的W签证，以及其他一系列措施。在这里最重要的是，该法案还提出了各种扩大和改革技术移民的规定。[160]

首先，EB签证计划实现了大幅扩张。虽然维持了140 000个签证的限制，但该法案重新获得了前几年未使用的签证，取消了对每个国家的限制，并创造了几项重要的豁免。其中包括对签证接受者的配偶和子女、EB-1签证接受者和在美国大学获得STEM领域的高级学位或任何领域的博士学位的外国学生的豁免。该法案还为技术移民创造了一条新途径：基于绩效的积分系统，根据教育、经验和其他证书，每年可分配120 000~250 000个签证。这些签证中有一半是为高技能移民保留的，另一半是为低技术移民保留的。此外，该法案还针对创业企业家创建了新的EB签证（EB-6）和新的非移民签证（X签证）。[161]

其次，该法案还对H-1B签证计划进行了修改。根据市场需求和失业数据，签证的上限提高到每年115 000个，并进一步扩大到180 000个。原始法案包含一系列保护措施，以确保国内的劳动力不会受到这种扩张的不利影响——这是商业和劳工之间谈判的结果。为了应对来自高科技公司的压力，以及AFL-CIO的反对意见，最终法案放松了其中一些要求，同时仅将其他要求应用于依赖H-1B签证的公司。[162] 此外，对依赖H-1B签证的计算被修改，使得接近限制的主要美国公司（例如脸书）可以避免属于该类别，特别是通过赞助H-1B工作人员获得EB签证。[163] 正如劳工的主要谈判代表后来所说的，"美国领先的公司很特立独行"。[164] 在这些变化之后，AFL-CIO继续支持该法案的通过，但是一些附属公司现在开始反对它或不再那么热情地支持它。[165]

使用该计划的印度公司不希望通过该项法案，因为它们通常认为H-1B签证是值得信赖的。在其他变化中，依赖H-1B签证的公司被禁止将H-1B签证的劳工安排到其他公司——这是印度公司广泛使用的一种做法。此外，虽然新的三级工资结构旨在提高所有H-1B签证劳工的工资，但是依赖H-1B签证的公司也被单独挑选出来，并要求按照二级或以上的工资标准来支付H-1B签证的劳工的工资。该法案还将H-1B签证和L-1签证劳工的总数的上限设置为占美国公司劳动力的75%，这一数字在 2017 年下降到 50%。持 H-1B 签证和 L-1 签证的劳工占比为 30%~50% 的公司需要为每一位新的申请者支付 5 000 美元的申请费。总之，这些规定将使低成本的 IT 外包市场从依赖 H-1B 签证的公司转移走，包括印孚瑟斯、塔塔咨询和威普罗等印度公司，转而面向拥有足够多的美国雇员的美国竞争对手，例如埃森哲和 IBM，以避开这些门槛。[166] 印度主要软件贸易机构的主席谴责这些条款是"歧视性的"，但它们仍然被包含在该法案中。[167]

事实上，HTC 总体上是支持该法案的，并希望它通过。英特尔政府关系总监 2013 年 5 月表示："我们对这一进展非常满意，对该法案中的内容也很满意。"[168] 6 月，来自高科技公司和行业协会的 100 多位高管共同签署了一封信呼吁参议院通过"这项至关重要的立法"。[169] 同时，在 ACE 的带领下，十四个高等教育团体"强烈赞同"该法案，称其为"建立具有两党支持的能够更好地满足国家需要的移民体系的历史性机会"。[170] 6 月 27 日，参议院以 68：32 的比例通过该法案，共有 52 名民主党人、14 名共和党人和 2 名独立人士投赞成票。

然而，在共和党领导的众议院中，彻底修改的工作将面临更大的阻力。反对的原因很复杂。反移民组织再次提出反对。但是他们在 2006 年和 2007 年组织同样的基层抵制行动时遇到了麻烦。NumbersUSA 的主席甚至也承认，2013 年的反移民运动不如 2007 年那样容易动员。[171] 然而，如果反移民群体不如以往活跃，另一股反对力量——茶党——就会更加活跃。茶党运动在 2010

年中期选举中发展成熟,当时它帮助共和党赢回了众议院的控制权,并且它有助于在共和党中激发更强烈的财政保守主义形象。虽然开始于基层运动,但茶党的一部分合并为一系列专业活动组织,包括茶党爱国者队(Tea Party Patriots)和茶党国家队(Tea Party Nation)。其他几个保守团体也与这一运动保持密切的联系,包括繁荣美国(Americans for Prosperity)、增长俱乐部(Club for Growth)、自由工作(FreedomWorks)和美国遗产行动(Heritage Action for America)。2012年总统大选中,奥巴马得以连任,许多由茶党支持的参议院挑战者被击败,这场运动遭受了挫折。然而,在2013年春季,美国国家税务局披露,其已经对一些保守团体的免税地位要求进行了额外的审查,尤其关注那些名称中包括茶党等词语的团体,这使得茶党运动重整旗鼓。[172] 截至2013年底,茶党团体已经拥有大约500 000名个人"核心会员",并在推特上拥有382 000名粉丝。[173]

茶党很快成为反移民改革的重要来源。可以肯定的是,在2013年上半年,一些保守派团体对此问题的态度犹豫不决。尤其是繁荣美国、增长俱乐部和自由工作保守团体表示他们对参与这场特殊的立法斗争犹豫不决。[174] 此外,《茶党快报》(the Tea Party Express)的联合创始人萨尔·鲁索(Sal Russo)建议,他将移民改革,包括为无证移民开辟获得公民身份的道路,视为是不可避免的。[175] 然而,通俗地讲,茶党团体的反对被描述为"激烈而喧嚣"。[176] 其中最大的团体之一——茶党爱国者队——强烈地反对。茶党爱国者队是一个伞式组织,截至2014年已有2 000多个地方分会，该团体认为，移民政策改革，特别是为无证移民提供公民身份，将导致联邦政府的支出大幅度增加。[177] "在移民方案生效后，目前的非法移民群体将多快获得奥巴马医改福利？" 茶党爱国者队于 5 月质问道。[178] 遗产基金会也认为该法案的成本极高，美国遗产行动称其为"坏消息"。[179] 另一个团体，麦迪逊计划（the Madison Project）称这项法案是"彻彻底底的错误"。[180] 此外，反对者比旁观者更加活跃。正如共和党民意测验专家惠特·艾尔斯（Whit Ayres）在 7 月所提出的，众议院成员"正在对那些花时间写信、打电话和发电子邮件到他们办公室的人做出回应。没有任何共和党人会写信给他们的国会议员要求开辟途径获得公民身份。这并不是那种会让你冲锋在前的事情"。[181]

NumbersUSA 部署的基础筹备工作为茶党的反对行动赋予了更多的自主权。2010 年中期选举之后，NumbersUSA 将茶党团体作为反对移民改革的盟友，甚至在 2011 年聘请茶党"联络员"与茶党领袖合作，并在茶党活动中发表演讲。[182] NumbersUSA 的许多成员也加入了茶党。因此，每个运动的基层基础都有显著的重合。[183] 这意味着许多茶党成员从 NumbersUSA 收到有关移民问题的信息和更新。这些运动之间的重合在众议院也很明显。截至 2011 年 3 月，众议院大约 70% 的茶党核心小组成员也是反移民改革核心小组的成员。[184]

反对者将这种能量和组织引导到阻止众议院领导层进行移民改革上。支持移民的团体在众议院寻求支持，他们将多数党党鞭凯文·麦卡锡（Kevin McCarthy）视为 2013 年的重要潜在支持者。[185]麦卡锡不仅是众议院中排名第三的共和党人，还来自一个拥有37%西班牙裔且依赖移民劳工的地区。这位国会议员也因与硅谷的关系，并且赞成扩大H-1B签证计划而闻名。为了实现这个目标，2013年底，支持移民的团体通过集会、电话、信件和其他有针对性的举措围攻麦卡锡。作为回应，反对派动员民众抵制支持移民运动。当地茶党举办活动，并与国会议员会面以强调他们的反对意见。NumbersUSA也参与进来，要求其活动人士给麦卡锡的办公室打电话和留言，传达他们的担忧。NumbersUSA主席罗伊·贝克后来解释道："我们确实对麦卡锡做出了回应，因为他真的在开玩笑。"[186]最后，麦卡锡身边的一名工作人员告诉《华尔街日报》，强烈冲突的压力使他对在此问题上起带头作用保持警惕。[187]

更大的考验出现在2014年。1月初，《纽约时报》报道称，众议院议长约翰·博纳（John Boehner）"据说支持移民改革"，特别是在他聘请了曾为参议员约翰·麦凯恩（John McCain）工作的移民顾问丽贝卡·塔伦特（Rebecca Tallent）之后。[188] 1月30日，博纳和其他共和党领导人发布了一系列移民"原则"，不仅包括要求加强边境安全和就业核查，还要求给予一些无证移民法律地位。[189]博纳随后在众议院共和党撤退中组织了针对这些原则的讨论。

对手蓄势以待。博纳将在共和党撤退时提出移民问题的事实已经众所周知，所以反对者在开始之前进行游说。NumbersUSA鼓励"对博纳冷淡"的众议院共和党人，考虑跳过此次活动并向发言人施加压力。[190] 茶党爱国者队组织了一场自动电话留言运动，根据该组织的介绍，这造成了 41 046 名选民打电话向 90 位国会议员抗议。[191]

包括美国遗产行动和 ForAmerica（为了美国）等在内的保守派团体，也敦促其支持者给国会打电话。ForAmerica 声称它留下了 5 500 多条语音留言，在留言中称参议院中投票赞成通过该移民改革法案的人都是"叛徒"，并会产生不良的后果。[192] 最后，博纳的原则并没有被采纳，反对派所采取的压力策略是一个很重要的原因。正如一位密切参与其中的高等教育说客所回忆的那样："有很多国会议员希望在移民改革中获得肯定，包括在众议院共和党核心小组内，但是由于面临的压力越来越大，还是无法实现"。[193] 或者正如 Compete America 的斯科特·科利（Scott Corley）后来所说的那样，许多众议院共和党人"坚持这样的原则：他们的工作不是要领导选民了解真相，而是默许民粹主义"。[194] 撤退一周后，博纳宣布众议院不太可能在 2014 年通过移民改革。[195]

尽管看似移民改革在 2014 年处于濒临死亡的状态，但在当年的春季却出现了复兴的迹象。分析师早些时候曾指出，博纳可能会等到 5 月或 6 月来推动这个议题，因为到那个时候，大多数众议院共和党人都会完成初选。[196] 3 月，据报道称，博纳告诉捐助者和行业团体，他决意要在 2014 年通过移民改革。[197] 博纳还公开抨击反对改革的众议院共和党人，这引发了不同反对群体的谴责。[198] 但是，如果那年仍然有机会通过法案，那么这个机会在 6 月就会消失。6 月 10 日，众议院多数党领袖埃里克·康托尔（Eric

Cantor）在一场重要的挑战中失去了席位，败给了茶党一位不起眼的人物大卫·布拉特（David Brat），他曾攻击康托尔支持博纳推动移民改革。[199] 康托尔的失败震惊了共和党，当年的全面法案也石沉大海。

随着国会行动的停滞，奥巴马决定单方面对该体系进行改革。为此，2014年下半年，白宫官员就可能的政府行为与HTC和无证移民的支持者进行了密切磋商。HTC的支持者提出了许多关于政府部门如何从他们的角度使该系统更友好的想法。[200] 正如一位白宫官员之后所说的，政府一般都表示支持，并且愿意变得"非常有创造力"。[201] 但是这种行为也受到相关立法的限制，这些立法做出的一些改变——例如改变H-1B签证的数量或分配——结果证明是不可行的。

从2014年11月开始，奥巴马政府采取了一系列行动，为合法化倡导者和HTC提供了一些事项。[202] 对于前者，政府宣布了一项推迟将美国公民或合法永久居民父母驱逐出境的计划。政府还扩展了一项计划，推迟将一些无证的儿童移民驱逐出境。对HTC，政府允许某些H-1B签证持有者的配偶工作，使家庭生活更加轻松，前提是H-1B签证持有者已经申请了绿卡。管理部门还为绿卡申请经过批准的高技能工人提供便携式工作授权，使H-1B签证劳工更容易晋升或换工作。如前所述，政府还将STEM毕业生在OPT计划中的期限延长至24个月，并利用政府的"紧急决策权"使外国创业企业家更容易在美国工作。然而，其他措施仍然无法实现。美国政府谨慎考虑允许"重获"前几年未使用的 EB 签证，这一举措很受微软等高科技雇主的青睐。然而，政府官员最终决定，根据法律规定，该举措并不明确可用。[203]

事实上，该命令及其后果表明美国政府在改变美国移民政策方面的权力有限。得克萨斯州和其他二十五个州立即对延期驱逐出境的措施提出质疑，随后在司法系统中审议了这些措施的执行情况。与此同时，HTC 对美国的移民制度非常沮丧。H-1B 签证的上限和分配制度保持不变，绿卡积压的问题仍未解决。在 2014 年底宣布奥巴马的计划后，Compete America 的斯科特·科利说道："多年来，每个人都在说好话，但毫无表示。我们希望看到实际的行动，看到具体的结果。国会必须做出重要举措。"[204] 简而言之，这场战斗远未结束。

结　论

过去 20 年，美国针对技术移民政策的波动反映了 HTC 与其反对者之间不断变化的拉锯战。高科技公司和大学普遍支持自由主义政策并不断为之而战。反过来，抗争的成败取决于其他利益群体是否抵制。当 HTC 面临的阻力主要来自劳工时，它已经在很大程度上占了上风，尽管它必须在 1998 年和 2000 年接受临时措施以及上限的持续存在。相比之下，当 HTC 面临的阻力来自组织良好的大型公民团体时，无论劳工的立场如何，它们都未能提高开放程度。

对美国政策的另一种解释形成了令人不满意的结果。根据本书第2章所概述的战略性霸权假设,如果限制美国与中国和印度进行合作是可行的并且成本低的话,美国应该就会这样做。但是,目前尚不清楚这种方法如何解释自20世纪90年代中期以来H-1B签证上限的上升和下降。调整上限的可行性并未随着时间的推移而明显改变。虽然限制合作的成本已经发生变化,但这无法解释美国政策变化的原因。从21世纪初到2008年,随着美国经济从互联网泡沫的破灭中复苏,美国限制H-1B签证上限的成本增加。然而,在此期间,H-1B签证的上限却大幅下跌,特别是在2000年临时提高的上限失效后。更通俗地讲,如果某种现实政策推动了美国的政策,人们会认为政府部门的偏好在推动H-1B签证上限波动方面发挥了重要作用。但事实并非如此。克林顿政府对于在1998年提高H-1B签证上限并不热心,但仍然在当年提出来了。作为全面移民改革的一部分,布什政府和奥巴马政府都在试图提高H-1B签证上限,均未成功。简而言之,很难用H-1B签证上限的上升和下跌来反映国家战略。

针对移民的公众舆论也难以解释美国政策的波动。1998年9月,哈里斯民意调查(Harris Poll)针对1 000名美国成年人进行的调查显示,82%的人反对大幅提高H-1B签证的上限,只有16%的人表示赞成。[205]尽管IEEE-USA立即对这项民意调查的结果进行大范围宣传,但随后不久,众议院就通过了H-1B签证上限提高的议案。自2004年以来,公众舆论也没有为美国对技术移民的开放程度的下降提供令人信服的解释。事实上,20世纪90年代末到2008年,公众对技术移民的看法有所缓和。2007年底和2008年初进行的一项调查发现,只有40%的受访者反对增加技术移民。[206] 2013年,盖洛普民意调查(Gallup Poll)显示,76%的受访者赞成为短期技术工人增加签证。[207] 同样的民意调查也发现,如果满足某些条件,大多数人都支持为无证移民提供成为公民身份的机会。简而言之,舆论无法解释为什么美国1998—2004年扩大了技术移民,但此后却没有这样做。

那么,个别政党的兴衰是如何变化的呢?优先党派假设预测,抵制HTC的劳工和公民团体的势力会随着时间的推移而发生很大的变化,这取决于主要政党的相对实力。这种观点为美国的政策提供了一定程度的参考。与2006年共和党控制参议院和众议院时相比,在2007年民主党控制两院时,劳工明显有更强的能力与HTC抗衡。相比之下,反移民公民群体在试图影响共和党控制的商会方面最难对付。但是,总体而言,即使民主党控制了白宫,劳工也一直在努力阻止HTC实现其目标。相比之下,自2005年以来,公民团体一再阻止HTC。

现状假设预测HTC在捍卫现存政策时最为成功,在尝试改变时最不成功。这种方法也难以解释本章讨论的不同结果。HTC试图在审查的这两个阶段里改变美国移民法,但在第一阶段比在第二阶段更成功。现状偏见却无法解释这些不同的结果。

在这种情况下,联盟力量假说也表现不佳。第一个联盟力量假说预测,在高科技公司和学术机构都积极参与的情况下,HTC将取得最大成功。这种联合的重要性在2000年和2004年的胜利中很明显，当时研究型大学积极支持ICT公司推动提高H-1B签证上限的计划。即便如此，2004年之后高等教育机构仍然参与其中，但在此期间开放技术移民的努力失败了。第二个联盟力量假说预测，当HTC与其他商业利益结盟时，将会大获成功。2006—2014年，当高科技公司与其他商业团体（以及拉丁裔团体和其他组织）结盟时，这种情况最为明显。然而，这些努力都没有成功。当然，关键原因在于这一时期的反对派更加强大。HTC所面临的反对派的变化能够对本章所观察的结果进行解释，其联盟实力的变化则不能。

第 4 章
开放的大门：外国留学生

第4章 开放的大门：外国留学生

高等教育的全球化正在蓬勃发展。1975—2012年，高等教育海外学生人数从80万激增到450万。[1] 这一趋势在21世纪尤其令人印象深刻：2000—2012年，国际学生流动的年增长率平均为7%。[2] 美国继而顺应了这一趋势。几十年来，美国政府没有对赴美留学的外国学生数量设定限制，美国招收的外国学生人数超过任何国家。截至2016年，已有100多万国际学生就读于美国的大学和学院。[3] 自20世纪90年代末以来，中国和印度已成为这些国际学生最重要的来源。1999年和2000年，中国留学生的数量超过日本，位居榜首，2001年和2002年中国被印度超越。[4] 2009年和2010年，中国留学生的数量再次领先。[5] 总体而言，外国留学生在美国大学本科生中所占比例相对较小，但研究生占比很大，尤其是在科学与工程领域。[6]

本章将探讨21世纪初美国对留学生开放的政策和政治活动。本章第一节介绍美国如何对外国学生开放，特别是自20世纪60年代中期以来的情况。过去几十年，赴美留学的中国学生和印度学生人数急剧增加。第二节将介绍由高等教育团体主导的HTC如何成功地维持这种开放性，尤其是在缺乏有组织的反对势力的情况下。首先考虑的是美国在"9·11"恐怖主义袭击事件发生后立即制定的政策，当时的国会议员提出了临时禁止外国学生准入的议案。其次考虑的是袭击发生后的几年里美国政策的制定，当时外国学生和学者的准入相当困难。在这两种情况下，高等教育团体都实现了自己的目标，不仅仅是因为富有激情的游说，而且还因为缺乏有组织的反对势力。

大量外国学生进入美国学习

自《1924年移民法案》颁布以来，美国已经明确允许外国学生到美国教育机构学习。第二次世界大战以后，学生群体通过三大签证的其中之一得到准入。F-1签证是使用最多的签证，专为接受全日制学术教育的外国学生而设计，M-1签证专为高职学生设计，J-1签证专为参加美国国务院指定的文化交流计划的访客而设计。其中一部分国际访客是学生，另一部分是教授、博士后研究人员、医学毕业生和互惠生等。与H-1B签证不同的是，这些类别的签证没有年度上限。[7]

在没有年度上限的情况下，近几十年来，大量的外国学生进入美国。2014年，美国国务院批准了644 233个F-1签证、332 540个J-1签证和11 058个M-1签证。[8]在这三类签证中，中国和印度获得的F-1签证数量最多。2015年，中国获得的签证数量占J-1签证总量的12%，M-1签证总量的18%，以及F-1签证总量的43%。印度获得的签证数量占J-1签证总量的2%，M-1签证总量的6%，F-1签证总量的12%。如图4.1所示，中国和印度的F-1签证份额在2007年之前很相近，当时两国各占总数的10%~15%。2007年以后，中国所占的F-1签证份额迅速飙升，直观反映了在美国接受本科教育的中国学生数量的增加。中国学生数量最多的大学是加州大学洛杉矶分校、得克萨斯大学奥斯汀分校、华盛顿大学和"十大联盟"（Big Ten）等知名公立大学。[9]

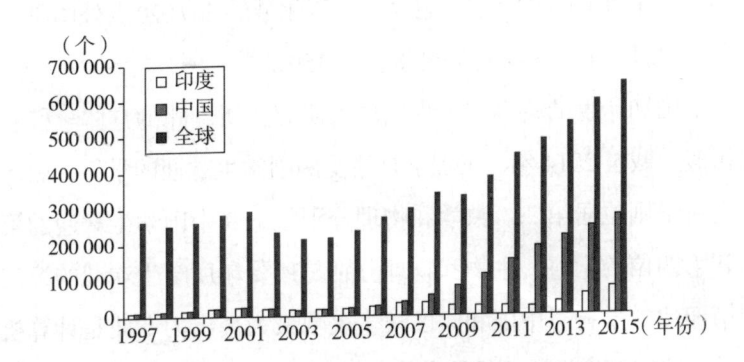

图4.1　1997—2015年由美国国务院发行的F-1签证数量

资料来源：美国国务院，"根据签证类别和国籍发行的非移民签证"（Nonimmigrant Visa Issuances by Visa Class and by Nationality），国务院领事局，访问于2016年9月9日。https://travel.state.gov/content/visas/en/law-and-policy/statistics/non-immigrant-visas.html.

在研究生阶段，在美留学的外国学生在科学与工程领域尤为突出。尽管来自海外的本科生大规模涌入，特别是来自中国的本科生，但是在2013年和2014年，外国学生的数量仅占美国高等教育入学总人数的4.2%，然而近几年来，一些学校外国学生的数量占入学总人数的15%以上。[10] 如果关注科学与工程领域的研究生教育，外国学生在学生总人数中所占的比例更高。

2000年，在美国大学获得科学与工程领域博士学位的人中，获得临时签证的外国学生人数占 31%，到 2013 年，这一数字已跃升至 37%。[11] 在某些领域，特别是工程、计算机科学和经济学领域中获得博士学位的学生中一半及以上都是外国学生。迄今为止，中国和印度已成为科学和工程领域外国研究生的最大来源国。2014 年 11 月，在美国大学注册的科学与工程领域的 209 020 名外国研究生中，中国学生占 33%，印度学生占 35%。[12]

中国和印度的科学与工程领域的研究生所青睐的具体学科非常相似。截至 2014 年，工程学是最受两国学生欢迎的学科，而计算机科学则位居第二。数学和物理分别是最受中国学生欢迎的第三和第四位的学科，生物和物理分别是最受印度学生欢迎的第三和第四位的学科。中国和印度学生表现最为突出的专业是计算机科学，他们在该学科的成绩令其余 83% 的外国研究生望尘莫及。[13]

随着外国学生的数量越来越多，他们已经成为美国学术创新的重要贡献者。[14] 2008 年的一项研究估计，美国大学中外国研究生的数量增加 10%，可以使专利申请的数量增加 4.7%，大学专利授权增加 5.3%，非大学专利授权增加 6.7%。之后的研究报告指出，外国和美国研究生都对学术创新做出了重大且积极的贡献，该报告认为，无论国籍是什么，限制高水平的学生入学，都会对大学创新产生有害影响。[15] 此外，当时的研究估计外国学生毕业后通常会留在美国。2013 年，获得临时签证的印度籍博士中，有超过 80% 的人毕业后有意留在美国。[16]

第4章 开放的大门：外国留学生

"9·11"事件后为开放而进行的抗争

美国对外国学生的持续开放不仅仅是出于政府的自愿，还反映了HTC为维持开放系统所做出的积极努力，同时也是因为缺乏有组织的反对势力。事实上，HTC（尤其是学术界）对国外学生的涌入产生了浓厚的兴趣。对于许多美国大学来说，外国学生已成为重要的收入来源。事实上，美国教育的国际收入从1999年的130亿美元增长到2015年的近360亿美元。[17]这一收入在2008年之后变得尤为重要，因为当时美国经济下滑导致许多公立大学的资金被削减。如前所述，科学与工程领域的外国学生也是许多美国研究型大学受过良好教育的劳动力的重要来源。科技公司也对来自国外的科学与工程领域学生的涌入产生了浓厚的兴趣。正如第3章所介绍的，外国学生可以在毕业后通过OPT在有限的时间内到美国工作，之后可以获得H-1B这样的工作签证。有些公司甚至在学生还未毕业的时候就与科学或工程领域有前途的外籍学生建立联系，希望在毕业后雇用这些学生。[18]

尽管HTC的企业和学术机构都对国际学生感兴趣，但学术部门通常会在这个问题上进行游说。虽然外国学生是大学的首要关注点，但却是科技公司的次要问题。因此，正如一位高等教育代表所说，企业倾向于在游说外国学生上"搭便车"，这使得企业游说者可以将资源集中用于其他问题。[19]正如第2章所述，大学的利益传统上已经被在华盛顿的一系列集团所代表。最为突出的是"六巨头"：美国社区学院协会、美国州立大学协会、

ACE、AAU、APLU 及全国独立学院与大学协会。ACE 为伞式组织，组织华盛顿高等教育秘书处的会议，华盛顿高等教育秘书处成员包括约 50 个与高等教育相关的团体。同时，全国外国学生事务协会代表国际教育专业人士提供建议，COGR（政府关系委员会）代表研究型大学、医疗中心和研究机构提供建议，联邦政府每年至少资助其 1 500 万美元进行研究。主要研究型大学通常还在华盛顿设有办事处，并开展自己的游说活动。

避开禁令

虽然美国大学对国际学生的涌入产生了浓厚的兴趣，但在 20 世纪 90 年代，"六巨头"对待此事则相对平静。正如两位学者在 1998 年所说的，美国高等教育尚未"在美国政府代表推动国际项目和学术交流的倡议之前，成为一个组织良好的倡导者"。[20] 1996 年，当富布赖特项目（the Fulbright Program）的资金被削减时，美国学术界没有大肆宣传。[21] 同年，当国会通过立法为国际学生建立监督系统时，全国外国学生事务协会领导了针对新系统的反对活动。[22] 相比之下，更加大型的高等教育机构要么起到支持作用，要么并不参与其中。[23]

2001 年"9·11"事件对美国的外国学生的准入政策产生了重大影响，也极大地影响了高等教育机构的活动。19 名基地组织劫机者中有 18 人是以旅游和商业签证进入美国的。[24] 其中一个人哈尼·汉朱尔（Hani Hanjour）以 F-1 学生签证的身份进入美国学习英语，但从未上课，也从未有过失踪的报告。此外，另外两名劫机者将他们的签证成功地转换为职校学生身份。[25]袭击事件之后,暴露出来的这些问题导致移民政策明显变得更为严格,学生签证是一个特别令人担忧的问题。正如《华盛顿邮报》2001年10月所报道的:"近期发生的恐怖袭击事件彻底改变了移民问题的辩论,取代了特赦议程,提出了重新规范美国边境的建议,严格限制了学生签证,增加了对美国境内外国人的追踪。"[26] ACE 副主席特里·哈特尔(Terry Hartle)后来说道:"一切都在争夺中。"[27]

尽管如此,未来几年内,HTC 在维持国际学生流动方面取得了巨大成功,尤其是因为它几乎没有遭到有组织的反对。它面临的第一个挑战特别严重:临时禁止所有外国学生准入。2001 年 9 月 27 日,参议员戴安娜·范斯坦(Dianne Feinstein)提议暂停学生签证 6 个月,以便美国移民与归化局有充足的时间解决该系统存在的问题。[28]范斯坦的建议并不是最严苛的:众议院提出了更长的暂停时间。但是范斯坦的建议特别重要,因为她是参议院司法委员会技术、恐怖主义和政府信息小组的主席。范斯坦还呼吁建立基金、建立跟踪学生的电子系统、建立新的入学程序、提高入境口岸的安全性并采取其他措施。高等教育官员"非常认真地"采取了所提出的暂停计划,他们认为这些措施会在新的政治环境中被实施。[29]

正如《波士顿环球报》援引的一位高等教育官员的话,这些措施所造成的结果是一轮"激烈的游说"。[30] 10 月 2 日,为了对范斯坦的提议做出回应,ACE 主席大卫·沃德(David Ward)给参议院司法委员会写了一封信，由 29 家高等教育机构联合签署。[31] 这封信"强烈反对暂停计划"，认为这项禁令"不符合国家的战略或经济利益"，并且"在知识素养、善意和失去的经济活动方面对美国造成的损失将是巨大的"。它还认为由于学生签证仅占总体签证的 2%，因此此项禁令的效果不佳。这封信进一步指出，要消除这种禁令，即使是很短期的禁令所造成的损害也需要"数十年"来修复。这封信所提到的要点成为范斯坦和高等教育官员之间的会议重点，这些官员包括来自范斯坦所在的加州的公立和私立大学代表。[32]

作为回应，范斯坦的提议很快就被搁置了。10 月 5 日，在与大学领导层会面后不久，范斯坦说暂停"可能没有必要"。[33] 她的新闻秘书说，与高等教育代表对话后，范斯坦已经决定"退缩"。[34] 范斯坦之所以这样做，是因为她理解大学将支持为外国学生引入监控系统。正如其办公室所做出的解释："如果我们能够就学生签证申报要求得到学校的合作，那么暂停就没有必要。"[35] 但是，ACE 从未反对过建立学生监督系统。[36] 相反，理事会已经针对如何资助这种系统的发展表达了担忧。范斯坦为实现此目标提出了全额联邦资金——ACE 和其他协会对此表达了"强有力的支持"。[37] 新闻报道将此次提出的暂停计划的撤销称为高等教育界的"重大胜利"。[38]

这次胜利并不令人惊讶。简单地说，这样的反对意见微乎其微。最明显的反对派来自反移民组织——FAIR。如第 3 章所述，FAIR 的势力相对较小，调动基层对抗的效果较差。10 月 24 日，也就是范斯坦退出 2 周以后——FAIR 主席丹尼尔·斯坦（Daniel Stein）出现在美国有线电视新闻网（CNN）的一档时事辩论节目 Crossfire（"交叉火力"）中，称其反对现在的既成事实。[39] 但是，FAIR 不仅行动过晚，而且在反对派中也显得势单力薄，没有进行任何基层运动来对范斯坦施压。[40]

实际上，FAIR 很少得到其他团体的支持。特别需要注意的是，"9·11"事件发生后，国内学生团体更关注学生自由而不是外国学生涌入所带来的竞争。例如，在 2001 年 10 月底的一次采访中，美国学生协会的立法主任对"针对国际学生的怀疑"表示担忧，并且指责学生的隐私"明显受到损害"。[41] FAIR 也没有得到其他反移民组织的支持。2002 年，反移民智库移民研究中心的马克·克里科良（Mark Krikorian）针对这一情况进行了总结："实际上，我们对外国学生并没有做太多的事情……我认为，在对整个移民政策的考察中，一个很大的漏洞实际是几乎没有人关注过外国学生。"[42]

HTC 在反对暂停学生签证的过程中并没有面临严重的反对意见。多年以后，据 ACE 高层回忆，并没有其他有组织团体的反对。[43]

建立可行的系统

"9·11 事件"之后还有更多的挑战。虽然没有暂停学生签证的计划，但政府部门在对待外国学生的方式上更加谨慎，学生和学术访问者的签证发放更加困难。作为回应，HTC 与政府部门和国会进行接洽以解决其担忧。虽然打击暂停令会对国会施加压力,但是 HTC 现在发现自己正在与政府部门就如何确保国家安全进行对话。如第 2 章所述,这超出了本书研究的理论范围。即便如此,我还是在这里探讨一下 HTC 的相对有效性,尤其是在无其他群体反对的情况下。

"9·11"事件之后,政府部门的担忧表现在多个方面。F-1 签证的拒绝率从 2000 年的 20% 上升到 2002 年的 27%,并且在 2003 年保持在 25% 以上。[44] 中国和印度的 F-1 签证和 J-1 签证申请的拒绝率特别高,2003 年中国达到 42%,印度达到 43%。[45] 一些被拒签的中国学生在美国驻北京大使馆外举行抗议活动。[46] 一般来说,申请经常被推迟会导致学生的学习很晚开始或完全错过他们的课程,回国的学生在重新进入本国的过程中经常会遇到挑战。学术机构发现很难预测哪些申请需要更多时间,这使由于签证造成的延误难以管理。[47] 严格执行现有的规则也为外国学生抵达美国后带来了新的挑战。[48] 加之美国经济疲软和来自其他国家学生的竞争加剧,这种挑战打破了美国的海外研究领先地位。[49] 实际上,2001—2004 年,F-1 签证的申请数量下降了近 10 万。2004 年,用于研究生学习的签证申请数下降了 28%,2005 年又下降了 5%,中国学生和印度学生的申请签证数量下降得尤为显著。[50] 工程类研究生项目受到严重影响,因为这些课程严重依赖来自中国和印度的学生。[51]

这些挑战引起了大学和科技公司的极大关注。2003 年底,耶鲁大学校长理查德·莱文(Richard Levin)表示,消除学生签证的障碍已成为华盛顿及美国大学的头等要事。[52]科技公司担心美国大学科学与工程领域外国学生数量减少会限制它们获得更多优秀的外国人才。2002年11月，一位跨国高科技公司的主管对《远东经济评论》说道："我们担心这可能会损害未来几年工程硕士和博士的培养。"[53] ITAA主席哈里斯·米勒当年早些时候告诉美国有线电视新闻网："这可能会对行业产生严重的影响，（美国的）数学和科学研究生项目中，有一半学生来自国外。当一家公司正在寻找最优秀和最聪明的人，特别是拥有学士学位、硕士学位和博士学位的人时，很多候选人也都来自国外。"[54]

尽管高等教育机构和科技企业面临着共同的问题，但是高等教育显然冲锋在前，带头应对这一挑战，这不仅是因为大学优先吸引外国学生，还是因为他们直接参与招生过程。为此，高等教育团体多管齐下。2004年5月12日，来自24个高等教育组织、科学和工程组织的负责人联合发表了一篇《关于损害美国科学、经济和安全利益的签证问题的声明和建议》。该声明指控"签证相关问题正在阻止最优秀和最聪明的国际学生、学者和科学家在美国学习和工作"。该声明预测，在没有其他行动纠正的情况下，"美国不欢迎国际学生、学者和科学家的错误认知将会继续扩大"。它警告称，美国"高等教育和科学企业，经济和国家安全受到的损害将是无法弥补的"。该声明接着提出六大具体问题，并就如何解决这些问题提出建议。为了将这些问题阐释清楚，在10月举办参议院外交委员会之前，多个大学的校长在证词中强调了这一说法，该声明全文以官方的名义进行发表。[55]

高等教育团体还与国会进行了各种合作。ACE 为国会工作人员组织了一次伦敦之旅,以便让他们更好地了解获得签证的过程。选择伦敦不仅是出于情况接近,还因为在当时,伦敦发放的学生签证数量比任何地方都多,包括向许多印度学生发放的签证。[56] 美国外国学生事务协会也努力谋求国会的帮助。当一所大学因延迟申请而遇到特殊麻烦时,协会会通知那所大学所在州的国会议员。[57] 高等教育团体还与美国国务院和政府部门就学生签证问题进行直接对话。ACE 副主席特里·哈特尔后来回忆,"我们正在推动它们"来解决这些问题。[58] 美国外国学生事务协会还与国务院和参与机构间审查过程的其他部门进行合作,以确定问题领域并加快进程。协会还会提醒注意申请需要特别长时间的特定案例。在某些情况下,这很有帮助,因为华盛顿的官员并不总会将延误上升到领事层面。[59]

虽然这些努力正在进行,但高等教育团体还强调了针对外国学生计划的另一个问题:新的监控系统。2002 年底,美国国土安全部建立了 SEVIS(学生和交流访问者信息系统)。从 2003 年 2 月 15 日起,学校新入学的学生和访客必须使用该系统,并从 2003 年 8 月 1 日开始让所有学生和访客使用。2003 年 3 月,ACE 主席大卫·沃德在国会抱怨政府部门没有对高等教育对新系统的担忧做出足够的回应。[60] 沃德接着概述了 SEVIS 的一系列问题。由于系统仓促推出,并不完善,所以该系统遇到了各种问题,包括数据丢失、奇怪的违规行为和认证教育机构的措施不足等。[61] 全国外国学生事务协会随后与国土安全部密切合作以改进系统。[62]

高等教育官员致力于应对各种挑战，他们所面临的有组织的反对微不足道。在此期间，FAIR 在其网站上提出了学生签证的年度上限，认为在招生和资助方面，外国学生对国内学生造成了更大的竞争。[63] 但是，并没有基层运动来支持这一行动。尽管 NumbersUSA 可能在这方面为 FAIR 提供了帮助，但是在 21 世纪初，这方面力量仍然很弱，而且在任何情况下，该组织都会对外国学生持不同的看法。NumbersUSA 主席罗伊·贝克后来表示，NumbersUSA 并没有设法限制在美国留学的外国学生人数，并称高等教育是"美国最好的出口产品之一"。[64] 当然，还有一些针对外国学生计划的个人批评者。例如，2002 年，哈佛大学经济学家乔治·博尔哈斯（George Borjas）在《国家评论》杂志上发表文章，质疑接纳这么多外国学生的价值。[65] 这篇文章以国家安全为由批评外国学生项目，并指责它正在腐蚀大学的入学标准，并带来诸多问题。博尔哈斯还为反移民智库移民研究中心撰写了一份报告，对外国学生计划提出了强烈批评。[66] 然而，这些孤立的论点未能引起更普遍的反对。当高等教育机构的官员在 2003 年 3 月和 2004 年 10 月国会前就外国学生问题进行做证时，专家组并没有批评该计划。[67]

高等教育面对的阻力微乎其微，成功实现其目标近在咫尺。F-1 签证的拒签率从 2002 年的 27% 下降至 2006 年的 20%。[68] 国务院也一致努力减少签证申请延迟的问题。事实证明，评判签证申请所需的时间在很大程度上取决于申请人是否必须接受名为

Visas Mantis("签证螳螂")的机构的安全检查。该程序于1998年首次推出,旨在确保拒签某些人,这些人被认为可能会将管制技术转让给恐怖主义国家或其他利益相关的国家。"9·11"事件后,此类检查的数量直线飙升,因此审查过程进展缓慢。2003年,美国审计总署指出,Visas Mantis 审查平均需要67天才能完成。[69]来自中国、印度和俄罗斯的申请人审查速度特别慢。2004年底,经过多方努力,Visas Mantis 提高了审查效率,审查的平均时间缩减到15天。[70]拒绝率也保持在很低的水平,仅为2%。[71]此外,还有更多的举措来提升学生签证的申请速度:2004年7月,美国国务院发布了一份电报,表明F-1签证、J-1签证和M-1签证的申请人会安排优先面签,因为这些申请人经常会面临抵达美国的最后期限的问题。[72]SEVIS的问题也得到了改善。截至2004年10月,全国外国学生事务协会主席马琳娜·约翰逊(Marlene Johnson)称SEVIS为次要问题,因为"其余问题主要是技术问题"。[73]截至2005年,美国审计总署将该系统描述为"得到了改进"。[74]虽然此后SEVIS的工作仍在继续,但它俨然已经不是焦点问题了。

2005年,情况趋于稳定,HTC突然面临着一个针对外国学生和研究人员流动的不同挑战:出口管制。从传统来讲,如果该学术研究工作可定性为"基础研究",则可以免除政府的许可要求。2005年3月,美国商务部就拟议的规定征求公众意见,该规定将大大增加大学的许可负担。[75]该规定旨在扩大"视同出口"的规章,其控制着将技术转让给在美的外国公民。[76]该规定重新定义了受控设备的使用,包括简单地操作它,然而在过去,必须满足多个标准才能被认为其已经发生。该规定还将根据外国人的出生国家而不是其国籍或居住国家实施控制。

高等教育团体对此迅速做出反应。6月下旬，AAU和COGR分别向商务部提交了一份19页和16页的信件，提出了一系列问题和担忧。[77]这些问题包括在欢迎外国学者和学生方面对美国大学形象的影响，外国学生和学者在美国科学研究中的重要性，拟议规定将产生的许可负担的程度，通过这些措施改善国家安全的可能性不大，以及对科学研究的负面影响。ACE和其他高等教育团体对此也提出了批评，公众也纷纷发表自己的观点。针对该拟议规定，总共有307条公众意见，其中200多条是由学术科学家和研究人员提交的，这些意见显然也对该规定持否定态度。[78]

2006年5月，美国商务部工业和安全局宣布撤销拟议的规定。[79]使用的定义将保持不变，但认为出口管制不适用于出生国。很明显，这是高等教育集团的胜利。然而，还有其他的阻碍。工业和安全局规定，即使研究结果的报告不受控制，在进行研究时也可能需要许可证才能使用受控设备。这与AAU和COGR所采取的立场背道而驰，后者认为研究的行为和报告是不可分割的。即便如此，鉴于其他提案的撤回，这一变化的实际影响非常有限。事实上，高等教育机构的官员对整体结果非常满意。正如COGR一份内部备忘录所说："在大多数情况下，这对大学和研究机构来说是个好消息。"[80]许可的负担仍然可控，美国高等教育的形象不会因新的烦琐监控技术而受到损害。此外，当需要许可证时，商务部也不可能食言。[81]

ACE 副主席特里·哈特尔后来回忆说，2006 年围绕外国学生准入的政策环境再次趋于"稳定"。[82] 在此背景下，外国学生入学率将在未来几年再创新高。尽管在 2004 年 F-1 签证的申请量下降到 211 497，但是根据图 4.1 的数据，在此之后，这些数据的涨幅也令人印象深刻。2008 年，美国国务院收到了 504 607 份 F-1 签证申请，其中有 340 711 份得到了许可。[83] 申请美国研究生院的人数也有所增长，2005 年和 2006 年度增长了12%，之后一年增长了 9%。[84] 实际上，2008 年，申请数量的不断增加使得美国国务院不堪重负，出现了大量审核延迟的情况，高等教育机构进行投诉，问题再次得到解决。[85] 虽然 2009 年申请放缓，但是随着美国陷入全球金融危机的泥沼中，这种增长于 2010 年再次恢复。2013 年，国务院首次签发了 50 多万张 F-1 签证。

结 论

"9·11"事件发生后的几年，由高等教育集团主导的 HTC 致力于确保美国对外国学生保持开放。在袭击事件发生后不久，高等教育集团的官员面临暂停学生签证的提议，该签证将在短期内阻止外国学生流入，并对美国长期致力于国际化教育的承诺提出严重质疑。面对这一提议，HTC 所面临的来自其他团体有组织的反对微不足道。因此，HTC 的努力非常成功。在接下来的几年，外国学生的涌入将不可避免地呈下降趋势，部分原因是签证的拒签率提高、审核延误以及这些问题在国外产生的负面影响。2005年出现了新的出口管制的可能性。为了应对这些挑战，高等教育团体直接与政府部门合作，后者被迫在国家安全问题与全球化教育和学术研究的现实之间寻找平衡。HTC与政府部门之间的这种接触不在第2章所述的理论范围之内。尽管如此，HTC在此项工作中成功地引人注目，它表明高科技利益团体在影响政府部门对国家安全的态度方面非常强大。

美国针对外国学生的政策还有没有其他解释呢？战略霸权假设表明美国已经在战略上采取了行动。具体而言，战略霸权假设可以对美国的政策进行解释，这种观点解释了美国排除外国的学生将要付出多大的代价，以及美国并没有垄断高等教育，虽然这些观点似乎是合理的，但是它们忽略了一些重要因素。首先，美国有许多选择，且这些选择比全面禁止或限制外国学生的成本低很多。例如，美国的政策制定者可以限制来自某些国家的学生人数，但不限制其他国家的学生人数，以确保这些限制的成本在学生派遣国不成比例地下降。其次，尽管美国并没有垄断高等教育行业，但它确实在科学和工程学教育中占据主导地位。根据《泰晤士高等教育》2014年和2015年公布的排名，工程和技术领域全球排名前20位的大学里，美国大学占据了14位；在物理科学领域全球排名前20位的大学里，美国大学占据了13位。[86]尤其是研究生阶段的学习，美国有着很多优势。最后，针对外国学生的战略性方法意味着要为在美留学的学生创造更多就业机会。

但是，正如第3章所阐述的，自2004年以来，这种机会已经被削减。综上所述，很难用战略的术语来解释美国对待外国学生的政策。

在这种情况下，舆论假设也难以阐明这一变化。"9·11"事件发生后，美国公众反对移民，并通过舆论影响政府的决策。例如，2001年10月的一项民意调查发现，58%的美国人希望移民水平下降，与4个月前的41%相比已经急剧上升。[87] 在这种情况下，针对外国学生签证计划的临时暂停或限制年度上限会很受欢迎。然而，HTC依然成功地接收了大量外国学生。

在这种情况下，优先党派的假设无关紧要。劳工或公民团体对HTC没有持明显的反对意见，因此我们无法评估不同政党的相对权力如何影响他们对抗HTC的能力。

在美国政府面向外国学生的政策方面，联盟力量假设尤其无益。其中第一种假设，当HTC的双翼都积极参与时，它是最成功的。在这种情况下，高等教育部门起了带头作用，而企业部门则在后台发挥了支持作用。此外，更广泛的商业利益在此问题上并没有发挥积极的作用。但即使在一方比另一方更活跃的情况下，HTC还是取得了巨大的成功。第二种联盟力量假设——当HTC的企业联盟与其他商业利益结盟时，HTC最为成功——在这里根本不相关。

最有用的可选解释似乎来自现状假设。美国传统上并没有限制美国大学的外国学生人数，所以即使对这些学生实施临时禁令，也会与现存的政策形成明显的背离。即便如此，由于难以对外国学生实施禁令，HTC在这里没有取得成功，而HTC最后的成功是因为其劝阻了一位重要的立法者实施这样的禁令。此外，"9·11"恐怖袭击事件以后，学生签证的处理成为一项严峻的挑战，HTC面临的任务从捍卫有利的现状转变为试图改变不利的现状。HTC也成功地完成了这项任务，尽管它需要在国家安全问题上与政府部门达成合作。

如果说在"9·11"恐怖袭击事件后，高等教育团体在学生签证问题上占据了主导地位，那么在21世纪初，HTC的企业部门将会负责另一个领域：全球研发。下一章将对此进行讨论。

第 5 章

基本开放：全球研发活动

第 5 章 基本开放：全球研发活动

人才的跨境流动是创新全球化的关键因素，而企业和大学从事研发的方式也是全球化的。跨国公司的研发中心已经越来越多地在全球不同的地方蓬勃发展，公司、大学和独立研究人员之间的跨境合作也越来越多。过去，这项活动主要为发达国家主导。但是，当今的发展中国家，特别是中国和印度，在全球研发中扮演着越来越重要的角色。美国公司也成为中国和印度最重要的研发投资者之一。美国也是中国和印度在研发联盟上的主要合作伙伴。因此，在把中国和印度纳入全球研发的方面，美国的开放发挥着至关重要的作用。

对于美国来讲，对全球研发这一现象进行监管是很有挑战性的。就其本质而言，高科技研发非常复杂，需要高水平的专业知识才能理解。美国科学家和工程师的野心以及美国社会的开放性也在克服跨境交流障碍和与外国同事的合作方面发挥了作用。由于这些原因，美国一直并且仍然在很大程度上对全球研发持开放态度。尽管如此，美国政府以各种方式监管全球研发的一个重要方面——外国投资。CFIUS（美国外国投资委员会）对外国的投资进行审查，特别是可能导致外国人控制美国业务的投资，并可以向总统建议以国家安全为由阻止该交易。[1] 反过来，美国的海外投资受到美国法律法规的约束，特别是有关税收、贸易和出口管制的法律法规。虽然对全球研发进行监管具有挑战性，但它并非不受监管，特别是在外国投资领域。

出于两个原因，本章重点关注美国针对OFDI（对外直接投资）的监管。一是该政策领域对全球研发构成了迄今为止最严峻的挑战。21世纪初以来，为了限制研发和其他服务业向海外的流动，已经有多方努力来改变与OFDI有关的美国法律。相比之下，CFIUS虽然近年来对改革的兴趣有所增加，但仍然没有限制投资。二是高科技集团已经进入OFDI领域。由于OFDI广泛的国际化投资和运营，其所面临的挑战尤其受到领先的高科技公司的关注。因此，这些公司积极应对这些挑战。相比之下，对作为一个集团的美国高科技公司来说，通过CFIUS对投资进行审查一直不是一个问题，尽管有时候对个别公司来讲这是个需要关注的问题。[2] 因此，围绕投资的政治讨论超出了本研究的范围。

本章将会概述与OFDI相关的美国关键政策。我将专注于几项针对外商投资的政策。我将解释美国传统上在这方面是如何开放的，但近些年却出现了一系列问题，特别是关于离岸外包对美国就业和技术领先的影响方面的问题。尽管存在这些担忧，美国立法者却很少有机会改变美国的政策。为了解释这一结果，我深入研究了这些政策的政治背景，以期展示HTC中的企业部门如何与其他商业盟友合作，以抵制联邦和州一级的反离岸外包立法。本章还探讨了高科技公司在这些努力中遇到的反对，尤其是有组织的劳工的反对。因为在这场斗争中，劳工基本上是没有形成组织的，所以高科技公司通常占据上风。

开放对外直接投资的三大支柱

美国对于 OFDI 的开放传统由来已久，这种开放性取决于几大不同的支柱。第一大支柱是税收政策。20 世纪上半叶，税收抵免和税收延期成为美国应对 OFDI 政策的重要组成部分。[3] 税收抵免指的是允许向外国政府缴纳的税款抵扣在美国缴纳的公司税款。税收延期指的是允许针对国外收入缴纳的税款延迟到收入收回本国后缴纳。延期的理由是，这使得美国公司能够在低税收国家与当地的竞争对手竞争。然而，批评者指责美国公司使用延期支付降低其有效税率，而且延期支付会鼓励美国公司在国外而不是在国内扩张。[4] 这些税收规定与领先的美国科技公司的全球业务密切相关。包括苹果、戴尔、惠普、IBM 和微软在内的公司被称为其中的"主要例子"，它们在国外享有高额的利润和很低的有效税率。[5]

第二大支柱是贸易政策。几十年来，随着全球创新和生产网络的兴起，美国 OFDI 政策的另一个关键方面是其对国外生产的商品和服务的开放性。美国对 ICT 行业的开放尤其体现在支持世界贸易组织下的《信息技术协定》，包括近年来针对该协定扩展的内容。[6] 贸易开放对 OFDI 来讲至关重要，因为美国公司有时依赖外国子公司和更广泛的国际网络来为美国市场生产，特别是在 ICT 领域。基于这个原因，工会不仅关注国际税收政策，还关注与贸易有关的措施，并将其作为打击离岸外包的手段。[7]

第三大支柱是美国的出口管制，特别是那些处于军民两用领域的管制。美国的《商业管制清单》列出了十类军民两用的技术，包括电子、计算机、电信和信息安全，在不同的国家，这些技术受到不同程度的管控。即便如此，20世纪90年代以来，包括高性能计算机和半导体在内的ICT关键领域的管控已经逐步实现自由化。[8]在其他领域，例如软件开发和云计算，很少有管控措施。该系统也越来越关注受控技术的最终用途，可以允许民用，而军用可能受到限制。因此，除少数例外情况外，目前美国的管控措施并不是制约ICT研发全球化的主要因素。[9]正如一位知识渊博的IBM高管在中国所观察到的，在公司决定是否进行国内研发的时候，有些情况下出口管制仍然是"相关因素"，但通常情况下并不是"首要因素"，[10]更重要的考虑因素包括当地人才的可用性和知识产权的安全性。其他公司，例如谷歌，选择不为美国军方开发产品，而是专注于民用从而避免了对新技术的控制。[11]

简而言之，美国针对国际税收、贸易和出口管制的政策普遍支持OFDI，特别是对外国研发的发展。这种开放性继而使得美国跨国公司在过去几十年中扩大了其在国外的研发活动。正如第1章所介绍的，2013年，美国公司通过其海外子公司在海外进行研发的投入超过490亿美元。尽管大部分（61%）的支出是针对欧洲的，但在中国和印度的支出份额正在增长。事实上，在中印两国进行投资研发的美国ICT公司名单现在看起来像是美国顶级高科技公司的集合，包括苹果、思科、戴尔、谷歌、惠普、IBM、英特尔、微软、甲骨文及高通等。事实上，美国企业已成为在中印进行研发的主要外国投资者之一。在中国，美国和日本是两大主要的外国投资者，但美日之间的差距却很大：2005—2013年，美国公司在中国的研发投入是日本公司的2.7倍。[12] 美国公司在印度的投资也大幅度领先。根据最新获得的数据，2003—2009年，在印度进行研发投资的外国企业中，美国所占的份额为53%，遥遥领先于其他国家，而德国在印度的投资比例为8%，位居第二。[13]

20世纪70年代以来，虽然美国一直对OFDI存在担忧，但是在21世纪初，出现了对于服务性工作及研发的转移的担忧。2002年11月，弗雷斯特研究公司发布的一份报告预测，截至2015年，美国将有330万个服务性工作岗位转移到海外。该报告补充道，ICT行业将"引领早期的外流"。[14] 这份报告引发了关于美国技术竞争力前景的恐慌，特别是针对中国和印度。正如英特尔首席执行官所说："世界结构发生变化……美国不再只关注高科技白领工作。"[15] 有些人担心海外建厂的危险，还有人谴责离岸外包。正如一些评论员指出的那样，两者是截然不同的现象：海外建厂指的是公司将业务转移到其海外子公司，而离岸外包则指的是将业务职能外包给海外地区的外国公司。[16] 无论使用何种措辞，这种恐慌都是真实的。2004年3月，盖洛普民意调查显示，61%的美国人担心自己、亲戚和朋友可能因为雇主将工作机会转移到海外而失业。同样的民意调查显示，58%的美国人表示，在决定投票支持谁当总统时，这个问题"非常重要"。[17]

有些人担心海外建厂会对美国如何定位自己与中国和印度的

关系造成影响。例如，2004年5月参议员约瑟夫·利伯曼（Joseph Lieberman）办公室发布的一份报告认为，在高科技领域，美国"输给了"这两个国家：

> 基础设施、劳动力、资本、技术和信息的外包不仅不利于我们的劳动力，也威胁着我们的知识经济支柱。中国和印度等新兴国家已经意识到技术领先会带来经济的繁荣。中印两国的政府致力于通过产业政策、补贴和商业激励措施吸引商业投资、技术转让和知识流入。[18]

该报告进一步指出："中国和印度庞大的人口规模及其较低的生活成本意味着他们的低工资将在未来很长一段时间内给美国的劳动力带来压力。"[19] 从那以后，关于离岸外包对美国竞争地位的影响的担忧持续存在。正如一位著名评论员在2016年6月所观察到的："虽然离岸外包业务最初意味着失业，但是随着时间的推移，它会导致更多资产（包括研发能力）的流失，从长远来看，这将削弱我们的竞争力。"[20]

面对这些问题，政府开始宣扬离岸外包的潜在好处。2004年，经济顾问委员会主席格雷戈里·曼昆（Gregory Mankiw）称离岸外包是"经济学家所谈论的贸易收益的最新表现"，因此是件"好事"。[21] 虽然曼昆的言论极具争议性，但是即使是艾伦·布林德（Alan Blinder）这种强调破坏可能性的经济学家也不支持为离岸外包设置障碍的想法。[22] 一些人认为，美国可以从服务贸易中获益，并且应该寻求开放这种贸易的可能性，而不是阻止它。[23] 其他人认为，在海外更加活跃的美国跨国公司在美国也要更加活跃，无论是专注于就业、销售、资本支出还是研发。[24] 甚至是像 IEEE-USA 这样一些批评海外建厂的机构所指出的，试图做太多限制它的行为是很危险的。"离岸外包是一个很复杂的问题，"IEEE-USA 主席约翰·斯特德曼（John Steadman）在 2004 年 3 月表示，"很明显，在某些领域，如果禁止任何级别的离岸外包，公司就可以'弃牌'。"[25]

面对这场复杂而持久的辩论，美国的政策基本上仍然对离岸外包开放。这并不是因为缺乏关于如何限制它的想法：自 21 世纪初以来，联邦和州一级都有各种各样的建议来限制离岸外包。然而，其中很少有成为法律的。例如，2004 年 1 月，国会通过立法限制了该财年联邦合同工作的外包，但是一项使该条款永久化的提案后来被否决了。自 2010 年以来，国会还考虑了几项限制离岸外包的法案，但没有一项成为法律，只有一个例外。许多州政府也考虑过限制离岸外包的措施，但大多数措施也被否决了。

现在让我们转向美国对离岸外包保持开放背后的政治因素。

针对离岸外包的斗争

2002 年末，随着争议日益激烈，美国政府在 2003 年开始正视离岸外包现象。正如美国政府所做的那样，立法者将面对两大对立方的游说。在支持开放的一方中，技术公司早就主动采取了措施，因为围绕离岸外包的争议主要涉及 ICT 行业。ITAA 特别积极地试图影响这场辩论。该组织向媒体表示，离岸外包对美国就业的影响被夸大了，对美国公司来讲，保持竞争力和盈利是至关重要的。该组织还强调，如果美国变得不那么开放，其他国家将会采取报复行动。2004 年 3 月，ITAA 主席哈里斯·米勒在国家公共广播电台上做了解释：

> 许多公司通过在国外销售获得了丰厚的利润。当我们赢得比赛的时候，当我们在该领域纵横驰骋的时候，当我们大获成功的时候，说出"让我们停止比赛并改变规则，以使自己处于劣势"，这是非常愚蠢的行为。[26]

ITAA 在推动其法案的同时与其他商业团体联手，2004 年初，这些团体创建了一个新的组织：经济增长与美国就业联盟。该组织有大约 200 个商业协会，包括 ITAA、美国银行家协会、商业圆桌会议、全国制造商协会和美国商会。[27] 该组织的声望、财富和组织能力是显而易见的，当时媒体也注意到了它的力量。[28]

辩论的另一方是有组织的劳工，包括 IEEE-USA 和 AFL-CIO。工党领袖了解他们在限制离岸外包时所面临挑战的严重程度。AFL-CIO 首席国际经济学家西娅·李（Thea Lee）是这样描述反对派的："这是一个极其富裕的企业集团，如果他们（在这个问题上）花费大量资源，那将需要认真对待这件事情了。"[29]

李希望来自公众舆论的支持以及公司站在"错误的一方"这样的事实能够使劳工赢得胜利，或者至少是赢得一部分胜利。不过，这是一场不平衡的竞赛。正如某位作者在2004年所提出的："反对反离岸外包立法的力量在利用影响力方面更有组织性、更富有，并且更复杂，他们将阻止限制作为首要任务。"[30]

针对离岸外包的政治斗争类似于20世纪90年代末针对H-1B签证计划的斗争。科技公司游说支持开放，而有组织的劳工则反对开放，力量的对比更有利于科技公司。事实上，在这种情况下，随着技术公司与其他有着共同关注点的商业群体进行更加密切的合作，力量对比更加不利于劳工。在联邦和州两级的立法斗争中，力量的不平衡将会发挥重要作用。虽然有组织的劳工已经赢了一些战斗，但HTC及其盟友却赢了整个战争。

联邦级别的抗争

从2003年开始，AFL-CIO开始与国会开展针对打击离岸外包措施的合作。[31]虽然劳工巨头顺理成章地与民主党立法者展开密切的合作，但是双方都有担忧。这些努力加上更广泛的公众关注，开始在年底得到回应。国会理所当然地会关注最容易影响业务的一方面：政府采购。

2003年10月，参议院以95∶1的票数比例通过了一项反离岸外包修正案，对针对若干部门和机构的拨款法案进行了修正。该修正案要求在2004年内，让在美国行政管理和预算局通告A-76下进行的联邦契约工作都能得到回报。[32]该法案于2004年1月由布什总统宣布通过。

这项特殊的措施并没有引起 HTC 的大规模反对。该法案的影响可能很有限，公司担心打击这项方案会损害他们良好的企业公民形象。[33] 然而，有人担心该法案将导致更广泛的限制。ITAA 主席哈里斯·米勒解释了1月份采购限制通过后的担忧："我担心公司方面，因为即使这项法案的影响有限，离岸外包的反对者也会寻求更大的保护。"[34] 商界领袖不相信政府会找到办法阻止离岸外包，但他们确实担心政府可能会使离岸外包变得更加困难且成本更高。[35]

人们担心提出更大的限制是有根据的。2004年2月，康涅狄格州参议员克里斯托弗·多德（Christopher Dodd）的工作人员与 AFL-CIO 专家会面之后，多德提出了《美国工人保护法》。[36] 早先修正案所施加的限制仅限于2004年，但多德的法案使其成为永久性限制。多德的法案还将限制扩大到具有联邦资金的州合同。[37] 该法案将对中国和印度产生影响，许多欧洲国家不会受到该法案的限制，因为它们是世界贸易组织针对政府采购契约的27个签署国之一。[38] 多德随后同意在与两党的其他参议员的谈判中调整该法案的语言，这些参议员包括马克斯·博卡斯（Max Baucus）、约翰·麦凯恩和米奇·麦康奈尔（当时的多数党党鞭）。虽然新语言创造了一些例外条件，但永久性禁止离岸外包合同工作的核心理念仍然存在。[39]

多德的努力得到了一个自称为 JTN（就业和贸易网络联盟）的联盟的热烈支持。尽管该联盟将自己描述为反对离岸外包的商业和劳工团体联盟，但它本质上是一项劳工倡议。15个赞助商包括来自AFL-CIO各部门的代表，包括造纸、联合工业、化学和能源工人（PACE）国际联盟和美国钢铁工人协会。[40] 相比之下，少部分支持JTN的商业团体都是小型组织，例如宾夕法尼亚州制造商协会和康涅狄格州制造联盟。其中一些人选择支持JTN，因为他们无法影响国家商业团体，例如全国制造商协会和美国商会，这些全国性商业团体对小型机构的担忧毫不关心。[41] 虽然IEEE-USA不是JTN的一部分，但是它也支持反离岸外包工作。3月中旬，IEEE-USA发布了一份声明立场的文件，认为美国政府采购规则应该有利于在国内完成的工作，并且对于"在任何情况下，如果支持该项工作对国家没有明显的长期经济利益，或者不是支持我们国家经济或军事安全至关重要的技术，都要限制离岸外包"。[42]

作为经济增长和美国就业联盟的一部分，科技公司为了击败多德的提议做出了更大的努力，这种努力比它们1月份针对影响更有限的法案所做的努力还要大。即便如此，科技公司也不希望它们的反对会损害自身形象，或者是失去美国政府这个客户。因此，ITAA及其盟友在如何阻止修正案通过时非常谨慎。如果多德的提议成为法律，那么科技公司就会与国会和政府当局的盟友合作，悄悄向主要立法者通报它们的业务将如何受到影响。[43] ITAA主席哈里斯·米勒也要求印度IT公司保持冷静，让它们的美国同行负责游说。[44] 科技公司还努力重新构建公众辩论。在与白宫、商务部和美国贸易代表办公室的官员会面时，科技公司领导人建议使用全球采购而非离岸外包这一术语，他们强调了回顾历史的重要性，历史上，人们曾多次担忧新技术或者外来竞争会导致本国就业机会消失，结果证明，这些担忧是毫无根据的。[45] ITAA 赞助了一项名为《离岸 IT 软件和服务外包对美国经济和 IT 行业的影响》的研究，该研究描述了离岸外包的好处。报告指出，离岸外包不是 IT 服务部门失业的主要原因，即使是有离岸外包的情况，美国的 IT 工作岗位数量也会增加。[46] 这一报告还提到，限制与其他国家的贸易会产生不良后果。AeA（前身为 AEA）的官员认为，外国公司可以通过减少对美国的投资来应对美国的保护主义政策。[47]

科技公司的努力不足以阻止参议院通过该提案。2004 年 5 月，参议院通过了一项税收法案，多德的提案以 92∶5 的票数比例作为修正案通过。[48] 然而，科技公司最终将成功地使该修正案悄然消亡。6 月，众议院以 251∶78 的票数比例通过了自己的税收法案。[49] 众议院和参议院谈判代表在秋季召开会议调解两项法案，行业将在这里施加影响力。正如《华盛顿邮报》所报道的那样："在极大的游说压力下，共和党谈判代表一般支持众议院。"[50] AFL-CIO 专业雇员部门主席保罗·阿尔梅达（Paul Almeida）后来回忆说，该行业"大力推动了多德修正案的消亡"。[51] 这些努力取得了成功，多德修正案没有出现在会议产生的最终法案中。

2004 年之后联邦政府已经不再限制离岸外包，但是在 2008 年奥巴马当选美国总统之后，这一问题卷土重来。这次的重点不是政府采购，而是税收优惠政策。这不是一个新想法。2004 年 3

月,AFL-CIO 执行委员会辩称:"鼓励美国海外就业的联邦税收政策必须由专注于创造就业机会的税收激励措施取代。"[52] 参议员约翰·克里在 2004 年总统竞选期间也多次提出这一问题,并且特别提到了从事离岸外包的"本尼迪克特·阿诺德(Benedict Arnold)①式的公司"。[53] 在 2008 年的竞选活动中,奥巴马再次提到海外税收和离岸外包问题。[54]

奥巴马上任后对离岸外包问题的态度并不明确。2009 年 2 月,奥巴马承诺在国会联席会议之前结束"向海外派遣工作的公司的税收优惠"。[55] 但是,在接下来的一个月里,奥巴马试图让公众意识到这一措施的影响力有限。在白宫的一次市政厅会议上,奥巴马承认离岸外包并没有消失。"并非所有的就业机会都会回来,"奥巴马说道,"我们要做的就是创造一些无法外包的新工作。"[56] 然而,同年 5 月,美国政府发起了一项名为《平衡竞争环境:遏制避税港并取消海外转移税收激励措施》的倡议。[57] 政府要求公司在扣除与海外费用有关的扣除额之前就其海外收入进行纳税。[58] 政府预计这项激励措施将使联邦政府的收入在 10 年内增加 2 100 亿美元。

为了反对该提案,一些商业团体组成了促进美国竞争优势联盟。该联盟不仅包括全国制造商协会和美国商会,还包括 ITAA、TechAmerica、TechNet 和技术 CEO 委员会这样的高科技团体。[59] TechAmerica 拥有大约 1 200 名成员;该集团是由 AeA、网络安

---

① 美国独立战争期间的叛徒。——译者注

全产业联盟、电子政务和 ITAA 以及信息技术产业委员会合并而成的。由于大规模的海外投资，这些技术公司尤其感到恐慌。[60]

经过联盟短暂但激烈的游说，2009 年秋，奥巴马政府搁置了该计划。[61] 在与政府官员的私下会晤中，商界强调该计划对推动奥巴马提出的首要任务——在全球金融中稳定经济危机没有什么作用。此外，他们认为该计划将很难实施，它将以不受欢迎的方式影响许多企业，而且对减少离岸外包几乎没有作用。[62] 科技公司的抵制是非常重要的，其中许多公司都在 2008 年的总统竞选中支持了奥巴马。由于政府对经济的重视，人们特别不愿意对一个拥有巨大增长潜力的行业进行修补。一位官员后来回忆道："我们不会花费大量的政治资金来解决他们反对的事情，特别是在它看起来不会对经济产生积极的影响的情况下。"[63]

然而，这个问题并没有直接消失。2010 年 2 月，奥巴马政府的预算要求提议改变对海外公司收入的税收的计算方式，这将在 10 年内筹集 1 220 亿美元——这与 2009 年的 2 100 亿美元的目标相比大幅度下降，但仍是一笔不小的数目。[64] 虽然这些变化措施并不会被采用，但是已经进行了几次更加集中的尝试来变革海外公司的税收。5 月下旬，参议院财务委员会主席马克斯·博卡斯和众议院筹款委员会主席桑德·列文（Sander Levin）联合提出了《美国就业和关闭税收漏洞法案》。该法案包括各种税收和支出措施，包括提高风险资本家税收的条款，并在 10 年内将海外公司的收入增加 140 亿美元。[65] 这两项措施都令科技公司十分不快，并联合起来抵制这些措施。然而，如果科技公司讨厌该法案，劳工就会钟爱该法案。虽然 IEEE-USA 对此法案没有表态，但 AFL-CIO 主席理查德·特鲁姆卡（Richard Trumka）称这项立法"严厉打击身家百万的对冲基金经理以及将工作转移到海外的公司的税收漏洞"。[66] 工党也发表言论对其进行支持。民主党民意测验专家杰夫·加林（Geoff Garin）说："在这个问题上站错方向是很危险的。我们相信，为了阻止失业，我们能够做的最重要的事情就是阻止就业机会流向海外。"[67] 凭借劳工和公众舆论的支持，5 月 28 日，由民主党控制的众议院以 215∶204 的票数比例通过了该项法案，投票结果主要沿着党派路线进行。

然而，该法案却在参议院遭遇失败。6 月中旬，PACE 联盟致函参议院所有成员，解释说外国税收条款将损害美国公司在国外的竞争力。共和党参议员基特·邦德（Kit Bond）和约翰·图恩（John Thune）支持其提出的观点，邦德提出了一项修正案，要求撤销该法案中的外国税收条款。[68] 尽管该修正案被否决，民主党人现在却面临着共和党的阻挠。参议院的民主党领导人多次尝试在 6 月结束对该法案的辩论，但每次尝试都失败了，最后只获得了三票。在最后一次失败后，多数党领袖哈里·里德搁置了该法案。[69]

工党及其民主党盟友最终在夏季结束时取得了小范围胜利。8 月初，一些民主党参议员修改了最初引入的促进联邦航空管理局现代化的法案。修订后的法案为各州提供了 260 亿美元的资金，以防止教师裁员并且支持医疗补助金。[70] 该法案得到了劳工的大力支持，特别是教师工会对此表达了强烈的兴趣。与此同时，HTC 的联盟也开始出现裂缝。8 月 2 日，包括惠普、美国国家半导体公司、高通和得州仪器等科技公司在内的 22 家公司共同签署了一封寄给参议院领导层的信，称如果收入用于资助已经失效的税收抵免，他们将支持针对海外收入税收政策的变革。虽然美国联邦航空局的法案没有恢复信用，这封信却显示了商界对于维持海外税收政策现状的重要性的不同意见。正如《华尔街日报》的报道，这封信标志着"企业内部分裂的第一个迹象，可能会鼓舞民主党人"。[71] 民主党人此次抓住了机会。8 月 4 日，参议院同意结束对该法案的辩论，温和派共和党人奥林匹亚·斯诺（Olympia Snowe）和苏珊·柯林斯（Susan Collins）与其党派中的其他人分道扬镳，对此投赞成票。[72] 8 月 5 日，参议院以同样的比例通过该法案。8 月 10 日，众议院通过了该法案，奥巴马也于当天签署了该法案。[73] 胜利实现了，但是规模很小：该法案曾经的目标是税收改革后将增加 2 100 亿美元的新收入，如今只能实现 100 亿美元。

民主党领导人试图在秋季基于这次小规模的成功继续前进。实际上，在 2010 年 11 月的中期选举前夕，选民仍然非常担心工作机会外流。一项民意调查让受访者选择政府为加速经济复苏而可能采取的最重要的行动。排名第一的结果是：减少针对外国的外包并提高自身技能。[74]

民主党立法者为利用这一发展立刻采取行动。2010 年 9 月，参议院提出了《创造美国就业机会，中止离岸外包法案》。[75] 该法案为公司雇用美国劳动力以取代外国雇员提供税收优惠。如果公司在海外开办或扩展类似业务，该法案还禁止公司收到与在美国进行的业务结束有关的扣减。最后，该法案废除了针对一些公司的海外税收延迟政策，这些公司在美国减少或关闭贸易或业务，并在海外开展或扩大类似业务以便向美国出口产品。该法案再次得到劳工的支持，特别是 AFL-CIO，但是遭到 TechAmerica 和美国商会等商业团体的抵制。TechAmerica 主席菲尔·邦德写了一封信给参议院全体成员，声称"增加的税收成本……最终将由美国员工、消费者或股东承担"。[76] 考虑到该法案预计遭遇的阻力，一些民主党支持者私下承认该法案很难通过。[77] 9月，参议院以 53∶45 的票数比例同意不停止围绕该法案的辩论，不久后，该法案被否决。

投票结束后，AFL-CIO 继续反对离岸外包，并且希望能够影响 11 月的选举。11 月，AFL-CIO 的主席理查德·特鲁姆卡指责参议院的共和党人在休会之前"最后一次打击工薪家庭"，并在强调"工薪阶层正面临艰难选择"。[78] 10 月初，AFL-CIO 推出了一个新网站，这一网站让选民能够从邮政编码中辨认出有离岸外包工作的公司，部分是基于工人是否因为失去工作而获得联邦贸易调整援助以应对外国竞争。[79] AFL-CIO 还与其附属组织 Working America（工作美国）发表了名为《海外就业：美国经济和工作家庭成本》的报告，强调这一现象的严重程度。除其他措施外，该报告呼吁重整旗鼓推动《创造美国就业机会，中止离岸外包》这项法案的通过。[80]

然而，中期选举的结果对有组织的劳工来讲是一个极大的挫折，劳工寄希望于通过国会获得一项反离岸外包法案。共和党人在众议院获得了惊人的 63 个席位，收回了控制权，同时在参议院获得了 6 个席位，减少了民主党的多数席位。共和党人还在州立法机构中取得了重大进展，提高了他们影响重新划分国会选区的能力。因此，批评离岸外包的人士放弃了通过联邦立法可以实现目标的看法。[81]

可以肯定的是，自 2010 年以来一直有一些反离岸外包的活动。这些活动通常是在选举年关注"哗众取宠的法案"，正如一位密切观察者所描述的那样，这些法案并没有可能被通过。[82] 2012 年，密歇根州的民主党参议员黛比·斯塔贝诺（Debbie Stabenow）提出了《工作岗位回国法案》，这项法案得到了劳工组织的支持。该法案为公司提供税收优惠，以便将工作机会从海外转移回美国，并且拒绝对将美国企业迁往外国地区所产生的外包费用进行税收减免。同年 7 月，该法案在参议院停滞不前，当时一项停止辩论的提议只获得了 56 票。[83] 2014 年，该法案重新被提及，但遭遇了同样的命运。[84]

尽管人们对 21 世纪初期出现的离岸外包存在担忧，但反离岸外包立法一般都难以成为联邦级别的法律。劳工在反离岸外包方面取得了一些胜利，总体而言，HTC 及其盟友成功地抵制了会限制离岸外包的立法。即便在 2009 年和 2010 年，当民主党控制白宫和国会两院时，情况也是如此。然而，劳工与 HTC 之间的斗争并不仅限于联邦层面，这场斗争也在各州发挥作用。

各州的抗争

HTC 在 2004 年与多德的修正案进行抗争的同时,还在州一级抵制一批反离岸外包立法。根据一项统计,2003 年和 2004 年,40 多个州立法机构提出了 200 多项反离岸外包法案。[85] 2005 年和 2006 年,又提出了 190 项类似法案。有组织的劳工在全美国开展工作,以推动这项立法。《华盛顿邮报》报道称:"AFL-CIO 已动员全国各地支持此类法案,不仅要求彻底禁止海外承包,而且要求结束鼓励海外工作的税收优惠政策,并结束迫使承包商披露员工所在位置的措施。"[86] 正如在联邦一级所做的那样,劳工领导了州一级的反抗离岸外包的运动。

HTC 及其在商界的盟友积极反击。2004 年 7 月,ITAA 主席哈里斯·米勒告诉媒体:"离岸外包是迄今为止最耗时的问题……我们正在积极打击这些法案。"[87] 或者,正如米勒在国家公共广播电台说的:"我们就像是一场肆虐的干旱中的志愿消防部门。我的意思是,到处都有余烬,我们只能不停地奔跑来消灭它们。"[88]

最后,ITAA 及其盟友在很大程度上取得了成功。虽然提出了数百项反离岸外包法案,但只有少数成为法律。例如,在 2003 年和 2004 年,只有亚拉巴马州、科罗拉多州、印第安纳州、北卡罗来纳州和田纳西州通过了法案,赋予了在美国的承包商政府采购工作的优先权。[89] 此外,通过的法案的限制性通常是相当强的。印第安纳州的法律赋予国内公司 1%~5% 的价格优惠。北卡罗来纳州的法律建立了对国内产品和服务的偏好,但前提是价格和质量有保证。亚拉巴马州通过了一项决议,该决议仅鼓励各州和地方实体使用国内服务,对采购决策没有任何授权或要求。工党领袖对此结果非常失望。华盛顿技术工人联合会主席马库斯·考特尼(Marcus Courtney)说:"在此问题上,公司利益所受到的束缚是难以置信的。"[90]

什么能够对这种不平衡的结果进行解释?简单地讲,经济增长和美国就业联盟不仅富有且组织良好,而且在影响和阻止立法方面也很精明。在各州级别的工作中,该小组采用了几种特别的策略:招募大型雇主告诉立法者他们会受到拟议限制的伤害,并且警告称如果离岸外包受到限制,并且要花很多的时间去开会,纳税人的成本会增加。该联盟还强调立法会如何违反贸易协定并减少外商投资。正如美国商会的一位高管所称,这些"封锁和攻击"技术会通过商业会议和其他方式传达给联盟成员。[91]

ITAA领导层后来回顾了在各州级别成功的几个关键因素。[92]首先,由于许多公司在几乎所有州都进行了游说,最有效的方法是说服企业成员,他们的立法重点是停止反离岸外包立法。许多告诉立法者这个问题对他们来说很重要的公司会发出强烈的信号。其次,重要的是要防止外包辩论成为通过媒体传播出去的高度公开的争论比赛。公众辩论得越激烈,就越难说服立法者让反离岸外包法案悄然消亡。最后,一些公司非常精明,做出了有助于化解问题的调整。例如,在国外设有呼叫中心的公司设计了他们的系统,使得听起来焦虑的客户可以立即切换到美国呼叫中心。

总之，科技公司及其盟友在各州取得了成功，他们不仅拥有巨额财富和组织良好的体系，还能发动全国性运动，机智地利用这些资源。HTC 的失败有时是由于异常情况。例如，2005 年，新泽西州通过了美国最严格的反离岸外包法，禁止政府合同工作在美国境外进行。[93] 该法律为 HTC 设置了一个不寻常的障碍，因此，其通过的环境值得进一步研究。

该法案于 2002 年由参议员雪莉·特纳（Shirley Turner）在新泽西州参议院首次提出。12 月，该法案以 40∶0 的结果在州参议院全票通过。这一发展引起了 ITAA 的注意，然后又上升到《华尔街日报》所称的"激烈的游说运动"以在州议会中拖延该法案。[94] 此外，印度新德里的一家贸易集团——全国软件和服务公司协会（National Association of Software and Service Companies）代表 850 家公司，聘请了游说公司伟达公关（Hill & Knowlton）来打击新泽西州法案以及其他反离岸外包法案。这些努力似乎得到了回报。该法案于 2003 年在州议会停滞不前，没有举行听证会或投票。[95] 联盟成员淹没了大会，发出数千封愤怒的电子邮件要求采取行动，但无济于事。[96]

2004 年，参议员特纳重新提出这项法案，希望 1 月通过的联邦反离岸外包立法能够推动其前进。[97] 正如 ITAA 主席哈里斯·米勒后来所说，联邦法案给了"那些正在试图提出相似立法的人一定程度的援助和安抚：'联邦政府做到了，我们为什么不能？'"[98] 6 月，特纳的法案又一次在参议院成功通过，但是，该法案再次在立法机构中停滞不前。作为回应，特纳向一名民主党州长詹姆斯·麦格里维（James McGreevey）求助。选择麦格里维非常合乎逻辑：AFL-CIO主席约翰·斯威尼将麦格里维政府描述为该国最亲劳工的州政府之一。[99] 但是，特纳发现这位州长对此漠不关心。"他说：'我能怎么办？'"她后来回忆道。"他多少有点缺乏兴趣"。[100] 特纳后来推测麦格里维担心他在重新选举的时候遇到商界的反对。[101] 该法案又一次陷入僵局。

这种情况在8月发生了变化。当月，麦格里维承认自己与一名男子发生婚外情并宣布他打算在11月15日辞职。延期辞职消除了进行特别选举的必要性，这使得其民主党同僚，州参议院议长理查德·科德（Richard Codey）接任麦格里维成为新泽西州州长。麦格里维还表示，他希望采取一些可以巩固其遗留政策的行动。[102] 9月，他采取了一项行动，签署了一项限制政府合同工作外包的行政命令。该命令允许州政府机构与雇用海外工人的公司合作，但提前是雇用美国工人的公司无法提供服务，或者使用美国劳工的成本会给该州经济带来困难，或者州财务部长宣布该合同最有利于公众。[103] 虽然这并不像特纳的法案那么严格，但是该措施已经与州长早先的立场大有不同。

在签署该命令后，特纳说："恕我直言，我们需要一部法律而不是行政命令。[104] 州长换来换去，新的继任者只需用一支钢笔就可以取消前任的行政命令。"11月15日，麦格里维下台，理查德·科德成为代理州长。正如特纳后来所说，过渡时期对于通过反离岸外包法律"非常有帮助"。[105] 科德代表了一个相对自由的地区，他已经在州参议院支持这项法案。[106] 2005年3月14日，议会以 68∶5 的票数比例通过了该法案。5 月 5 日，该法案由科德签署成为法律。

新泽西州严格的反离岸外包法是在非常特殊的情况下才出现的。麦格里维州长曾被吹捧为民主党内冉冉升起的新星。[107] 然而，迫使他辞职的丑闻使他成为一名不再关注连任或国家职务的"跛脚鸭"州长。只有在丑闻发生后，麦格里维才会发布行政命令以限制离岸外包。此后不久，他的辞职反而促进了反离岸外包法的通过。

2006 年以后，对反离岸外包立法的兴趣在州一级逐渐减弱。如图 5.1 所示，2006 年，州立法机构针对离岸外包引入的法案数量达到峰值，为 209 个。但是，在 2007 年之后，这类法案引入的数量降至每年不足 100 个，当然，这是一个粗略的指标，只是基于法案概要是否包括"离岸外包"一词或"外包"一词。并非所有法案都是反离岸外包措施，而一些反离岸外包法案并未包含"离岸外包"一词或"外包"一词。此外，2006 年之后，仍然有一些值得注意的行动来限制各种级别的离岸外包。例如，2010 年，田纳西州通过了一项法律，禁止州政府将使用海外呼叫中心的服务外包。[108] 同年，俄亥俄州州长泰德·斯特里克兰（Ted Strickland）发布了一项行政命令，禁止将公共资金用于海外提供的服务。[109] 即便如此，自 2006 年以来，各种级别限制离岸外包活动的下降非常惊人，这一趋势与来自媒体报道的数据一致。[110] 这种下降表明，在 2008 年大选中进行的联邦级别抗争之后，有组织的劳工已经不断为反离岸外包进行努力。

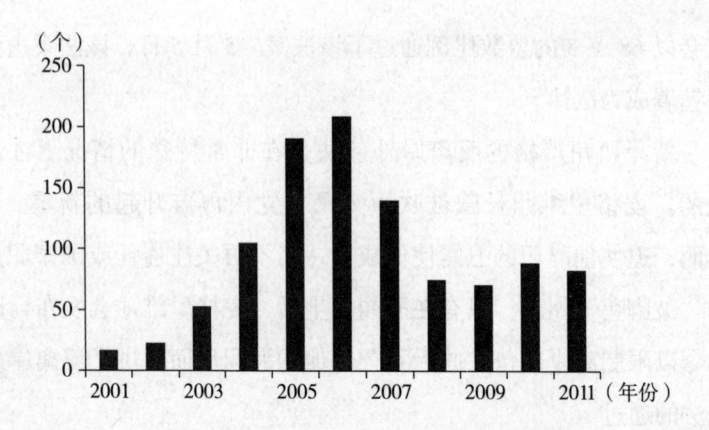

图 5.1　2001—2011 年法案概要中包含
"离岸外包"一词或"外包"一词的州议案数量

资料来源：律商联讯（LexisNexis State Net）数据库，访问于 2015 年 8 月 4 日。

结　论

21 世纪初以来，美国全球研发的主要挑战是反离岸外包立法。特别是 2003—2006 年，以及 2009—2010 年联邦层面的斗争，有组织的劳工主导了一系列行动来降低离岸外包的程度，而不是完全停止这种行为。总的来说，这些努力集中在税收和贸易政策上，而不是出口管制。虽然重点不仅仅在于高技能工作岗位，但是许多提案都会使高科技公司的海外研发工作变得更加复杂。

高科技公司一直担心反对离岸外包运动，他们通过高效的行动来限制其影响。通过与其他商业团体合作，高科技公司在与劳工的斗争中取得了很大成功。2004年初，国会通过立法限制政府合同工作在当年接下来的时间内的外包，高科技公司在联邦级别遭受了较小的挫折，但他们成功地阻止了这一变化成为永久性的立法。高科技公司在2010年8月遭遇了一次小规模的挫折，当时它们内部的混乱导致国际公司税制发生了微小的变化。然而，在随后的2010年、2012年和2014年，科技公司帮助击败了联邦反离岸外包法案。在美国，2003—2006年引入了许多反离岸外包法案，但HTC及其商业盟友的阻止让其中大部分都没有成为法律。在新泽西州，通过的限制性最强的法律出现在非比寻常的情况下，这使科技公司很难取得成功。因此，美国对离岸外包主要保持开放态度，这一结果与第2章概述的理论吻合。

在这种情况下，可选解释是如何奏效的呢？战略性霸权假设预测，如果这样做是可行的并且成本更低，美国将限制与中印两国的合作。就可行性而言，在这种情况下，限制合作肯定比限制移民更加困难。美国政府可以监控和监管合法移民，但企业到外国投资很难管理，特别是当大公司在海外保留充足的资金时。尽管如此，美国联邦和州政府确实拥有可用于解决离岸外包的工具，但它们不会轻易使用。虽然专家在本章讨论的各种法案的经济影响上存在分歧，但是显而易见的是，奥巴马政府正在积极地应对其中几项法案，其中一些法案承诺会增加联邦收入。相比之下，反离岸外包立法对中国和印度没有明显的好处，因此很难将成本分配视为决定性因素。

在这种情况下，舆论假设显然缺乏支持。虽然公众舆论通常站在劳工一边，但是其政治效用有限。如前所述，相当多的公众担心2004年的离岸外包，也是在当年多德的修正案被打败了。在2010年中期选举之前，公众舆论也有利于反离岸外包立法，但此时通过反离岸外包立法的努力也失败了。

优先党派假设也很难找到很多支持的证据。在这种观点中，当民主党占据主导地位时，劳工反对HTC的能力应该远远大于支持商业的共和党。然而，在这段时间内，无论哪一方更为突出，劳工基本上是不成功的。即便在2009年和2010年，当民主党控制政府部门和国会两院时，情况也是如此。虽然民主党确实试图在2010年通过《创造美国就业，中止离岸外包法案》，但这一努力在参议院被击败——有四名民主党人和由民主党转为独立人士的约瑟夫·利伯曼投票反对。

现状假设更加有用，它是我在本章中进行的利益集团分析的补充。高科技公司在很大程度上取得了成功，不仅因为它们的力量比有组织的劳工大很多，而且还因为它们在劳工试图改变现状的同时捍卫现状。2010年、2012年和2014年，联邦反离岸外包法案的失败就很好地证明了这种情况。这些法案都在参议院中夭折，其中绝大多数人需要前进，这使得高科技利益集团特别容易阻止变革。即使如此，在有些情况下，高科技公司一开始就成功地阻止了立法被引入，如成功搁置了2009年奥巴马税制改革提议。这表明，对现状的偏见是造成这种情况的部分原因，但不是全部原因。

本章中提出的证据对两种联盟力量假设有着截然不同的含

义。第一种假设——当企业和学术机构都积极参与时，HTC 是最成功的——并未得到证实。尽管学术界没有参与，HTC 还是在很大程度上取得了成功。相比之下，第二种假设——关于其他企业的支持程度——得到了证实。高科技公司显然与其他商业集团进行了结盟，包括全国制造商协会和美国商会，这有助于解释为什么在这种情况下，HTC 非常成功。但值得注意的是，即使是这个令人印象深刻的商业联盟也遭遇了一些失败。这一结果与前一章所述的外国学生争夺战中的结果形成鲜明对比。在前一章的情况下，HTC 拥有的盟友较少，但面临的反对较少，其胜利也更具决定性。

总 结

创新全球化

总　结　创新全球化

　　本书前面的章节中有三大发现。第一大发现是，创新是全球化的。无论是技术劳工还是科学与工程领域的学生，现在司空见惯的大规模跨境人才流动尤其显著。研发活动也在走向全球化。无论是研发联盟、风险投资活动、大学合作伙伴关系还是科学论文合著，不断增加的跨境合作显而易见。尽管美国跨国公司仍在国内进行大部分研发工作，但是在海外研发中心不断增长的投资也很明显。这些变化已经使得发展中国家，特别是中国和印度，能够在从未参与过的创新中发挥作用。这些变化也迫使美国思考如何在其长期占据主导地位的经济领域与新兴大国开展合作。

　　第二大发现是，美国对全球创新的开放性是由能够体现该国技术领导地位的组织推动的。在面向人才流动和全球研发的开放性方面，美国高科技公司和研究型大学有着重要的共同利益。然而，作为一个有组织的政治力量，HTC 相对较新。直到 20 世纪末，非政府组织才成为美国研发的主要资助者。此外，仅在 20 世纪 90 年代，ICT 公司开始组织起来影响支持全球创新的政策。HTC 的企业端和学术机构端之间的合作范围和性质也各不相同。无论是非正式的方式还是正式的方式，公司和大学都在技术移民方面进行了最密切的合作，在此领域，它们的利益密切相关。2001 年"9·11"事件之后，美国大学率先行动维持国际学生的流动，因为它们本就倾向于这样做并且也在这件事情上处于优势地位，尽管企业对这种做法产生的结果也感兴趣。由于全球研发领域出现的特殊挑战（反离岸外包立法）已经严重威胁企业的利益，所以企业率先维持对全球研发的开放性。

第三大发现是，正如第 2 章所述，美国政策中的开放程度大致反映了 HTC 面临的有组织的抵制的性质。当 HTC 面临其他群体微不足道的阻力时——正如"9·11"事件后外国学生项目受到挑战时它的应对措施一样——HTC 成功地维持了外籍人才的无限制流动。当 HTC 面临的抵制主要来自劳工时，HTC 很大程度上是成功的。在 1998—2004 年进行围绕 H-1B 签证上限以及反离岸外包立法的斗争中，情况确实如此。当 HTC 面临的抵制来自大型公民团体时，它未能实现其目标。这些团体构成了 HTC 未能克服的挑战，这就是 2004 年以来，HTC 未能促成技术移民增加的原因。HTC 的力量强大但并非不可阻挡，因此，迄今为止，HTC 最强大的对手不是劳工，而是公民团体。

第 2 章中列出的可考虑的解释都难以解释美国政策的变化。正如第 3 章所介绍的，战略性霸权假设强调现实政治中的相对收益计算，但这并不能解释随着时间的推移，H-1B 签证的上限上下起伏。正如第 4 章和第 5 章介绍的，这种假设也难以解释美国对外国学生和离岸外包的开放程度的变化。更笼统地说，这种说法很难解释以下事实：政府部门的首选政策经常得不到通过。1998 年，克林顿政府对于提高 H-1B 签证上限并不热衷，但是那年的上限提高了。布什总统和奥巴马总统对增加技术移民更感兴趣，但他们通过全面立法而为此做出的努力没有成功。最后，尽管奥巴马政府支持反离岸外包立法，但他们的尝试也没有成功。

公众舆论对美国政策的影响微乎其微。正如第3章所介绍的，20世纪90年代末到2013年，公众对技术移民的态度似乎已经有所缓和，但在此期间，美国的政策变得不那么开放。此外，如第4章所介绍的，"9·11"事件之后，公众舆论几乎没有阻碍学生签证的暂停发放。正如第5章所介绍的，公众舆论在离岸外包方面的态度显然是消极的，但美国很大程度上仍然对此持开放态度。

优先党派假设在案例研究中得到了更多支持。与共和党相比，劳工显然在影响民主党立法者的能力上更强，而反移民群体在试图影响共和党时最有效。即便如此，无论哪个政党更为突出，劳工一直都在努力与HTC就其在华盛顿的影响力进行竞争。甚至在20世纪90年代末，民主党当政之时，当劳工试图捍卫现状时情况也是如此。2010年，当民主党掌控白宫和国会两院时，劳工未能让反离岸外包立法获得通过，这种结果令人震惊。相比之下，大型公民团体一直是HTC强硬的反对者。

现状假设也提供了对案例的一些见解。在打击反离岸外包立法的斗争中，高科技公司正在捍卫立法现状，这显然使它们的工作更容易。由于HTC最初试图保留对外国学生的现行政策，因此现状偏见似乎也与第4章相关。然而，HTC不仅在2001年试图保持良好的现状时取得了成功，还在此后几年努力改变日益不利的现状时也取得了成功。这表明，在这种情况下，针对HTC

有组织的反对的确比现状偏见的存在更加重要。此外，现状偏见无法解释美国在技术移民政策上的变化。HTC一直试图改变这一领域的现状，但是随着时间推移，其成功的程度发生了翻天覆地的变化。

这两个关于联盟力量的假设试图以不同的方式解释美国的政策。第一种假设预测，当企业和学术机构积极参与时，HTC将获得最大的成功，这种情况并未得到证据的证实。在外国学生的问题上，当学术机构更加活跃时，HTC才是最成功的；在离岸外包的问题上，只有企业参与的情况下才会大获成功。显而易见的是，当其他群体的反对势力缺席或者力量微弱时，HTC的每一支翼都能占上风。第二种假设预测，当HTC的企业联盟与其他商业利益集团结盟时，HTC是最成功的。这种观点得到了证实，特别是因为高科技公司与其他商业团体的联盟有助于解释它们在击败反离岸外包措施上的相对成功。然而，在其他情况下，高科技公司与其他商业集团进行的联盟却失败了。2004年之后，HTC与一些商业利益集团联盟，希望在全面移民改革的战斗中取得胜利，但是这个强大的联盟一直没有成功，因为它遇到的反对力量太强大了。

这些发现所带来的深远影响是什么？在本章的其余部分，我将从几个不同的角度来回答这个问题。首先，介绍这项研究对国际关系的影响，特别是对全球创新研究的影响。其次，将重点关注美国政策对美国的影响，特别是美国对中印两国的立场。最后，介绍了2016年美国联邦选举的影响以及美国政策未来的走向。

对国际关系的影响

几年前,罗伯特·基欧汉(Robert Keohane)[①]指出,近几十年来,国际政治经济领域的学术研究"非常不愿意关注世界政治中发生的重大变化"。[1]创新全球化是一种非常值得认真研究的新现象。正如本书开始时所指出的,全球创新对于21世纪的财富分配、权力平衡和经济相互依赖具有重要意义。然而,在全球创新崛起的背景下,美国政策并未受到国际关系学者的认真研究。尽管有学者们已经开始探索美国技术移民政策或离岸外包政策中的政治因素,但是本书强调的是,这两大政策领域紧密相连,都对一个更宏观的现象进行了补充。此外,它表明美国在这两大领域的政策可以通过一个共同的分析框架来理解,该框架关注一系列特定的社会行动者:HTC、劳工和公民团体。通过关注美国与中国和印度的关系,本书为权力转型中的政治经济学提供了新的见解——这一主题在过去很少受到关注。

本书还解释了美国在全球创新政策方面所做的具体工作。关于美国离岸外包的政治方面的一些初始工作已经集中到了针对这种现象的公众舆论上。[2]这项工作很重要,但是正如我所表明的,到目前为止,公众舆论在这一领域还不是驱动美国政策的因素。近期关于技术移民的工作反而关注了高技能本国人对高技能移民

[①] 美国学者,以其著作《霸权之后:世界政治经济中的合作与冲突》闻名于国际关系学界,是国际关系学界中新自由制度主义的重要学者,目前在普林斯顿大学的威尔逊学院担任政治科学教授。——译者注

政策的偏好，学者对此一直在争论高技能本国人是否会将技术移民视为经济上的威胁。[3]本书表明，即使在经济相对繁荣的情况下，同一产业中高技能本国人也可能会将这种移民视为经济上的威胁。然而，本书还表明，高技能本国人在抵制美国技术移民扩大方面的能力非常有限。虽然先前的研究已经展示了地方级别的有效抵制，但是本研究表明，高技能本国人很难影响国家政策，即使已经有国家劳工运动支持他们的工作。[4]相比之下，公民团体可能会更加有效。

本书还阐明了美国高技能移民和低技能移民政策之间的关键区别。有研究已经表明，出于对贸易开放和资本流动的回应，企业对低技能移民的需求降低，造成的结果是国家政策变得更加严格。[5]本书的研究结果表明，同样的效果并不适用于高技能移民。近几十年来，尽管贸易开放程度很高，并且公司流动性很大，但是美国高科技公司一直致力于扩大技术移民。对技术移民持续存在的兴趣可能反映了这一类工作的复杂性。离岸外包中的高技能劳工比离岸外包中低技能劳工面临更多的挑战。此外，当需要将高技能的技术工作外包时，高科技公司会发现，在将外籍劳工送回海外之前让其进入美国是更有利的。这也就是为什么H-1B签证有时被称为"外包签证"。通过这种方式，某些种类的技术移民可能会支持离岸外包，而不是替代它。

展望未来，我们仍然需要更多地了解全球创新中的政治。虽然书主要关注HTC及与其对立的利益集团之间在美国政策制定方面的争论，但是未来的研究应该探讨在面临国家行政机关的阻力时，HTC是如何应对的。具体而言，当HTC追求的开放性与政府确保国家安全的努力冲突时，我们需要更深入地了解政策背后的原因。人们很容易想象出国家政治领导层将在任何此类冲突中占上风。在现实情况中，这种相互影响更可能类似于谈判，可能有多种结果产生。正如第4章所讨论的，2001年之后，HTC与政府部门针对外国学者和学生问题的相互影响非常值得注意。在维持开放体系方面，即使美国商务部在2005年试图收紧出口管制措施，HTC仍然获得了成功。但是，在其他情况下，高科技利益集团可能不太成功。未来的研究工作应该致力于解释这种差异。

大体上，未来的研究应该思考其他国家如何应对全球创新。从历史的角度来看，美国作为这一领域的先驱者脱颖而出。从一开始，美国就在吸引国外知识型工作者方面发挥了主导作用，并且几乎没有其他发达国家的竞争。[6] 美国在开拓全球研发的某些方面也发挥了关键作用。包括IBM、微软和得州仪器在内的美国公司在开发发展中国家的研发设施和离岸外包方面一直处于领先地位。[7] 在国际研发联盟和国际科学合作方面，美国的表现也引人注目。但是，美国并不是唯一一个参与全球创新的发达国家。这就引发了一个问题，其他发达国家如何应对这一现象呢？

最近的研究探讨了发达国家如何采用新的技术移民政策，而不是更普遍的全球创新政策。即便如此，该研究也表明在未来的研究中有几种值得学习的方法。第一种方法将国家视为理性和单一的行为者。[8] 在这一点上，国家可以被理解为"跟随霸权"以发展自己的高科技产业。该领域的一些研究将发达国家锁定在高科技人才的竞争中，这场竞争的关键工具是针对高技能移民的政策。[9] 第二种方法强调国内政治。这方面的研究强调政策结果中的跨国差异，并认为这种差异反映了本国制度和利益。[10] 第三种方法也强调政策结果的差异，但关注的是用不同的意识形态和移民历史来解释它们。[11] 结合外部和内部力量后形成的方法也是可能的。[12] 未来的研究应该在这些方面继续进行，但是大体上，研究中应该考虑针对技术移民和全球创新政策。未来的研究还可以探索判断各种理论方法有效性的条件。

未来的研究还应该思考中等收入国家和发展中国家针对全球创新的政策。越来越多的政策研究关注的"后期创新者"（late innovators）成为全球创新网络中更重要的参与者。此外，这些研究还强调了解决市场失灵、吸引外商投资以及将本国公司与全球市场联系起来的政策。[13] 本书的研究已经强调了后期创新者如何在改革天平之间保持平衡，一端的改革鼓励更大的研发力度，另一端的改革限制政府对研发的监督。[14] 中等收入国家和发展中国家对全球创新政策的不同选择很少受到关注。[15] 此外，当学者关注政策选择时，他们通常会考虑外商投资政策或移民政策。全面的解释应该将两个领域的政策都考虑在内。

对美国、中国和印度造成的影响

为了解释美国的全球创新政策，我强调了特定利益集团的游说和政治斗争。这些团体在政治上的力量饱受诟病。事实上，学者已经强调了特殊利益的运作在世界主要大国的兴衰中发挥的作用。例如，曼瑟尔·奥尔森（Mancur Olson）所著的《国家的兴衰》（The Rise and Decline of Nations）一书提出了著名的假设，稳定的民主国家最终屈服于"制度硬化"（institutional sclerosis），其中特殊利益的积累使政策制定偏离"国家"利益且不利于经济增长。[16] 实际上，故事不太可能如此简单。利益集团在民主中履行多种职能，包括向决策者提供信息——即使这些信息是利己的。一些学者强调，关键问题是某个国家的既得利益群体是否会抑制技术变革并扼杀创新，而不是看这些利益群体是否占多数。[17] 在全球化世界中，我要补充一点，我们必须思考既得利益群体和国家政策如何影响其他国家的发展。或者借用吉尔平所说的，我们必须思考既得利益群体如何影响"创造性"的传播。在这种背景下，本书中介绍的利益集团斗争以及由此产生的政策，是否进一步缩小了美国与中国和印度等新兴大国之间的差距？

本书篇幅有限，无法明确回答如此广泛而复杂的问题。但是，总结出一些宽泛的观察评论是有可能的。从保持创新领导力的角度来看，美国对于外国学生保持稳定的开放政策总体上是发挥了美国的优势。正如第 1 章所介绍的，从美国大学获得科技与工程领域博士学位的中国和印度学生传统上可能在毕业后至少留在美国五年。[18]这使得近几十年来，在美国大学获得科学与工程专业博士学位的外国学生的比例有了明显上升，2013年，这一比例达到42%。即便如此，我们也不应该认为美国在将来也会保持相当大的吸引力。正如第1章所介绍的，随着时间的推移，中国和印度学生留美的比例逐渐下降。特别是中国，中国政府仍不断吸引最聪明的学生归国，中国学生回国的人数已经大幅增加了。例如，北京大学化学系中有加州理工学院、哥伦比亚大学、哈佛大学、麻省理工学院、加州大学伯克利分校、芝加哥大学和宾夕法尼亚大学等美国顶级大学的毕业生。如果中国对学术侨民的相对吸引力继续增加，那么外国学生项目对美国未来的技术领导力产生的影响更加难以确定。

这使得我们开始思考技术移民的问题。在这个领域，有明确的证据表明美国政治体制存在功能失调的问题。简而言之，阻碍美国改革其技术移民制度的政治活动，无论是通过有针对性的法案还是全面立法都损害了美国在争夺科技与工程领域高技能人才的能力。作为一种客工计划，正如它的创造者之一所说的那样，H-1B签证"不是美国最有效的欢迎人才的方式"。[19]甚至一些主张扩大该计划的人也承认该计划有严重的问题，包括用有害的方式限制劳工流动。[20]与此同时，批评者指出了更多的问题。[21]然而，更严重的是美国政府未能改革EB签证计划。作为一种永久移民的方式，EB签证计划是美国吸引优秀人才的强大工具。然而，针对每个国家的限额以及已经形成的大量积压工作，特别是来自中国和印度的申请的积压，可能会使很多优秀的人才在是否留在美国的问题上多年来一直举棋不定。事实上，对一些申请人来说，已经无法估计他们需要等待多长时间才能获得签证，甚至是否会获得签证。[22] 在某些时候，优秀的人才可能会认为他们在其他地方有更好的选择。正如第 3 章所介绍的，未能解决这一问题，是 21 世纪围绕美国移民改革的利益集团政治斗争的直接结果。

美国对离岸外包采取的相对开放的做法更难以评估。大多数美国企业的研发支出仍然发生在美国，而大多数美国海外研发支出都发生在欧洲而不是亚洲。[23] 尽管美国公司在中国和印度的研发活动正在增加，但是它对这些国家当地创新能力的影响仍然很难评估。最近的研究表明，随着时间推移，外国跨国公司在中国的研发工作更加富有成效。[24] 但是，这种发展对中国企业有多大帮助或伤害尚不清楚。一项针对中国企业的研究发现，外国研发活动的增加实际上对这些企业的技术变革产生了消极影响。[25] 然而，其他研究提供了更多的积极评估。[26] 外国研发对印度产生的影响也难以衡量。2010 年发表的一项研究发现，寻求创造新技术的外国研发对国内企业产生了积极影响，而将现有技术用于当地市场则产生了负面影响。[27] 值得关注的是，随着外国公司在印度研发活动的增加，情况是否仍然如此？现在是否可以在中国看到同样的效果？简而言之，外国研发在中国和印度的整体影响仍不明朗。

展望未来，全球研发对中国和印度的影响仍有很大的变数。这肯定取决于中国和印度在未来几年所采取的经济改革方式。正如我在其他地方所提到的,这可能会增强或限制中国和印度公司从全球研发中获利的能力。[28] 但这也取决于美国政府和美国公司所采取的方法。以往的研究表明,旨在限制美国公司海外投资的法案不太可能在国会通过。更有成效的方法需要公共和私营部门之间加强合作,以保护跨国网络中的知识产权。这样的工作已经在进行,但仍然任重道远。2007 年,美国商务部的两位重要官员表示,美国政府需要新的思路来实施出口管制,他们建议公司应该根据特定技术和预期的终端用户,思考指定根据具体情况制订有针对性的风险缓解计划以供政府考虑。[29] 问题的关键不是要建立一个新的出口管制制度,而是要帮助公司更好地掌控其长期的脆弱性,同时解决 21 世纪所面临的日益复杂的技术控制问题。[30] 虽然这种定制化的讨论尚未普及,但是已经有少数公司与美国政府就其在中国的运营问题进行了此类对话。[31] 来日方长,这种合作方式可能面临其自身的挑战,但是与限制海外研发相比,这种方式更有可能成功。[32]

总之,各种依据纷乱繁多。美国的全球创新方法在某些方面存在功能失调的迹象,在其他方面却没有。美国政策的影响难以评估,并可能在未来发生改变。实际上,这种评估非常简短并且是暂时性的,显然需要更多的研究。但是,我们不应该就此得出结论,美国技术移民政策中的问题代表了美国无法逃脱的奥尔森式"硬化"形式。自 19 世纪以来,包括企业、工会和反移民团体在内的各大利益集团一直为美国的移民政策而争论不休,而且随着时间的推移,美国的政策发生了大幅度的变化。[33] 此外,不同群体,特别是公民团体的力量会随着大众对于特定目标的热情不断起伏而盛衰不定。考虑到这一点,接下来讨论美国全球创新政策的未来。

观往知来

2016年11月,唐纳德·特朗普当选美国总统,打破了美国政治制度的传统智慧。特朗普竞选活动中值得注意的主题是反移民、反全球化和反少数种族,甚至是众议院议长保罗·瑞安所称"教科书式"的种族主义。[34]特朗普的胜利似乎将美国的反移民运动推向了白宫,同时也标志着HTC在政治上面临巨大的失败,因为HTC主要支持希拉里·克林顿。[35]截至2017年5月,特朗普的当选对美国政策制定的全面影响仍不明朗。政府部门的许多空缺职位仍未填补,鉴于特朗普与俄罗斯关系的争议以及其他问题,人们纷纷猜测他将留任多久。即便如此,值得一提的是,在全球创新的政策上,美国的政策制定是否正在转向一个新的阶段?在新阶段里,政府的影响力是否会使社会利益集团,尤其是HTC的影响力不断减小?

基于以下几点原因,这不太可能实现。第一个原因是美国政策在这一领域的最重大变化通常要求白宫与国会合作。事实上,正是出于这个原因,奥巴马政府试图通过立法修改美国的离岸外包和移民政策。反过来,国会需要为强大的利益集团创造大量机会，以阻止不受这些集团欢迎的变革。高科技公司以及更广泛的商业利益集团，已经在近十几年成功地阻止了大多数修改美国离岸外包政策的尝试，即使这些变化得到了白宫的支持。同一时期，公民团体也阻止了多次企图改变美国移民政策的行动。特朗普政府仍然有可能设法通过立法推进其部分议程，特别是在共和党控制国会两院时。然而，大部分忽视 HTC 集体利益的重大立法是不可能实现的。

当然，政府部门可以单方面采取行动，但这种行动可能会面临限制。正如第 3 章所介绍的，尽管奥巴马政府确实通过行政行为对技术移民政策做出了一些改变，但是它避免了做出根据法律不能明确提出的更广泛的改变。事实上，奥巴马的改变让 Compete America 的执行主席大为恼火，称仍然需要许多"行动"和"具体结果"。[36] 特朗普政府可以根据更广泛的行政权力概念行动，但是如果这样做，也会面临法律诉讼的威胁。例如，2017 年上半年，特朗普对某些穆斯林占多数的国家实施旅行禁令，高科技公司和大学对此都积极支持动用法律手段来反对特朗普的这种行为，这使特朗普政府大受打击。[37] 然而，这一争端最终得到解决，这突出表明，政府部门并不拥有随意重塑美国政策的权力，即使试图这样做可能会损害美国的形象。

第二个原因是特朗普政府和 HTC 之间的关系更复杂，二者之间既有冲突也有合作的可能性。可以肯定的是，双方存在很多冲突，关于旅行禁令的争议就是一个明显的例子。特朗普政府早期改变 H-1B 签证计划的举措也使技术公司大为失望，特别是暂停加急申请处理并禁止入门级计算机工作被视为"专业性工作"（specialty occupation）。[38]特朗普撤销了奥巴马的一些政策规定，包括H-1B签证获得者配偶的工作授权，以及针对科学、技术、工程和数学领域的毕业生的实习工作许可证。与此同时，媒体报道声称硅谷正在努力"推翻"特朗普，包括通过组建"科技的运动"（Tech for Campaigns）这样的新团体来支持民主党候选人的工作。[39]特朗普与科技行业的冲突非常尖锐，并且在将来有可能升级。

然而，特朗普政府也与HTC进行了对话，他们可以在一些领域进行合作。2017年4月，白宫启动了针对H-1B签证计划的审查，该计划旨在确保签证"授予最熟练或收入最高的请愿受益人"。[40]撰写本书时，这次审查是否会导致立法者或政府为此而立法尚不清楚。但是，审查将有可能产生使HTC大部分成员接受的提案。根据具体细节，许多领先的美国ICT公司可以从更加基于绩效的系统中受益，因为这些公司通常雇用受过更多教育的H-1B签证获得者并支付比其他公司更高的工资。这种制度是否也会使美国大学受益将由具体情况决定。强调技能可以使新毕业生受益，但新的工资门槛或其他要求可能不会对新毕业生有利。相比之下，一个更加基于绩效的系统可能会减少IT外包公司的签证，不仅包括印度公司，还包括从事这项业务的美国公司（例如IBM）。这不仅会影响IT外包公司，也会影响它们的客户，其中很多客户都是美国领先的ICT公司。[41]美国各类公司也可能会担心国外对这些变化的反应，特别是印度。总体来说，美国HTC的一些成员可能会支持一个更基于绩效的系统，而其他成员则抵制这一改变。

税制改革是特朗普政府与美国高科技公司之间可能进行合作的领域。作为候选人，特朗普反对美国就业机会的离岸外包，并威胁称要通过某种边境税的政策来惩罚这种行为。但是，边境税理念在特朗普政府内部引发了争议，并且到目前为止，边境税还没有成为税制改革工作的重点。[42] 相反，政府一直专注于激励企业在美国进行投资，特别是通过降低企业收入税率和提供免税期以鼓励跨国公司从国外汇回利润，[43] 这些想法自然会吸引一些高科技公司。[44] 即便如此，如果政府期望通过免税期来刺激在美国进行新的高科技投资，那么他们会大感失望。大型的 ICT 公司不受资本约束，汇回的利润更有可能用于减少债务、支付股东股息和进行股票回购。[45]

第三个原因是持久力。虽然特朗普当选标志着美国发展进程中的惊人变化，但是这并没有抹去过去 20 年来推动美国政策的基本社会利益。在特朗普离开白宫很久之后，高科技利益集团仍将是一股强大的政治力量，它们将继续敦促更大程度的面向全球创新的开放。HTC 成功的程度将在很大程度上受到其所面临的抵制的性质的影响。这种抵制在未来可能会更加强大，特别是如果特朗普离任后反移民运动加剧的话。抵制也可能变弱，因为反移民运动可能会随着时间的推移而逐渐萎缩，反对零敲碎打式改革的团体在某些情况下也可能会放松警惕或者被排除在外。如果是这样，美国对将来与中国和印度的合作可能会更加开放。美国是否会以更加有智慧的方式开展此类合作，以弥补其当前方式的缺点，尚有待观察。

注　释

引　言

1. 对于此功能是如何创造出来的，我很感谢微软亚洲研究院高级通信经理（2011—2014年）Joy Ann Lo 能够在 2015 年 9 月 22 日与我进行私人沟通。
2. National Science Foundation, *Science and Engineering Indicators 2016* (Arlington, VA: National Science Foundation, 2016), chapter 3, 101.
3. National Science Foundation, *Science and Engineering Indicators 2016*, chapter 2, 71.
4. IBM, "IBM Research: Global Labs," *IBM*, April 3, 2015, www.research.ibm.com/labs/; Sujit John, "Cisco Needs to Align with Indian Government's Goals," *Times of India*, July 2, 2014.
5. James D. Fearon, "Rationalist Explanations for War," *International Organization* 49, no. 3 (1995): 405; Dustin H. Tingley, "The Dark Side of the Future: An Experimental Test of Commitment Problems in Bargaining," *International Studies Quarterly* 55, no. 2 (June 2011): 521–44.
6. Susan K. Sell, *Private Power, Public Law: The Globalization of Intellectual Property Rights* (Cambridge: Cambridge University Press, 2003); Jonathan D. Aronson, "International Intellectual Property Rights in a Networked World," in *Power, Interdependence, and Nonstate Actors in World Politics*, ed. Helen V. Milner and Andrew Moravcsik (Princeton, NJ: Princeton University Press, 2011), 185–203.
7. Vivek Wadhwa et al., *Losing the World's Best and Brightest: America's New Immigrant Entrepreneurs, Part V* (Kansas City, MO: Ewing Marion Kauffman Foundation, March 2009). Evidence regarding reverse migration is discussed in chapter 1.
8. Colin Powell, "Remarks at the Elliott School of International Affairs," (speech, George Washington University, Washington, DC, September 5, 2003), https://2001-2009.state.gov/secretary/former/powell/remarks/2003/23836.htm.
9. Gary P. Freeman and David K. Hill, "Disaggregating Immigration Policy: The Politics of Skilled Labor Recruitment in the U.S.," *Knowledge, Technology & Policy* 19, no. 3 (2006): 7–26; Lucie Cerna, "The Varieties of High-Skilled Immigration Policies: Coalitions and Policy Outputs in Advanced Industrial Countries," *Journal of European Public Policy* 16,

no. 1 (January 2009): 144–61; Lucie Cerna, "Attracting High-Skilled Immigrants: Policies in Comparative Perspective," *International Migration* 52, no. 3 (June 2014): 69–84; Monica Boyd, "Recruiting High Skill Labour in North America: Policies, Outcomes and Futures," *International Migration* 52, no. 3 (June 2014): 40–54; Chris F. Wright, "Why Do States Adopt Liberal Immigration Policies? The Policymaking Dynamics of Skilled Visa Reform in Australia," *Journal of Ethnic and Migration Studies* 41, no. 2 (January 28, 2015): 306–28.

10. Edward D. Mansfield and Diana C. Mutz, "US Versus Them: Mass Attitudes Toward Offshore Outsourcing," *World Politics* 65, no. 4 (2013): 571–608; Kerry A. Chase, "Moving Hollywood Abroad: Divided Labor Markets and the New Politics of Trade in Services," *International Organization* 62, no. 4 (2008): 653–87.

11. Mark Zachary Taylor, *The Politics of Innovation: Why Some Countries Are Better Than Others at Science and Technology* (Oxford: Oxford University Press, 2016); Joel W. Simmons, *The Politics of Technological Progress* (Cambridge: Cambridge University Press, 2016); Linda Weiss, *America Inc.? Innovation and Enterprise in the National Security State* (Ithaca, NY: Cornell University Press, 2014); Joseph Wong, *Betting on Biotech: Innovation and the Limits of Asia's Developmental State* (Ithaca, NY: Cornell University Press, 2011); Dan Breznitz, *Innovation and the State* (New Haven, CT: Yale University Press, 2007).

12. 本书中"高科技"通常特指 ICT 产业。第 3 章对 HTC 的概念进行了解释。

13. 在定性研究中进行对照比较所面临的挑战，参见 Alexander George and Andrew Bennett, *Case Studies and Theory Development in the Social Sciences* (Cambridge, MA: MIT Press, 2005), 151–79。

14. 其中一些访谈纯粹是在背景基础上进行的。其他内容在后面的章节中引用。

15. Elhanan Helpman, *The Mystery of Economic Growth* (Cambridge, MA: Harvard University Press, 2004).

16. Christina L. Davis and Sophie Meunier, "Business as Usual? Economic Responses to Political Tensions," *American Journal of Political Science* 55, no. 3 (July 2011): 628–46.

17. Edward D. Mansfield and Brian Pollins, "Interdependence and Conflict: An Introduction," in *Economic Interdependence and International Conflict: New Perspectives on an Enduring Debate*, ed. Edward D. Mansfield and Brian Pollins (Ann Arbor: University of Michigan Press, 2003); John Ravenhill, "The Economics-Security Nexus in the Asia-Pacific region," in *Security Politics in the Asia-Pacific: A Regional-Global Nexus?*, ed. William Tow (New York: Cambridge University Press, 2009), 188–207.

18. Stephen G. Brooks, *Producing Security: Multinational Corporations, Globalization, and the Changing Calculus of Conflict* (Princeton, NJ: Princeton University Press, 2005).

19. Dale C. Copeland, *Economic Interdependence and War* (Princeton, NJ: Princeton University Press, 2014); Dale C. Copeland, "Economic Interdependence and War: A Theory of Trade Expectations," *International Security* 20, no. 4 (1996): 5–41.

20. Robert Gilpin, *U.S. Power and the Multinational Corporation: The Political Economy of Foreign Direct Investment* (New York: Basic Books, 1975), 67; Robert Gilpin, *War and Change in World Politics* (Cambridge: Cambridge University Press, 1983), 182.

21. William R. Thompson, "Long Waves, Technological Innovation, and Relative Decline,"

International Organization 44, no. 2 (1990): 201–33; George Modelski and William R. Thompson, *Leading Sectors and World Powers: The Coevolution of Global Politics and Economics* (Columbia: University of South Carolina Press, 1996).

22. Tai Ming Cheung and Bates Gill, "Trade Versus Security: How Countries Balance Technology Transfers with China," *Journal of East Asian Studies* 13, no. 3 (2013): 445.

第1章 全球创新的崛起

1. Andrew B. Kennedy, "Slouching Tiger, Roaring Dragon: Comparing India and China as Late Innovators," *Review of International Political Economy* 23, no. 2 (2016): 1–28. 关于中国和印度在创新方面的发展轨迹的争论，参见 Andrew B. Kennedy, "Powerhouses or Pretenders? Debating China's and India's Emergence as Technological Powers," *The Pacific Review* 28, no. 2 (2015): 281–302。

2. 为了能更好地理解"创新"这一概念，参见 Jan Fagerberg, "Innovation: A Guide to the Literature," in *The Oxford Handbook of Innovation*, ed. Jan Fagerberg, David C. Mowery, and Richard R. Nelson (Oxford: Oxford University Press, 2005), 4–9。

3. "对世界来讲新颖的"技术通常与"对国家来讲新颖的"技术和"对公司来讲新颖的"技术进行比较。参见 Organisation for Economic Cooperation and Development (OECD), *The Measurement of Scientific and Technological Activities (Oslo Manual)* (Paris: OECD, 1997)。

4. Fagerberg, "Innovation," 4–9.

5. 此外，当给定技术由以模块化方式组合的组件组成时，通常区分两种其他类型的创新。"模块式"创新是指单个组件的变化，而"架构式"创新是以新的方式组合以前存在的组件。参见 Dieter Ernst, *A New Geography of Knowledge in the Electronics Industry? Asia's Role in Global Innovation Networks* (Honolulu, HI: East-West Center, 2009), 7–12; Richard M. Henderson and Kim B. Clark, "Architectural Innovation: The Reconfiguration of Existing Product Technologies and the Failure of Established Firms," *Administrative Science Quarterly* 35, no. 1 (March 1990): 9–30。

6. Daniele Archibugi and Simona Iammarino, "The Globalization of Technological Innovation: Definition and Evidence," *Review of International Political Economy* 9, no. 1 (Spring 2002): 98–122; Rajneesh Narula and Antonello Zanfei, "Globalization of Innovation: The Role of Multinational Enterprises," in *The Oxford Handbook of Innovation*, ed. Jan Fagerberg, David C. Mowery, and Richard R. Nelson (Oxford: Oxford University Press, 2005), 318–45; Dieter Ernst, *Innovation Offshoring: Exploring Asia's Emerging Role in Global Innovation Networks*, East-West Center Special Report No. 10 (Honolulu, HI: East-West Center, July 2006).

7. 从这一点来看，这里所采取的方法与以下研究中采用的方法类似：William Lazonick, *Sustainable Prosperity in the New Economy? Business Organization and High-Tech Employment in the United States* (Kalamazoo, MI: W. E. Upjohn Institute, 2009)。

8. 这并不是说创新只是增加劳动力和资本投入的一个功能。正如关于国家和区域创新体系的文献所表明的那样，资本和劳动力运作的背景非常重要。参见 Christopher Freeman, *Technology, Policy, and Economic Performance: Lessons from Japan* (London: Pinter, 1987); Bengt-Åke Lundvall, *National Systems of Innovation: Toward a Theory of Innovation and Interactive Learning* (London: Pinter, 1992); Richard R. Nelson, ed., *National Innovation Systems: A Comparative Analysis* (Oxford: Oxford University Press, 1993); Bjørn T. Asheim and Meric S. Gertler, "The Geography of Innovation: Regional Innovation Systems," in *The Oxford Handbook of Innovation*, ed. Jan Fagerberg, David C. Mowery, and Richard R. Nelson (Oxford: Oxford University Press, 2005), 291–317。一个有趣的研究方向是探讨全球化如何改变国家创新体系。参见 David M. Hart, "Understanding Immigration in a National Systems of Innovation Framework," *Science & Public Policy* 34, no. 1 (2007): 45–53。

9. Paul M. Romer, "Endogenous Technological Change," *Journal of Political Economy* 98, no. 5 (1990): S71–S102.
10. 另外3%是自由职业者。参见 National Science Foundation, *Science and Engineering Indicators 2016* (Arlington, VA: National Science Foundation), chapter 3, 37。
11. National Science Foundation, *Science and Engineering Indicators 2016*, chapter 3, 40.
12. National Science Foundation, *Science and Engineering Indicators 2016*, chapter 5, appendix table 18.
13. National Science Foundation, *Science and Engineering Indicators 2016*, chapter 5, 76–78.
14. National Science Foundation, *Science and Engineering Indicators 2016*, chapter 5, 76.
15. Keith Pavitt, "Innovation Processes," in *The Oxford Handbook of Innovation*, ed. Jan Fagerberg, David Mowery, and Richard R. Nelson (Oxford: Oxford University Press, 2006), 95; David C. Mowery and Bhaven N. Sampat, "Universities in National Innovation Systems," in *The Oxford Handbook of Innovation*, ed. Jan Fagerberg, David Mowery, and Richard R. Nelson (Oxford: Oxford University Press, 2006), 221–24.
16. Barry R. Chiswick and Timothy Hatton, "International Migration and the Integration of Labor Markets," in *Globalization in Historical Perspective*, ed. Michael D. Bordo, Alan M. Taylor, and Jeffrey G. Williamson (Chicago: University of Chicago Press, 2003), 70.
17. Harm G. Schröter and Anthony S. Travis, "An Issue of Different Mentalities: National Approaches to the Development of the Chemical Industry in Britain and Germany Before 1914," in *The Chemical Industry in Europe, 1850–1914*, ed. Ernst Homburg, Anthony S. Travis, and Harm G. Schröter (Dordrecht, Netherlands: Kluwer, 1998), 100.
18. Petra Moser, Alessandra Voena, and Fabian Waldinger, "German Jewish Émigrés and US Invention," *The American Economic Review* 104, no. 10 (2014): 3222–55; Annie Jacobsen, *Operation Paperclip: The Secret Intelligence Program That Brought Nazi Scientists to America* (New York: Little, Brown, 2014).
19. "人才流失"一词最初用于描述英国科学家在20世纪60年代初流入美国的情况，但很快该词就用于表示发展中国家的人才流向发达国家。参见 Hart, "Understanding Immigration in a National Systems of Innovation Framework," 46。
20. Frédéric Docquier, Olivier Lohest, and Abdeslam Marfouk, "Brain Drain in Developing Countries," *The World Bank Economic Review* 21, no. 2 (January 1, 2007): 194.

21. Cansin Arslan et al., *A New Profile of Migrants in the Aftermath of the Recent Economic Crisis*, OECD Social, Employment and Migration Working Paper No. 160 (2014): 37, www.oecd.org/els/mig/WP160.pdf.
22. 作者的计算基于 Arslan et al., *A New Profile of Migrants*, 26。
23. AnnaLee Saxenian, *The New Argonauts: Regional Advantage in a Global Economy* (Cambridge, MA: Harvard University Press, 2006).
24. National Science Foundation, *Science and Engineering Indicators 2016*, chapter 3, 103.
25. Institute for Regional Studies, "Silicon Valley Index 2017," *Silicon Valley Indicators*, February 2017, 14, http://jointventure.org/images/stories/pdf/index2017.pdf.
26. OECD, *Education at a Glance 2014: OECD Indicators* (Paris: OECD, 2014), 344.
27. OECD, *Education at a Glance 2014*, 342.
28. OECD, *Education at a Glance 2014*, 350–51.
29. National Science Foundation, *Science and Engineering Indicators 2016*, chapter 2, 91.
30. Australian Government Department of Education and Training, "International Students Studying Science, Technology, Engineering and Mathematics (STEM) in Australian Higher Education Institutions," *Research Snapshots*, October 2015, https://international education.gov.au/research/Research-Snapshots/Documents/STEM%202014.pdf.
31. National Science Foundation, *Science and Engineering Indicators 2016*, chapter 2, appendix table 43.
32. National Science Foundation, *Science and Engineering Indicators 2004* (Arlington, VA: National Science Foundation, 2004), chapter 2, appendix table 27; National Science Foundation, *Science and Engineering Indicators 2016*, chapter 2, 71.
33. 第 4 章详细讨论了在美国进行科学与工程领域学习的中国和印度研究生的数量。
34. National Science Foundation, *Science and Engineering Indicators 2016*, chapter 5, 81.
35. National Science Foundation, *Science and Engineering Indicators 2016*, chapter 2, appendix table 33.
36. National Science Foundation, *Science and Engineering Indicators 2016*, chapter 5, appendix table 16.
37. National Science Foundation, *Science and Engineering Indicators 2016*, chapter 3, 105.
38. 第 2 章用了很大的篇幅对工业界研发的崛起进行了介绍。
39. National Science Foundation, *Science and Engineering Indicators 2012* (Arlington, VA: National Science Foundation, 2012), chapter 4, 15 and 55.
40. 如前所述，尽管我对学生流动的情况分开对待，但是此处介绍的全球研发的两个类别大致基于 Archibugi 和 Iammarino 以前的研究。参见 Archibugi and Iammarino, "The Globalization of Technological Innovation"。
41. Steve Fraser, "The Hollowing Out of America," *The Nation*, December 3, 2012, www.thenation.com/article/171563/hollowing-out-america#.
42. National Science Foundation, *Science and Engineering Indicators 2014* (Arlington, VA: National Science Foundation, 2014), chapter 4, 27.
43. Narula and Zanfei, "Globalization of Innovation," 326.
44. 跨国公司特别需要与薄弱的知识产权保护进行抗争。参见 Minyuan Zhao, "Conducting

R&D in Countries with Weak Intellectual Property Rights Protection," *Management Science* 52 (August 2006): 1185–99。

45. Bureau of Economic Analysis, "Foreign Direct Investment in the U.S., Majority-Owned Bank and Nonbank U.S. Affiliates, Research and Development Expenditures for 2013," *International Data: Direct Investment and Multinational Enterprises*, 2016, www.bea.gov/iTable/index_MNC.cfm.
46. Bureau of Economic Analysis, "U.S. Direct Investment Abroad, All Majority-Owned Foreign Affiliates, Research and Development Expenditures for 2013," *International Data: Direct Investment and Multinational Enterprises*, 2016, www.bea.gov/iTable/index_MNC.cfm.
47. Andrew B. Kennedy, "Unequal Partners: U.S. Collaboration with China and India in Research and Development," *Political Science Quarterly* 132, no. 1 (2017): 63–86.
48. Bureau of Economic Analysis, "U.S. Direct Investment Abroad.""信息"类包括软件发行。2013年还没有软件发行的数据，但前几年里，软件发行在"信息"类海外研发支出中占主导地位。
49. 对于这两种类型的讨论，参见 Narula and Zanfei, "Globalization of Innovation," 326–29。
50. 近年来，学者们已经注意到其他类型的海外研发。例如，参见 Jian Wang, Lan Xue, and Zheng Liang, "Multinational R&D in China: From Home- Country-Based to Host-Country-Based," *Innovation: Management, Policy & Practice* 14, no. 2 (June 2012): 192–202。
51. Melissa Schilling, "Technology Shocks, Technological Collaboration, and Innovation Outcomes," *Organization Science* 26, no. 3 (May–June 2015): 668–86.
52. Stephen G. Brooks, *Producing Security: Multinational Corporations, Globalization, and the Changing Calculus of Conflict* (Princeton, NJ: Princeton University Press, 2005), 32–33.
53. 注意，没有一个数据库包含创建的所有联盟，尽管这些数据库达成一致意见，即随着时间的推移，联盟数量会有所不同。因此，基于SDC白金数据库的数据应被视为具有启发性而非准确无误。参见 Melissa Schilling, "Understanding the Alliance Data," *Strategic Management Journal* 30, no. 3 (2009): 233–60。
54. Ernst and Young, *Globalizing Venture Capital: Global Venture Capital Insights and Trends Report*, 2012, 7, www.ey.com/Publication/vwLUAssets/Globalizing_venture_capital_VC_insights_and_trends_report_CY0227/$FILE/Globalizing%20venture%20capital_VC%20insights%20and%20trends%20report_CY0227.pdf.
55. KPMG and CB Insights, *Venture Pulse 2016* (New York: CB Insights, April 13, 2016), 55, https://www.cbinsights.com/research-venture-capital-Q1-2016.
56. KPMG and CB Insights, *Venture Pulse 2016*, 16.
57. "About SMART," *Singapore–MIT Alliance for Research and Technology*, 2013, http://smart.mit.edu/about-smart/about-smart.html.
58. Peter H. Koehn, "Developments in Transnational Research Linkages: Evidence from US Higher-Education Activity," *Journal of New Approaches in Educational Research* 3, no. 2 (2014): 53.
59. Jason Lane and Kevin Kinser, "Is Today's University the New Multinational

Corporation?" *The Conversation*, June 5, 2015, http://theconversation.com/is-todays-university-the-new-multinational-corporation-40681.

60. National Science Foundation, *Science and Engineering Indicators 2016*, chapter 5, appendix table 41.
61. 尤其是中国。参见 Denis Fred Simon and Cong Cao, *China's Emerging Techno- logical Edge: Assessing the Role of High-End Talent* (New York: Cambridge University Press, 2009), 238。
62. "Navigating China's Tech Jungle," *Business Times*, September 1, 2012.
63. "Guruduth Banavar," *LinkedIn*, accessed February 11, 2016, www.linkedin.com/in/banavar.
64. Prasad Ram, founder and chief executive officer, Gooru, interview by author, Palo Alto, California, July 15, 2014.
65. 第 4 章介绍中国在这些签证计划中的突出地位。
66. National Science Foundation, *Science and Engineering Indicators 2016*, chapter 5, appendix table 56.
67. Andrew B. Kennedy, *The International Ambitions of Mao and Nehru: National Efficacy Beliefs and the Making of Foreign Policy* (New York: Cambridge University Press, 2012); Andrew B. Kennedy, "India's Nuclear Odyssey: Implicit Umbrellas, Diplomatic Disappointments, and the Bomb," *International Security* 36, no. 2 (2011): 120–53.
68. 关于全球研发可能给发展中国家带来的危险，参见 Ernst, *A New Geography of Knowledge?*, 38–39。
69. 中华人民共和国国务院,《国家中长期科学和技术发展规划纲要（2006—2020 年）》, 第 2 部分第 2 节, 中国政府门户网站, 访问于 2006 年 2 月 9 日, www.gov.cn/jrzg/2006-02/09/content_183787.htm。
70. William C. Hannas, James Mulvenon, and Anna B. Puglisi, *Chinese Industrial Espionage: Technology Acquisition and Military Modernization* (New York: Routledge, 2013); Kennedy, "Slouching Tiger, Roaring Dragon."
71. David Zweig and Changgui Chen, *China's Brain Drain to the United States: Views of Overseas Chinese Students and Scholars in the 1990s* (Berkeley: Institute of East Asian Studies, University of California, 1995), 19.
72. David M. Lampton, *A Relationship Restored: Trends in U.S.–China Educational Exchanges, 1978–1984* (Washington, DC: National Academies, 1986), 23.
73. Leo A. Orleans, "China's Changing Attitude Toward the Brain Drain and Policy Toward Returning Students," *China Exchange News* 17, no. 2 (1989): 2.
74. Orleans, "China's Changing Attitude," 2.
75. Foreign Broadcast Information Service, "Foreign Schooling Policy Remains Unchanged," *FBIS-CHI-88-224*, November 14, 1988, 31.
76. 《中共中央关于建立社会主义市场经济体制若干问题的决定》, 1993 年 11 月 14 日, http://cpc.people.com.cn/GB/64162/134902/8092314.html。
77. United Nations Educational, Scientific and Cultural Organization (UNESCO), "Education Data," *UIS.Stat*, 2014, www.uis.unesco.org/datacentre/pages/default.aspx.
78. Zweig, "Learning to Compete," 194.
79. Zweig and Wang, "Can China Bring Back the Best?," 596.

80. "千人计划",千人计划网,2016 年,www.1000plan.org/qrjh/section/2.
81. Hong Liu and Els van Dongen, "China's Diaspora Policies as a New Mode of Transnational Governance," *Journal of Contemporary China* 25, no. 102 (2016): 15.
82. Huiyao Wang, David Zweig, and Xiaohua Lin, "Returnee Entrepreneurs: Impact on China's Globalization Process," *Journal of Contemporary China* 20, no. 70 (June 2011): 415.
83. Charlotte Liu et al., "Turning Point: Chinese Science in Transition" (Shanghai: Nature Publishing Group, November 2015), 8, www.nature.com/press_releases/turning_point.pdf; Chi Ma, "Famous Science Projects Face Axe in Funding Overhaul," *China Daily*, January 8, 2015, www.chinadaily.com.cn/china/2015-01/08/content_19275863.htm.
84. Yu Wei and Zhaojun Sun, "China: Building an Innovation Talent Program System and Facing Global Competition in a Knowledge Economy," *The Academic Executive Brief*, 2012, http://academicexecutives.elsevier.com/articles/china-building-innovation-talent-program-system-and-facing-global-competition-knowledge.
85. 《关于公布第一批青年千人计划引进人才名单的公告》,千人计划网,2011 年 11 月 11 日,http://1000plan.org/qrjh/article/18053。
86. 《第十一批千人计划青年人才、创业人才入选名单》,千人计划网,2015 年 5 月 13 日,http://1000plan.org/qrjh/article/61716;《关于公布第十二批国家千人计划青年人才、创业人才入选人员名单的公告》,千人计划网,2016 年 3 月 14 日,http://1000plan.org/qrjh/article/61716;《关于公布第十三批国家千人计划青年项目创业人才项目入选人员名单的公告》,千人计划网,2017 年 5 月 11 日,http://1000plan.org/qrjh/article/69239。
87. "ORISE Workforce Studies Infographics—StayRates," *Oak Ridge Institute for Science and Education*, March 31, 2017, https://public.tableau.com/views/ORISEWorkforceStudiesInfographics-StayRates-mobilefriendly/5-YearStayRates?%3Aembed=y&%3Ashowviz Home=no&%3Adisplay_count=y&%3Adisplay_static_image=y&%3AbootstrapWhen Notified=true.
88. 《入选中国千人计划外专项目的专家达 381 名》,科学网,2017 年 4 月 15 日,http://news.sciencenet.cn/htmlnews/2017/4/373557.shtm。
89. Jacques Gaillard and Anne-Marie Gaillard, "Introduction: The International Mobility of Brains—Exodus or Circulation?" *Science, Technology & Society* 2, no. 2 (1997): 195–228.
90. Zweig, "Learning to Compete," 192–93.
91. David Zweig, Chung Siu Fung, and Donglin Han, "Redefining the Brain Drain: China's 'Diaspora Option,'" *Science, Technology & Society* 13, no. 1 (2008): 1–33.
92. 引用自盛若蔚,《我国流失顶尖人才数居世界首位》,《人民日报》,2013 年 6 月 6 日,http://finance.people.com.cn/n/2013/0606/c1004-21754321.html。
93. 王辉耀,《人才战争》(北京:中信出版社,2009)。
94. 国家留学基金委员会,《2012 年国家留学基金资助出国留学人员选派简章》,2011 年 11 月,http://v.csc.edu.cn/Chuguo/739b1b8c118441e5bb211c388563f7da.shtml;国家留学基金委员会,《2017 年国家留学基金资助出国留学人员选派简章》,2016 年 12 月 12 日,www.csc.edu.cn/article/709。
95. 国家留学基金委员会,《2015 年国家公派出国留学选派计划确定》,2014 年 10 月 30 日,

www.csc.edu.cn/News/2acf973ba1a84ca69f5386a574771906.shtml。

96. Kennedy, "Slouching Tiger, Roaring Dragon," 71–72.
97. Colum Murphy and Lilian Lin, "For China's Jobseekers, Multinational Companies Lose Their Magic," *Wall Street Journal*, April 3, 2014, http://blogs.wsj.com/chinarealtime/2014/04/03/for-chinas-jobseekers-multinational-companies-lose-their-magic/?mod=chinablog. 关于这一点，我还有幸采访了一位中国政府官员。Interview by author, Beijing, June 25, 2013.
98. 《国家中长期科学和技术发展规划纲要（2006—2020年）》，第8部分，第8节。
99. 《国务院关于加快培育和发展战略性新兴产业的决定》，中国政府门户网站，2010年10月10日，第6部分，www.gov.cn/zwgk/2010-10/18/content_1724848.htm。
100. 《国民经济和社会发展第十二个五年规划纲要》，第20部分第52章第1节，中国政府门户网站，www.gov.cn/2011lh/content_1825838.htm。
101. Nick Marro, "Foreign Company R&D: In China, For China," *China Business Review*, June 1, 2015.
102. Matthew Miller, "Spy Scandal Weighs on U.S. Tech Firms in China, Cisco Takes Hit," *Reuters*, November 14, 2013, www.reuters.com/article/2013/11/14/us-china-cisco-idUSBRE9AD0J420131114.
103. People's Republic of China Ministry of Science and Technology official, interviewed by author, Beijing, July 3, 2013.
104. "China to Overtake US as New Frontier for Global R&D," *People's Daily Online*, January 27, 2014, http://english.peopledaily.com.cn/98649/8523078.html.
105. Gert Bruche, "The Emergence of China and India as New Competitors in MNCs' Innovation Networks," *Competition & Change* 13, no. 5 (2009): 276; Edward S. Steinfeld, *Playing Our Game: Why China's Rise Doesn't Threaten the West* (New York: Oxford University Press, 2010), 152.
106. Steinfeld, *Playing Our Game*, 152; Loren Brandt and Eric Thun, "The Fight for the Middle: Upgrading, Competition, and Industrial Development in China," *World Development* 38, no. 11 (November 2010): 1566–69.
107. Interview by author, Beijing, July 4, 2013. 受访者希望匿名。
108. Lee Branstetter, Guangwei Lee, and Francisco Veloso, "The Rise of International Coinvention," in *The Changing Frontier: Rethinking Science and Innovation Policy*, ed. Adam B. Jaffe and Benjamin F. Jones (Chicago: University of Chicago Press, 2015), 162.
109. Sylvia Schwaag-Serger, "Foreign Corporate R&D in China: Trends and Policy Issues," in *The New Asian Innovation Dynamics: China and India in Perspective*, ed. Govindan Parayil and Anthony P. D'Costa (New York: Palgrave Macmillan, 2009), 50–78.
110. Joy Ann Lo, senior communications manager, Microsoft Research Asia, interview by author, February 19, 2014.
111. "R&D Technology Center China," *GE Lighting Asia Pacific*, accessed April 16, 2014, www.gereveal.ca/LightingWeb/apac/resources/world-of-ge-lighting/research-and-development/china-technology-centre.jsp.
112. "Intel China Research Center," *Intel*, accessed May 6, 2014, www.intel.com/cd/corporate/

icrc/apac/eng/about/167066.htm.
113. Kennedy, "Unequal Partners," 78–79.
114. 《国家中长期科学和技术发展规划纲要（2006—2020 年）》。
115. American Enterprise Institute, "China Global Investment Tracker," *AEI*, April 30, 2017, www.aei.org/china-global-investment-tracker/.
116. Louise Lucas, "US Concerns Grow Over Chinese Chip Expansion," *Financial Times*, January 16, 2017, https://www.ft.com/content/fb2e4454-c36e-11e6-9bca-2b93a6856354.
117. 《国家中长期科学和技术发展规划纲要（2006—2020 年）》，第 8 部分第 8 节。
118. 《国务院关于加快培育和发展战略性新兴产业的决定》，第 4 部分。
119. Xiaolan Fu and Hongru Xiong, "Open Innovation in China: Policies and Practices," *Journal of Science and Technology Policy in China* 2, no. 3 (2011): 204–205, 207–208.
120. Thomson Reuters, SDC Platinum database, accessed April 27, 2015, access via subscription only.
121. Douglas B. Fuller, *Paper Tigers, Hidden Dragons: Firms and the Political Economy of China's Technological Development* (Oxford: Oxford University Press, 2016), 60; Di Guo and Kun Jiang, "Venture Capital Investment and the Performance of Entrepreneurial Firms: Evidence from China," *Journal of Corporate Finance* 22 (2013): 377.
122. Fuller, *Paper Tigers, Hidden Dragons*, 61.
123. Mark Humphery-Jenner and Jo-Ann Suchard, "Foreign Venture Capitalists and the Internationalization of Entrepreneurial Companies: Evidence from China," *Journal of International Business Studies* 44, no. 6 (2013): 607–21.
124. Government of India Department of Science and Technology, *Science, Technology and Innovation Policy 2013* (New Delhi: Ministry of Science and Technology, 2013), 4, www.dst.gov.in/sti-policy-eng.pdf.
125. Narendra Modi, "PM's Speech to 104th Session of the Indian Science Congress, Tirupati (Full Text)," *Microfinance Monitor*, January 3, 2017, www.microfinancemonitor.com/pms-speech-to-104th-session-of-the-indian-science-congress-tirupati-full-text/43799.
126. Devesh Kapur, *Diaspora, Development, and Democracy: The Domestic Impact of International Migration from India* (Princeton, NJ: Princeton University Press, 2010), 51–54.
127. Government of India, Passports Act of 1967, Pub. L. No. 15 (1967), 1, http://passportindia.gov.in/AppOnlineProject/pdf/passports_act.pdf.
128. Government of India, Passports Act of 1967, 6.
129. Government of India, Emigration Act of 1983, Pub. L. No. 31 (1983), 15, http://moia.gov.in/writereaddata/pdf/emig_act.pdf.
130. David Fitzgerald, "Inside the Sending State: The Politics of Mexican Emigration Control," *International Migration Review* 40, no. 2 (2006): 262.
131. 主要的例外是医疗领域，其中引入了一些限制，但有太多漏洞而无法奏效。参见 Binod Khadria, "Brain Drain, Brain Gain, India," in *The Encyclopedia of Global Human Migration*, ed. Immanuel Ness (New York: Wiley-Blackwell, 2013), 743。
132. J. Singh and V. V. Krishna, "Trends in Brain Drain, Gain and Circulation: Indian Experience of Knowledge Workers," *Science Technology & Society* 20, no. 3 (November 1, 2015): 302–6.

133. Kapur, *Diaspora, Development, and Democracy*, 180–81.
134. Rajiv Gandhi, "Revamping the Educational System," *Indian National Congress*, August 29, 1985, www.inc.in/resources/speeches/345-Revamping-the-Educational-System.
135. "Vajpayee Calls for Reversing Brain Drain, Cutting Red Tape," *Hindu Business Line*, January 4, 2003, www.thehindubusinessline.com/bline/2003/01/04/stories/2003010402410500.htm; "PM for Reverse Brain Drain of Scientists," *Economic Times*, January 4, 2011, http://articles.economictimes.indiatimes.com/2011-01-04/news/28424740_1_scientists-of-indian-origin-talent-pool-98th-indian-science.
136. Kapur, *Diaspora, Development, and Democracy*, 165. 移民率是某一教育层次群体中移民的人数除以该群体在原籍国的总人数。
137. 关于之前的三句话，参见 Sanjoy Chakravorty, Devesh Kapur, and Nirvikar Singh, *The Other One Percent: Indians in America* (Oxford: Oxford University Press, 2016), x, 30, 108。
138. UNESCO, "Education Data"; Devesh Kapur, "Indian Higher Education," in *American Universities in a Global Market*, ed. Charles T. Clotfelter (Chicago: University of Chicago Press, 2010), 326.
139. Institute for International Education, "International Student Totals by Place of Origin, 2013/14–2014/15," *Open Doors Report on International Educational Exchange*, 2015, www.iie.org/Research-and-Publications/Open-Doors/Data/International-Students/All-Places-of-Origin/2013-15.
140. National Science Foundation, *Science and Engineering Indicators 2016*, chapter 2, appendix table 27.
141. Australian Government Department of Education, "International Student Enrolments by Nationality in 2013," April 2014, 1, https://internationaleducation.gov.au/research/research-snapshots/pages/default.aspx; UNESCO, "Global Flow of Tertiary-Level Students," *UIS. Stat*, accessed December 10, 2014, www.uis.unesco.org/EDUCATION/Pages/international-student-flow-viz.aspx.
142. Rajiv Gandhi, "Keep Pace with Technology," *Indian National Congress*, December 19, 1985, www.inc.in/resources/speeches/315-Keep-Pace-with-Technology.
143. Singh and Krishna, "Trends in Brain Drain," 308–10.
144. 2001年，印度推出了示范教育贷款计划，为在印度或国外接受高等教育的学生提供软贷款。然而，该计划并不要求学生返回印度，一直被批评为烦琐且缺乏影响力。参见 Asian Development Bank, *Counting the Cost: Financing Asian Higher Education for Inclusive Growth* (Manila: Asian Development Bank, 2012), 16。
145. Kennedy, "Slouching Tiger, Roaring Dragon," 71–72.
146. Chakravorty, Kapur, and Singh, *The Other One Percent*, 56.
147. Chakravorty, Kapur, and Singh, *The Other One Percent*, 56; Vivek Wadhwa, *The Immigrant Exodus: Why America Is Losing the Global Race to Capture Entrepreneurial Talent* (Philadelphia: Wharton Digital, 2012); Singh and Krishna, "Trends in Brain Drain," 310–13.
148. Michael G. Finn, "Stay Rates of Foreign Doctorate Recipients from U.S. Universities, 2001" (Oak Ridge, TN: Oak Ridge Institute for Science and Education, November 2003), 9,

http://orise.orau.gov/files/sep/stay-rates-foreign-doctorate-recipients-2001.pdf.
149. Michael G. Finn, "Stay Rates of Foreign Doctorate Recipients from U.S. Universities, 2011" (Oak Ridge, TN: Oak Ridge Institute for Science and Education, January 2014), 7, http:// orise.orau.gov/science-education/difference/stay-rates-impact.aspx.
150. Fei Qin, "Global Talent, Local Careers: Circular Migration of Top Indian Engineers and Professionals," *Research Policy* 44, no. 2 (2015): 405–20.
151. Khadria, "Brain Drain, Brain Gain, India," 3.
152. High Level Committee on the Indian Diaspora, "The Indian Diaspora" (New Delhi: Ministry of External Affairs, 2001), xi, http://indiandiaspora.nic.in/contents.htm.
153. 有关印度侨民政策的有价值的概述，参见 Daniel Naujoks, *Migration, Citizen- ship, and Development: Diasporic Membership Policies and Overseas Indians in the United States* (New Delhi: Oxford University Press, 2013), 49–65。
154. Kapur, *Diaspora, Development, and Democracy*, 261–68.
155. Narendra Modi, "Modi Speaks in San Jose: The Indian Prime Minister in His Own Words," *SiliconValleyOneWorld*, September 27, 2015, www.siliconvalleyoneworld.com/2015/09/30/modi-speaks-in-san-jose-the-indian-prime-minister-in-his-own-words/.
156. Kapur, *Diaspora, Development, and Democracy*, 106–13.
157. World Bank Migration and Remittances Team, *Migration and Remittances: Recent Developments and Outlook*, Migration and Development Brief No. 23 (October 6, 2014): 4, 10, http://siteresources.worldbank.org/INTPROSPECTS/Resources/334934-1288990760745/MigrationandDevelopmentBrief23.pdf.
158. Ronil Hira, "U.S. Immigration Regulations and India's Information Technology Industry," *Technological Forecasting and Social Change* 71, no. 8 (October 2004): 837–54.
159. 同年，总部设在其他地方的六家外包公司（但也聘请了许多流动印度工人）获得了9 943 份 H-1B 签证。参见 Haeyoun Park, "How Out- sourcing Companies Are Gaming the Visa System," *New York Times*, November 10, 2015。
160. Nair Chendakera, "U.S., India Move to Boost Cooperation in R&D," *Electronic Engineering Times*, March 27, 2000; Bruce Stokes, "India's Paradox," *National Journal*, April 7, 2007; Amiti Sen, "India to Ask US for More H-1B Visas," *Economic Times*, October 19, 2009; Nirupama Rao, "America Needs More High-Skilled Worker Visas," *USAToday*, April 14, 2013, www.usatoday.com/story/opinion/2013/04/14/india-trade-technology-column/2075159/.
161. "India May Drag US to WTO for Hiking H-1B Visa Fee," *Times of India*, August 17, 2010, http://timesofindia.indiatimes.com/business/india-business/India-may-drag-US-to-WTO-for-hiking-H-1B-visa-fee/articleshow/6325497.cms.
162. "Obama Assures Modi on Concerns Over H-1B Visa Issue," *Times of India*, January 26, 2015, http://timesofindia.indiatimes.com/india/Obama-assures-Modi-on-concerns-over-H-1B-visa-issue/articleshow/46022377.cms.
163. Ronil Hira, "New Data Show How Firms Like Infosys and Tata Abuse the H-1B Program," *Economic Policy Institute*, February 19, 2015, www.epi.org/blog/new-data-infosys-tata-abuse-h-1b-program/.

164. Arun Janardhanan, "US Move to Lure Science Grads Worries India," *Times of India—Chennai Edition*, February 4, 2013.
165. Former high-ranking Indian official, interviewed by author. February 16, 2017, New Delhi. 受访者认为在不考虑签证限制的情况下，想要留在国外的人最终会找到一条路的。
166. Dinesh C. Sharma, *The Long Revolution: The Birth and Growth of India's IT Industry* (Noida: Harper Collins, 2009), 317–18.
167. "Research and Development," *General Electric*, 2017, www.ge.com/in/about-us/research-and-development.
168. Min Ye, *Diasporas and Foreign Direct Investment in China and India* (New York: Cambridge University Press, 2014), 177–204.
169. N. Mrinalini, Pradosh Nath, and G. D. Sandhya, "Foreign Direct Investment in R&D in India," *Current Science* 105, no. 6 (September 2013): 770–71.
170. Sujit John and Shilpa Phadnis, "For MNCs, India Still an R&D Hub and It's Growing," *Times of India*, March 2, 2017, http://timesofindia.indiatimes.com/city/bengaluru/for-mncs-india-still-an-rd-hub-and-its-growing/articleshow/57421665.cms.
171. Bruche, "The Emergence of China and India as New Competitors in MNCs' Innovation Networks," 276.
172. IBM India Research Lab, Bangalore, interviewed by author, January 13, 2014. 受访者希望匿名。
173. Nirmalya Kumar and Phanish Puranam, *India Inside: The Emerging Innovation Challenge to the West* (Cambridge, MA: Harvard Business Press, 2012), 109–14.
174. Government of India, "Science, Technology and Innovation Policy," 15.
175. Thomson Reuters, SDC Platinum database.
176. Narendra Modi, "PM's Address to the Nation from the Ramparts of the Red Fort on the Sixty-Eighth Independence Day," *PMIndia*, August 15, 2014, http://pmindia.gov.in/en/news_updates/text-of-pms-address-in-hindi-to-the-nation-from-the-ramparts-of-the-red-fort-on-the-68th-independence-day/.
177. Narendra Modi, "Text of PM Shri Narendra Modi's Address at the 102nd Indian Science Congress," *Narendra Modi*, January 3, 2015, www.narendramodi.in/text-of-pm-shri-narendra-modis-address-at-the-102nd-indian-science-congress.
178. Narendra Modi, "Modi Speaks in San Jose: The Indian Prime Minister in His Own Words," *SiliconValleyOneWorld*, September 30, 2015, www.siliconvalleyoneworld.com/2015/09/30/modi-speaks-in-san-jose-the-indian-prime-minister-in-his-own-words/.
179. 接下来的两句话参见 Rafiq Dossani and Martin Kenney, "Creating an Environment for Venture Capital in India," *World Development* 30, no. 2 (2002): 243–49。
180. Samarth Agarwal, interviewed by author, February 16, 2017. 阿加瓦尔是2016年成立的印度创业公司 Spaceboat 的创始人。
181. "One Year of Startup India: Report Card," *TechCircle*, January 16, 2017.
182. "RBI Eases Norms for Foreign Investment in Startups," *TechCircle*, October 21, 2016.

第 2 章 创新领导力与争议中的开放

1. 关于更早期的回顾，参见 G. John Ikenberry, David A. Lake, and Michael Mastanduno, "Introduction: Approaches to Explaining American Foreign Economic Policy," in *The State and American Foreign Economic Policy*, ed. G. John Ikenberry and David A. Lake (Ithaca, NY: Cornell University Press, 1988), 1–14。
2. Charles Poor Kindleberger, *The World in Depression, 1929–1939* (Berkeley: University of California Press, 1973); Stephen D. Krasner, "State Power and the Structure of International Trade," *World Politics* 28, no. 3 (1976): 322; David A. Lake, "Leadership, Hegemony, and the International Economy: Naked Emperor or Tattered Monarch with Potential?" *International Studies Quarterly* 37, no. 4 (December 1993): 459. 参见 G. John Ikenberry, *After Victory: Institutions, Strategic Restraint, and the Rebuilding of Order After Major Wars* (Princeton, NJ: Princeton University Press, 2001); Rafael Reuveny and William R. Thompson, *Growth, Trade, and Systemic Leadership* (Ann Arbor: University of Michigan Press, 2009); John Ravenhill, "US Economic Relations with East Asia: From Hegemony to Complex Interdependence?," in *Bush and Asia: America's Evolving Relations with East Asia*, ed. Mark Beeson (London: Routledge, 2006), 43–45。
3. Stephan Haggard, "The Institutional Foundations of Hegemony: Explaining the Reciprocal Trade Agreements Act of 1934," *International Organization* 42, no. 1 (1988): 91–119; Michael Mastanduno, *Economic Containment: CoCom and the Politics of East–West Trade* (Ithaca, NY: Cornell University Press, 1992); Hugo Meijer, *Trading with the Enemy: The Making of US Export Control Policy Toward the People's Republic of China* (Oxford: Oxford University Press, 2016).
4. Judith Goldstein, *Ideas, Interests, and American Trade Policy* (Ithaca, NY: Cornell University Press, 1993); James Ashley Morrison, "Before Hegemony: Adam Smith, American Independence, and the Origins of the First Era of Globalization," *International Organization* 66, no. 3 (2012): 395–428.
5. 更多示例参见 Helen V. Milner, *Resisting Protectionism: Global Industries and the Politics of International Trade* (Princeton, NJ: Princeton University Press, 1988), 103–58; Susan K. Sell, *Private Power, Public Law: The Globalization of Intellectual Property Rights* (Cambridge: Cambridge University Press, 2003), 75–120; Llewelyn Hughes, *Globalizing Oil: Firms and Oil Market Governance in France, Japan, and the United States* (New York: Cam- bridge University Press, 2014), 149–97; Margaret E. Peters, "Trade, Foreign Direct Investment, and Immigration Policy Making in the United States," *International Organization* 68, no. 4 (2014): 811–44; In Song Kim, "Political Cleavages Within Industry: Firm Level Lobbying for Trade Liberalization," *American Political Science Review* 111 (2017): 1–20。
6. 例如，参见 I. M. Destler, *American Trade Politics* (New York: Columbia University Press, 2005)。
7. Joseph A. Schumpeter, *Business Cycles: A Theoretical, Historical, and Statistical Analysis of the Capitalist Process* (New York: McGraw-Hill, 1939), 72–192.

8. Robert Gilpin, *U.S. Power and the Multinational Corporation: The Political Economy of Foreign Direct Investment* (New York: Basic Books, 1975), 69.
9. Robert Gilpin, *War and Change in World Politics* (Cambridge: Cambridge University Press, 1983), 182. 参见 Robert Gilpin, *Global Political Economy: Understanding the International Economic Order* (Princeton, NJ: Princeton University Press, 2001), 140–41。
10. William R. Thompson, "Long Waves, Technological Innovation, and Relative Decline," *International Organization* 44, no. 2 (1990): 201–33; George Modelski and William R. Thompson, *Leading Sectors and World Powers: The Coevolution of Global Politics and Economics* (Columbia: University of South Carolina Press, 1996).
11. Modelski and Thompson, *Leading Sectors and World Powers*, 70–71.
12. Daniel Drezner, "State Structure, Technological Leadership and the Maintenance of Hegemony," *Review of International Studies* 27, no. 1 (2001): 3–25; Espen Moe, "Mancur Olson and Structural Economic Change: Vested Interests and the Industrial Rise and Fall of the Great Powers," *Review of International Political Economy* 16, no. 2 (June 26, 2009): 202–30; Ashley J. Tellis et al., *Measuring National Power in the Post-Industrial Age* (Santa Monica, CA: RAND, 2000), 36–40. 其他学者指出了创新在支持国家实力上的重要性。参见 Mark Zachary Taylor, *The Politics of Innovation: Why Some Countries Are Better Than Others at Science and Technology* (Oxford: Oxford University Press, 2016)。
13. Reuveny and Thompson, *Growth, Trade, and Systemic Leadership*, 13.
14. William R. Thompson, "Systemic Leadership, Evolutionary Processes, and International Relations Theory: The Unipolarity Question," *International Studies Review* 8, no. 1 (2006): 4; Tellis et al., *Measuring National Power in the Post-Industrial Age*, 40.
15. ICT 行业通常被定义为包括 ICT 制造商和 ICT 服务提供商（包括软件、电信、数据处理和托管以及计算机系统设计公司）。参见 Brandon Shackelford and John Jankowski, "Information and Communications Technology Industries Account for $133 Billion of Business R&D Performance in the United States in 2013," *National Center for Science and Engineering Statistics*, April 2016, https://www.nsf.gov/statistics/2016/nsf16309/nsf16309.pdf。
16. Organisation for Economic Cooperation and Development (OECD), "Population," *OECD. Stat*, March 23, 2016, http://stats.oecd.org/Index.aspx?DatasetCode=POP_FIVE_HIST.
17. European Commission, "The 2016 EU Industrial R&D Investment Scoreboard," *Economics of Industrial Research and Innovation*, accessed March 13, 2017, http://iri.jrc.ec.europa.eu/scoreboard16.html.
18. 四个国家及地区包括：芬兰、以色列、韩国和中国台湾。参见 Shackelford and Jankowski, "Information and Communications Technology Industries Account for $133 Billion of Business R&D Performance in the United States in 2013"。
19. Times Higher Education, "World University Rankings 2014–2015," 2014, *Times Higher Education*, www.timeshighereducation.co.uk/world-university-rankings/2014-15/world-ranking.
20. Elhanan Helpman, *The Mystery of Economic Growth* (Cambridge, MA: Harvard University Press, 2004).
21. David S. Landes, *The Unbound Prometheus: Technological Change and Industrial*

Development in Western Europe from 1750 to the Present (Cambridge: Cambridge University Press, 2003), 47–50.
22. Paul Kennedy, *The Rise and Fall of the Great Powers* (New York: Vintage, 1987), 151; François Crouzet, *The Victorian Economy* (London: Methuen, 1982), 4–5.
23. Nicholas Bloom, Raffaella Sadun, and John Van Reenen, "Americans Do IT Better: US Multinationals and the Productivity Miracle," *The American Economic Review* 102, no. 1 (2012): 167–201.
24. Barry Jaruzelski, Volker Staack, and Aritomo Shinozaki, "Software-as-a-Catalyst," *Strategy+Business*, October 25, 2016, www.strategy-business.com/feature/Software-as-a-Catalyst?gko=7a1ae.
25. Michael C. Horowitz, *The Diffusion of Military Power: Causes and Consequences for International Politics* (Princeton, NJ: Princeton University Press, 2010).
26. Helen Milner and David B. Yoffie, "Between Free Trade and Protectionism: Strategic Trade Policy and a Theory of Corporate Trade Demands," *International Organization* 43, no. 2 (Spring 1989): 244; Dennis C. Mueller, "First-Mover Advantages and Path Dependence," *International Journal of Industrial Organization* 15, no. 6 (October 1997): 827–50.
27. 本段借鉴 Joel Mokyr, *The Lever of Riches: Technological Creativity and Eco- nomic Progress* (New York: Oxford University Press, 1990), 88, 117–19。
28. 接下来的四句话借鉴 Johann Peter Murmann and Ralph Landau, "On the Making of Competitive Advantage: The Development of the Chemical Industry in Britain and Germany Since 1850," in *Chemicals and Long-Term Economic Growth: Insights from the Chemical Industry*, ed. Ashish Arora, Ralph Landau, and Nathan Rosenberg (New York: Wiley, 1998), 31–34。
29. David A. Hounshell and John Kenly Smith, *Science and Corporate Strategy: Du Pont R&D, 1902–1980* (Cambridge: Cambridge University Press, 1988), 11.
30. Murmann and Landau, "On the Making of Competitive Advantage," 36–37.
31. Robert Friedel and Paul B. Israel, *Edison's Electric Light: The Art of Invention* (Baltimore, MD: Johns Hopkins University Press, 2010), 1.
32. "General Electric Research Lab History," *Edison Tech Center*, 2015, www.edisontechcenter.org/GEresearchLab.html.
33. 接下来的段落借鉴 David C. Mowery and Nathan Rosenberg, "The U.S. National Innovation System," in *National Innovation Systems: A Comparative Analysis*, ed. Richard R. Nelson (Oxford: Oxford University Press, 1993), 32–40。
34. Mowery and Rosenberg, "The U.S. National Innovation System," 48.
35. Mowery and Rosenberg, "The U.S. National Innovation System," 34.
36. Tony Borroz, "Chevrolet's Mouse That Roared," *Wired*, August 22, 2011, www.wired.com/2011/08/chevrolets-mouse-that-roared/.
37. "G.M. Earnings in '55 Go Over Billion Mark," *Chicago Tribune*, February 3, 1956; Steven Mufson, "Once a Recession Remedy, GM's Empire Falls," *Washington Post*, June 2, 2009; "Fortune 500: 1955 Full List," *Fortune*, 2015, http://archive.fortune.com/magazines/fortune/fortune500_archive/full/1955/.

38. T. A. Heppenheimer, *Turbulent Skies: The History of Commercial Aviation* (New York: Wiley, 1995), 162–69, 183.
39. National Science Foundation, *Science and Engineering Indicators 2012* (Arlington, VA: National Science Foundation, 2012), chapter 4, 13.
40. Mowery and Rosenberg, "The U.S. National Innovation System," 47.
41. Linda Weiss, *America Inc.? Innovation and Enterprise in the National Security State* (Ithaca, NY: Cornell University Press, 2014), 78.
42. 关于这段转变的回顾，参见 William Lazonick, *Sustainable Prosperity in the New Economy? Business Organization and High-Tech Employment in the United States* (Kalama- zoo, MI: W. E. Upjohn Institute, 2009), 1–113。
43. National Science Foundation, *Science and Engineering Indicators 2012*, chapter 4, appendix table 7.
44. 与其ICT同行相比，苹果公司的研发占比（研发支出除以总收入）传统上相对较低。然而，近年来，苹果公司收入颇高，所以即使是很少的份额也会使苹果在研发经费方面领先世界。
45. Barry Jaruzelski, Volker Staack, and Aritomo Shinozaki, "2016 Global Innovation 1000 Study," *PwC*, accessed March 15, 2017, www.strategyand.pwc.com/innovation1000. 请注意，亚马逊有时被归为一般零售商，有时被归为互联网公司。普华永道将其归为软件与互联网公司。
46. U.S. National Science Foundation, *Science and Engineering Indicators 2016* (Arlington, VA: National Science Foundation), chapter 4, appendix table 7.
47. Weiss, *America Inc.?*, 97.
48. Jacques S. Gansler and William Lucyshyn, *Commercial-Off-the-Shelf (COTS): Doing It Right* (College Park: University of Maryland Center for Public Policy and Private Enterprise, 2008), 55, www.dtic.mil/dtic/tr/fulltext/u2/a494143.pdf.
49. Jessi Hempel, "DOD Head Ashton Carter Enlists Silicon Valley to Transform the Military," *Wired*, November 18, 2015, www.wired.com/2015/11/secretary-of-defense-ashton-carter/.
50. Weiss, *America Inc.?*, 64–121.
51. 2016年，奥巴马政府提议在信息技术采购方面投入864亿美元，其中373亿美元用于国防机构。参见 John K. Higgins, "Proposed 2016 Federal Budget Plumps IT Spending by $2B," *E-Commerce Times*, March 11, 2015, www.ecommercetimes.com/story/81805.html。
52. Doug Cameron and Alistair Barr, "Google Snubs Robotics Rivals, Pentagon," *Wall Street Journal*, March 5, 2015, www.wsj.com/articles/google-snubs-robotics-rivals-pentagon-1425580734.
53. Olivia Solon, "US Tech Firms Bypassing Pentagon to Protect Deals with China, Strategist Says," *The Guardian*, March 2, 2016, www.theguardian.com/technology/2016/mar/02/us-tech-firms-pentagon-national-security-china-deals.
54. 除非另有说明，以下段落引用 David M. Hart, "Political Representation in Concentrated Industries: Revisiting the 'Olsonian Hypothesis,'" *Business and Politics* 5, no. 3 (2003): 261–86。

55. 关于 IBM 与美国政府关系的概述，参见 David Hart, "Red, White, and 'Big Blue': IBM and the Business–Government Interface in the United States, 1956–2000," *Enterprise and Society* 8, no. 1 (2007): 1–34。
56. Tony Romm, "Apple Takes Washington," *Politico*, August 27, 2015, http://politi.co/1Px6AWo.
57. 软资金是指对国家政党的捐款。这些捐款首次公开披露是在 1991—1992 年选举周期中，并在 2002 年选举后通过立法禁止。外部支出是指团体或个人独立于候选人委员会且不与候选人委员会协调而进行的政治支出。
58. 本段引用的数据，参见 Center for Responsive Politics, "Interest Groups," *OpenSecrets.org*, accessed March 16, 2017, www.opensecrets.org/industries/。请注意，关于政党方面的数据仅基于对候选人和政党的贡献。
59. 关于高科技行业协会的有用概述，参见 David Hart, "New Economy, Old Politics: The Evolving Role of the High-Technology Industry in Washington, D.C.," in *Governance Amid Bigger, Better Markets*, ed. Joseph S. Nye and John D. Donahue (Washington, DC: Brookings Institution, 2004), 247–50。
60. Michael A. Murray, "Defining the Higher Education Lobby," *The Journal of Higher Education* 47, no. 1 (January 1976): 82–83.
61. Washington Higher Education Secretariat, "About WHES," accessed February 3, 2016, www.whes.org/index.html.
62. 本段引用的数据，参见 Center for Responsive Politics, "Lobbying Spending Database," *OpenSecrets.org*, accessed March 3, 2017, www.opensecrets.org/lobby/。
63. David M. Hart, " 'Business' Is Not an Interest Group: On the Study of Companies in American National Politics," *Annual Review of Political Science* 7 (2004): 47–69; Kim, "Political Cleavages Within Industry."
64. David Hart, "High-Tech Learns to Play the Washington Game, or the Political Education of Bill Gates and Other Nerds," in *Interest Group Politics*, ed. Allan J. Cigler and Burdett Loomis, 6th ed. (Washington, DC: CQ, 2002), 293–312.
65. Lucie Cerna, "The Varieties of High-Skilled Immigration Policies: Coalitions and Policy Outputs in Advanced Industrial Countries," *Journal of European Public Policy* 16, no. 1 (January 2009): 144–61.
66. Shackelford and Jankowski, "Information and Communications Technology Industries Account for $133 Billion of Business R&D Performance in the United States in 2013," 5.
67. 例如，参见 Philip G. Altbach and Jane Knight, "The Internationalization of Higher Education: Motivations and Realities," *Journal of Studies in International Education* 11, no. 3–4 (2007): 292–93。
68. Lesleyanne Hawthorne, "The Growing Global Demand for Students as Skilled Migrants" (Washington, DC: Migration Policy Institute, 2008), 5–7, www.migrationpolicy.org/sites/default/files/publications/intlstudents_0.pdf.
69. 人们早已认识到资本在自由国际投资体制中对世界主导经济的兴趣，参见 *U.S. Power and the Multinational Corporation*, 44–78。
70. Rajneesh Narula and Antonello Zanfei, "Globalization of Innovation: The Role of

Multinational Enterprises," in *The Oxford Handbook of Innovation*, ed. Jan Fagerberg, David C. Mowery, and Richard R. Nelson (Oxford: Oxford University Press, 2005), 325–26; U.S. National Science Foundation, *Science and Engineering Indicators 2016*, chapter 4, 61–67.
71. Narula and Zanfei, "Globalization of Innovation: The Role of Multinational Enterprises," 328.
72. Gilpin, *U.S. Power and the Multinational Corporation*; Milner, *Resisting Protectionism*; Sell, *Private Power, Public Law*; Peters, "Trade, Foreign Direct Investment, and Immigration Policy Making in the United States."
73. "Fortune 500," *Fortune*, 2015, http://fortune.com/fortune500/.
74. Philip Elmer-DeWitt, "Apple as the Goose That Laid the Golden Eggs. Five of Them," *Fortune*, November 25, 2013, http://fortune.com/2013/11/25/apple-as-the-goose-that-laid-the-golden-eggs-five-of-them/.
75. Meijer, *Trading with the Enemy*, 145–64.
76. 关于游说信息的价值，参见 Frank R. Baumgartner et al., *Lobbying and Policy Change: Who Wins, Who Loses, and Why* (Chicago: University of Chicago Press, 2009), 123。
77. David Vogel, *Fluctuating Fortunes: The Political Power of Business in America* (New York: Basic Books, 1989); Mark A. Smith, *American Business and Political Power: Public Opinion, Elections, and Democracy* (Chicago: University of Chicago Press, 2000); Sheldon Kamieniecki, *Corporate America and Environmental Policy: How Often Does Business Get Its Way?* (Stanford, CT: Stanford University Press, 2006); Mark A. Smith, "The Mobilization and Influence of Business Interests," in *The Oxford Handbook of American Political Parties and Interest Groups*, ed. L. Sandy Maisel and Jeffrey M. Berry (Oxford: Oxford University Press, 2010), 451–67.
78. Baumgartner et al., *Lobbying and Policy Change*, 202–4.
79. Smith, *American Business and Political Power*, 8–11.
80. Baumgartner et al., *Lobbying and Policy Change*, 212.
81. Larry Sabato, *PAC Power: Inside the World of Political Action Committees* (New York: Norton, 1984), 135; R. Kenneth Godwin, *One Billion Dollars of Influence: The Direct Marketing of Politics* (Chatham, NJ: Chatham House, 1988), 131–36; Larry Sabato, *Paying for Elections: The Campaign Finance Thicket* (New York: Priority, 1989), 13.
82. Frank R. Baumgartner and Beth L. Leech, *Basic Interests: The Importance of Groups in Politics and in Political Science* (Princeton, NJ: Princeton University Press, 1998), 131.
83. Baumgartner et al., *Lobbying and Policy Change*, 79.
84. David C. Kimball et al., "Who Cares about the Lobbying Agenda?" *Interest Groups & Advocacy* 1, no. 1 (May 2012): 5–25.
85. 关于认知和框架在塑造外国经济政策偏好中的重要性，参见 Raymond Hicks, Helen V. Milner, and Dustin Tingley, "Trade Policy, Economic Interests, and Party Politics in a Developing Country: The Political Economy of CAFTA- DR," *International Studies Quarterly* 58, no. 1 (March 2014): 106–17。
86. George J. Borjas, *Immigration Economics* (Cambridge, MA: Harvard University Press, 2014).

87. Jens Hainmueller and Michael J. Hiscox, "Attitudes Toward Highly Skilled and Low-Skilled Immigration: Evidence from a Survey Experiment," *American Political Science Review* 104, no. 1 (February 2010): 61.
88. Gary Clyde Hufbauer, Theodore H. Moran, and Lindsay Oldenski, *Outward Foreign Direct Investment and US Exports, Jobs, and R&D: Implications for US Policy* (Washington, DC: Peterson Institute for International Economics, 2013).
89. Neil Malhotra, Yotam Margalit, and Cecilia Hyunjung Mo, "Economic Explanations for Opposition to Immigration: Distinguishing Between Prevalence and Conditional Impact," *American Journal of Political Science* 57, no. 2 (April 2013): 391–410; Brenton D. Peterson, Sonal S. Pandya, and David Leblang, "Doctors with Borders: Occupational Licensing as an Implicit Barrier to High Skill Migration," *Public Choice* 160, no. 1–2 (July 2014): 45–63.
90. Peterson, Pandya, and Leblang, "Doctors with Borders."
91. Baumgartner et al., *Lobbying and Policy Change*, 232.
92. Ken Kollman, *Outside Lobbying: Public Opinion and Interest Group Strategies* (Princeton, NJ: Princeton University Press, 1998).
93. Chase, "Moving Hollywood Abroad: Divided Labor Markets and the New Politics of Trade in Services," 660; Giovanni Facchini, Anna Maria Mayda, and Prachi Mishra, "Do Interest Groups Affect US Immigration Policy?" *Journal of International Economics* 85, no. 1 (September 2011): 114–28.
94. Laurie P. Milton, "An Identity Perspective on the Propensity of High-Tech Talent to Unionize," *Journal of Labor Research* 24, no. 1 (2003): 32; Robbert van het Kaar and Marianne Grünell, "Industrial Relations in the Information and Communications Technology Sector," *Eurofound*, August 27, 2001, www.eurofound.europa.eu/observatories/eurwork/comparative-information/industrial-relations-in-the-information-and-communications-technology-sector. 参见 Lazonick, *Sustainable Prosperity in the New Economy?*, 144–46。
95. 关于大规模动员的挑战，参见 Baumgartner et al., *Lobbying and Policy Change*, 156–57。
96. Janice Fine and Daniel J. Tichenor, "An Enduring Dilemma: Immigration and Organized Labor in Western Europe and the United States," in *The Oxford Handbook of the Politics of International Migration*, ed. Marc Rosenblum and Daniel J. Tichenor (Oxford: Oxford University Press, 2012), 532–72.
97. 我在这里遵循 Berry 的定义。参见 Jeffrey M. Berry, *The New Liberalism: The Rising Power of Citizen Groups* (Washington, DC: Brookings Institution, 1999), 2。
98. Berry, *The New Liberalism*; Baumgartner et al., *Lobbying and Policy Change*, 238. 虽然这些研究集中在美国政治上，但是公民团体在其他情况下能有效地反对商界。参见 Andreas Dür, Patrick Bernhagen, and David Marshall, "Interest Group Success in the European Union: When (and Why) Does Business Lose?" *Comparative Political Studies* 48, no. 8 (2015): 951–83; Andreas Dür and Gemma Mateo, "Public Opinion and Interest Group Influence: How Citizen Groups Derailed the Anti-counterfeiting Trade Agreement," *Journal of European Public Policy* 21, no. 8 (2014): 1199–1217。
99. Thomas T. Holyoke, "The Interest Group Effect on Citizen Contact with Congress," *Party Politics* 19, no. 6 (November 1, 2013): 937–40.

100. Kollman, *Outside Lobbying*, 58–100; Baumgartner et al., *Lobbying and Policy Change*, 127.
101. John R. Wright, *Interest Groups and Congress: Lobbying, Contributions and Influence* (Boston: Allyn and Bacon, 1996).
102. 关于结合不同自由国际关系理论的实用性，参见 Andrew Moravcsik, "Liberal Theories of International Law," in *Interdisciplinary Perspec- tives on International Law and International Relations: The State of the Art*, ed. Jeffrey L. Dunoff and Mark A. Pollack (Cambridge: Cambridge University Press, 2013), 85. 关于更多自由理论的研究，参见 Andrew Moravcsik, "Taking Preferences Seriously: A Liberal Theory of International Politics," *International Organization* 51, no. 4 (1997): 513–53。
103. David A. Lake, "Open Economy Politics: A Critical Review," *The Review of International Organizations* 4, no. 3 (September 2009): 225.
104. Joseph M. Grieco, "Anarchy and the Limits of Cooperation: A Realist Critique of the Newest Liberal Institutionalism," in *Neorealism and Neoliberalism: The Contemporary Debate* (New York: Columbia University Press, 1993), 129; John J. Mearsheimer, *The Tragedy of Great Power Politics* (New York: W. W. Norton, 2001), 401–2.
105. 最近的研究强调了国家的国内创新政策如何能够反映国家安全问题。参见 Weiss, *America Inc.?*；Taylor, *The Politics of Innovation*。
106. Dong Jung Kim, "Cutting Off Your Nose? A Reigning Power's Commercial Containment of a Military Challenger" (Ph.D. dissertation, University of Chicago, 2015); Dong Jung Kim, "Trading with the Enemy? The Futility of US Commercial Countermeasures Against the Chinese Challenge," *Pacific Review*, November 2, 2016, 1–20.
107. 关于"冷战"期间这些问题的普遍存在，参见 Mastanduno, *Economic Containment*。
108. Smith, *American Business and Political Power*, 9.
109. Baumgartner et al., *Lobbying and Policy Change*, 29–45.
110. David Nelson and Susan Webb Yackee, "Lobbying Coalitions and Government Policy Change: An Analysis of Federal Agency Rulemaking," *The Journal of Politics* 74, no. 2 (2012): 339–53.
111. Martin Gilens and Benjamin I. Page, "Testing Theories of American Politics: Elites, Interest Groups, and Average Citizens," *Perspectives on Politics* 12, no. 3 (2014): 575.
112. 关于测试因果机制的过程追踪的效用，参见 Alexander George and Andrew Bennett, *Case Studies and Theory Development in the Social Sciences* (Cambridge, MA: MIT Press, 2005), 205–32。
113. 如果需要，分析还可以考虑其他因素，例如，相关的签证费、入学是否取决于劳动力市场测试，以及是否允许配偶工作。参见 Lucie Cerna, "The EU Blue Card: Preferences, Policies, and Negotiations Between Member States," *Migration Studies* 2, no. 1 (March 1, 2014): 9–10。

第3章 旋转门：高技能劳动力

1. National Science Foundation, *Science and Engineering Indicators 2016* (Arlington, VA:

National Science Foundation, 2016), chapter 3, 101.
2. National Science Foundation, *Science and Engineering Indicators 2016*, chapter 3, 104.
3. Demetrios G. Papademetriou and Stephen Yale-Loehr, "Balancing Interests: Rethinking U.S. Selection of Skilled Immigrants" (Washington, DC: Carnegie Endowment for Inter- national Peace, 1996), 40–48.
4. 引用自 H. Rosemary Jeronimides, "The H-1B Visa Category: A Tug of War," *George- town Immigration Law Journal* 7 (1993): 369。
5. Papademetriou and Yale-Loehr, "Balancing Interests," 82.
6. 关于 H-1B 签证计划的起源，参见 Jeronimides, "The H-1B Visa Category"。
7. Bruce Morrison, testimony, *Hearing Before the Committee on the Judiciary of the United States House of Representatives Subcommittee on Immigration Policy and Enforcement*, 113th Cong. (March 5, 2013), 2.
8. 莫里森最初支持 H-1B 签证的上限为 25 000，但他随后在会议阶段将此数增加到 65 000。莫里森回忆说，最初的限制是基于有关移民和归化局目前使用情况的不准确数据，并且他增加了限制，以响应政府部门的额外信息，表明目前的使用量为每年 30 000-40 000 个签证。Bruce Morrison, former chair, House Judiciary Committee Subcommittee on Immigration, interviewed by author, February 27, 2016.
9. Bruce Morrison, interview. On the politics behind the Immigration Act of 1990 more generally, 参见 Daniel J. Tichenor, *Dividing Lines: The Politics of Immigration Control in America* (Princeton, NJ: Princeton University Press, 2002), 267–74。
10. Daniel Costa, "Little-Known Temporary Visas for Foreign Tech Workers Depress Wages," *The Hill*, November 11, 2014, http://thehill.com/blogs/pundits-blog/technology/223607-little-known-temporary-visas-for-foreign-tech-workers-depress.
11. Neil G. Ruiz, Jill H. Wilson, and Shyamali Choudhury, "The Search for Skills: Demand for H-1B Immigrant Workers in U.S. Metropolitan Areas" (Washington, DC: Brookings Institution, 2012), 4, 7, 14. 这些作者估计，高等教育、政府和非营利研究机构约占 2001—2010 年提交的 H-1B 签证申请数量的 10%。
12. Ruth Ellen Wasem, *Immigration: Legislative Issues on Nonimmigrant Professional Specialty (H-1B) Workers* (Washington, DC: Congressional Research Service, 2004), 6.
13. U.S. Immigration and Naturalization Service, *Report on Characteristics of Specialty Occupation Workers (H-1B): Fiscal Year 2000* (Washington, DC: U.S. Immigration and Naturalization Service, 2002), 8.
14. U.S. General Accounting Office, *Immigration and the Labor Market: Nonimmigrant Alien Workers in the United States* (Washington, DC: U.S. General Accounting Office, 1992), 34, www.gao.gov/assets/160/151654.pdf.
15. U.S. Immigration and Naturalization Service, *Report on Characteristics*, 5.
16. U.S. Citizenship and Immigration Services, *Characteristics of H-1B Specialty Occupation Workers: Fiscal Year 2015* (Washington, DC: U.S. Department of Homeland Security, 2016), 8.
17. Liz Robbins, "New U.S. Rule Extends Stay for Some Foreign Graduates," *New York Times*, March 9, 2016, www.nytimes.com/2016/03/09/nyregion/new-us-rule-extends-stay-for-

some-foreign-graduates.html.
18. Lynne Shotwell, executive director, Council for Global Immigration, interview by author, July 22, 2015.
19. Joan Sazabo, "Opening Doors for Immigrants," *Nation's Business*, August 1, 1989.
20. Daryl Buffenstein and Kevin Miner, Fragomen Worldwide, interview by author, February 12, 2016. Buffenstein 是美国移民律师协会（AILA）的前任主席，并在国会就1990年的移民法案做证。Miner 是 AILA 与美国劳工部联络委员会的副主席。引用自 Buffenstein。
21. Ronil Hira, "U.S. Immigration Regulations and India's Information Technology Industry," *Technological Forecasting and Social Change* 71, no. 8 (October 2004): 841.
22. 本句话和前一句话来自作者对 Daryl Buffenstein 和 Kevin Miner 的采访。引用自 Buffenstein。
23. Hira, "U.S. Immigration Regulations," 846.
24. American Immigration Lawyers Association, "Analysis of the American Competitiveness in the Twenty-First Century Act," accessed March 2, 2016, http://shusterman.com/h1b-analysisofac21.html。
25. 引用自 Cindy Rodriguez, "Foreign Workers Bill Approved," *Boston Globe*, October 4, 2000。
26. William Glanz, "High-Tech Lobbyist Counts Washington Successes," *Knight-Ridder Tribune Business News*, October 14, 2000.
27. Michael S. Teitelbaum, *Falling Behind? Boom, Bust, and the Global Race for Scientific Talent* (Princeton, NJ: Princeton University Press, 2014), 57–58.
28. Jason Zengerle, "Silicon Smoothies," *New Republic*, June 8, 1998.
29. Quoted in Glanz, "High-Tech Lobbyist Counts Washington Successes."
30. Zengerle, "Silicon Smoothies," 21.
31. John Simons, "Impasse on Bill to Boost Visas Persists Between Firms, U.S.," *Wall Street Journal*, August 6, 1998.
32. Zengerle, "Silicon Smoothies," 20.
33. Laurie P. Milton, "An Identity Perspective on the Propensity of High-Tech Talent to Unionize," *Journal of Labor Research* 24, no. 1 (2003): 32.
34. Quoted in Bill Pietrucha, "Labor Challenges High Tech Job Shortage Claims," *Newsbytes News Network*, March 19, 1998.
35. Paul Kostek, president, IEEE-USA, 1999, interviewed by author, June 29, 2015.
36. Ana Avendano, director of immigration, 2004 to 2009, and executive assistant to the president for immigration, 2009 to 2014, AFL-CIO, interviewed by author, February 21, 2015.
37. "FAIR Statement on the Pioneer Fund," *PR Newswire*, March 4, 1998; Devin Burghart and Leonard Zeskind, "Beyond FAIR: The Decline of the Established Anti-Immigration Organizations and the Rise of Tea Party Nativism" (Kansas City, MO: Institute for Research and Education on Human Rights, 2012), 4, www.irehr.org/issue-areas/tea-party-nativism/beyond-fair-report.
38. Roy Beck, president, NumbersUSA, personal communication, June 18, 2015. 参见 "Lott Wants Agreement with Dems on H-1B Visa Measure," *Congress Daily*, September 14, 2000。
39. Carolyn Wong, *Lobbying for Inclusion: Rights Politics and the Making of Immigration Policy* (Stanford, CA: Stanford University Press, 2006), 133–45.

40. 引用自 Miranda Ewell, "Clinton Opposes Higher Visa Cap; Focus on 'Home-Grown' Talent, Commerce Chief Says," *San Jose Mercury News*, January 13, 1998。
41. 引用自 Ewell, "Clinton Opposes Higher Visa Cap"。
42. U.S. General Accounting Office, *Assessment of the Department of Commerce's Report on Workforce Demand and Supply* (Washington, DC: U.S. General Accounting Office, 1998), 2, 6, http://gao.gov/assets/230/225415.pdf.
43. Pietrucha, "Labor Challenges High Tech Job Shortage Claims."
44. Simons, "Impasse on Bill to Boost Visas Persists Between Firms, U.S."
45. 保障措施限制了雇主将 H-1B 签证劳工转移到另一个雇主，要求雇主证明他们没有也不会取代美国工人，并要求雇主采取措施为需要 H-1B 签证的岗位招募同等或更高资格的美国工人。参见 Jessica F. Rosenbaum, "Exploiting Dreams: H-1B Visa Fraud, Its Effects, and Potential Solutions," *University of Pennsylvania Journal of Business Law* 13, no. 3 (2010): 802。注意，仅雇用"豁免 H-1B 签证劳工"（每年至少赚取 60 000 美元或相当于硕士学位或更高学历）的公司不受这些限制。参见 U.S. Department of Labor, "Fact Sheet 62: What Are 'Exempt' H-1B Nonimmigrants?" *Wage and Hour Division*, July 2008, 1, www.dol.gov/whd/regs/compliance/FactSheet62/whdfs62Q.pdf。
46. Tom Abate and Jon Swartz, "Eleventh-Hour Victory for Tech: Visa Increase, R&D Tax Measure in Budget Bill," *San Francisco Chronicle*, October 16, 1998, www.sfgate.com/business/article/11th-Hour-Victory-For-Tech-Visa-increase-R-D-2984825.php.
47. 有关立法程序和法案内容的实用总结，参见 Jung S. Hahm, "American Competitiveness and Workforce Improvement Act of 1998: Balancing Economic and Labor Interests Under the New H-1B Visa Program," *Cornell Law Review* 85 (1999): 1683–88。
48. Mark Leibovich, "High Tech Is King of the Hill," *Washington Post*, October 16, 1998.
49. 引用自 Leibovich, "High Tech Is King of the Hill"。
50. 引用自 Abate and Swartz, "Eleventh-Hour Victory for Tech: Visa Increase, R&D Tax Measure in Budget Bill"。
51. William Branigin, "Visa Deal for Computer Programmers Angers Labor Groups," *Washington Post*, September 27, 1998.
52. 引用自 Branigin, "Visa Deal for Computer Programmers Angers Labor Groups"。
53. 引用自 Branigin, "Visa Deal for Computer Programmers Angers Labor Groups"。
54. Harris Miller, president, Information Technology Association of America, 1995 to 2005, interview by author, July 1, 2015.
55. Teitelbaum, *Falling Behind?*, 113–14.
56. American Federation of Labor and Congress of Industrial Organizations (AFL-CIO), "Immigration," *AFL-CIO*, February 16, 2000, www.aflcio.org/About/Exec-Council/EC-Statements/Immigration.
57. "House Dems, AFL-CIO Discuss H-1B Visas," *Congress Daily*, March 14, 2000.
58. Jube Shiver, "Alliance Fights Boost in Visas for Tech Workers," *Los Angeles Times*, August 5, 2000, http://articles.latimes.com/2000/aug/05/business/fi-64994.
59. Terry Costlow, "Senate Set to Vote This Week on Visa-Cap Bill; High Noon Approaches for H-1B Friends, Foes," *Electronic Engineering Times*, October 2, 2000.

60. Paul Kostek, interview.
61. Robert Pear, "Clinton Asks Congress to Raise the Limit on Visas for Skilled Workers," *New York Times*, May 12, 2000.
62. Susan Bibler Coutin, *Nations of Emigrants: Shifting Boundaries of Citizenship in* El Salvador and the United States (Ithaca, NY: Cornell University Press, 2007), 184–87.
63. Bibler Coutin, Nations of Emigrants, 188.
64. American Competitiveness in the Twenty-First Century Act of 2000, Pub. L. No. 106-313, 114 Stat. 1251 (2000), www.gpo.gov/fdsys/pkg/BILLS-106s2045enr/pdf/BILLS-106s2045enr.pdf. 参见 Carolyn Lochhead, "Bill to Boost Tech Visas Sails Through Congress," San Francisco Chronicle, October 4, 2000, www.sfgate.com/news/article/Bill-to-Boost-Tech-Visas-Sails-Through-Congress-2735682.php。
65. 引用自 Lochhead, "Bill to Boost Tech Visas Sails Through Congress"。参见 Norman Matloff, "On the Need for Reform of the H-1B Non-Immigrant Work Visa in Computer- Related Occupations," University of Michigan Journal of Law Reform 36, no. 4 (Fall 2003): 815–914。
66. 引用自 "Analysis: Look at the Controversy Over H-1B Visas," National Public Radio: Talk of the Nation, September 26, 2000。
67. 引用自 Costlow, "Senate Set to Vote This Week on Visa-Cap Bill"。
68. 引用自 "Analysis: Look at the Controversy Over H-1B Visas"。
69. Marjorie Valbrun and Scott Thurm, "Foreign Workers Will Soon Get Fewer U.S. Visas," Wall Street Journal, October 1, 2003.
70. Jena Heath, "Congressman Switches Focus to High-Tech: Republican, New to Area, Softens Immigration Stance, Trumpets Tech," Austin American-Statesman, July 7, 2002.
71. Sandra Boyd, chair, Compete America, 2004 to 2006, interview by author, June 29, 2015.
72. Sara Schaefer Munoz, "Firms Push to Expand Visa Program," Wall Street Journal, March 11, 2004; Teitelbaum, Falling Behind?, 109.
73. Sandra Boyd, interview.
74. Danielle Belopotosky, "Lobbyists Push Congress for Action On H-1B Visas," Technology Daily, November 16, 2004.
75. Elizabeth Olson, "Congress Raises Limit on Skilled-Work Visas," International *Herald Tribune*, November 24, 2004.
76. Danielle Belopotosky, "Efforts to Change Visa Law for Skilled Workers Gains Steam," *Technology Daily*, October 1, 2004; Chloe Albanesius, "Outsourcing Controversy Influences Debate On H-1B Visas," *Technology Daily*, May 6, 2004.
77. Michael Posner, "Groups Jockey for Position On Possible Boost In H-1B Visas," *Congress Daily*, November 17, 2004.
78. Personal communication from Roy Beck, president, NumbersUSA, June 18, 2015.
79. Roy Beck, president, NumbersUSA, interview by author, June 13, 2015.
80. 总结内容参见 Richard Rulon, "Competing for Foreign Talent," *Legal Intelligencer*, December 15, 2004。
81. Glen Kessler and Kevin Sullivan, "Powell Cautious About Immigration Changes,"

Washington Post, November 10, 2004.
82. Michael Fletcher, "Bush Immigration Plan Meets GOP Opposition: Lawmakers Resist Temporary-Worker Proposal," *Washington Post*, January 2, 2005.
83. Michael Fletcher, "Bush Immigration Plan Meets GOP Opposition."
84. "Senator Kerry Delivers Democratic Hispanic Radio Address," *U.S. Fed News*, April 1, 2006.
85. "Compete America," *Technology Daily PM*, October 4, 2005.
86. "Compete America"; Edward Alden, "Emigrants to US Face Long Wait for Green Card," *Financial Times*, October 12, 2005.
87. Patrick O'Connor, "Anti-Immigration Groups Up Against Unusual Coalition," *The Hill*, February 28, 2006; Kate Phillips, "Business Lobbyists Call for Action on Immigration," *New York Times*, April 15, 2006, www.nytimes.com/2006/04/15/us/15lobby.html.
88. Nina Bernstein, "In the Streets, Suddenly, an Immigrant Groundswell," *New York Times*, March 27, 2006; Gerardo Lissardy, "Leading Hispanic Group Joins Immigrant-Rights Coalition," *EFE News Service*, May 12, 2006.
89. Jennifer Ludden, "Strange Bedfellows Join Forces for Immigration Reform," *National Public Radio: All Things Considered*, January 19, 2006.
90. Roy Beck, personal communication, June 18, 2015.
91. "NumbersUSA Activists Squash Amnesty in Senate: Senate Rejects Cloture on Amnesty Bill 46–53," *PR Newswire*, June 28, 2007.
92. Molly Ball, "The Little Group Behind the Big Fight to Stop Immigration Reform," *The Atlantic*, August 1, 2013, www.theatlantic.com/politics/archive/2013/08/the-little-group-behind-the-big-fight-to-stop-immigration-reform/278252/.
93. 引用自 Brian Mitchell, "Frist's Border Control-Only Bill Spurs Broad Immigration Deals," *Investor's Business Daily*, March 20, 2006。
94. 引用自 Mitchell, "Frist's Border Control-Only Bill Spurs Broad Immigration Deals"。
95. Comprehensive Immigration Reform Act of 2006, S.2611, 109th Cong. (2006), www.congress.gov/bill/109th-congress/senate-bill/2611. 参见 Wasem, *Immigration*, 24–25。
96. 引用自 Rachel L. Swarns, "Senate, in Bipartisan Act, Passes an Immigration Bill," *New York Times*, May 26, 2006, www.nytimes.com/2006/05/26/washington/26immig.html。
97. Suzanne Gamboa, "Senate Vote Sidetracks Immigration Compromise," *Associated Press*, April 7, 2006.
98. Jonathan Weisman and Jim VandeHei, "Immigration Bill Lobbying Focuses on House Leaders: With Senate in Hand, Bush May Face a Skeptical GOP Base," *Washington Post*, May 1, 2006.
99. Roy Beck, interview, April 3, 2015.
100. "Address by House Speaker J. Dennis Hastert: Reflections on Role of Speaker in Modern Day House of Representatives," *U.S. Newswire*, November 12, 2003.
101. Anne C. Mukem, "Firebrand Tancredo Puts Policy Over Party Line," *Denver Post*, November 27, 2005; "Rep. Tancredo Slams Senate's Compromise on Amnesty," *U.S. Fed News*, May 11, 2006.

102. 除注明的之外，以下句子基于 Roy Beck, interview, June 13, 2015。
103. Southern Poverty Law Center, "John Tanton Is the Mastermind Behind the Organized Anti-Immigration Movement," *Intelligence Report*, no. 106 (Summer 2002), www.splcenter.org/get-informed/intelligence-report/browse-all-issues/2002/summer/the-puppeteer?page=0,3.
104. Roy Beck, interview, June 13, 2015.
105. Jim VandeHei and Zachary A. Goldfarb, "Immigration Deal at Risk as House GOP Looks to Voters," *Washington Post*, May 28, 2006.
106. Charles Babington, "Immigration Bill Expected to Pass Senate This Week: Hastert May Block Version That Divides House GOP," *Washington Post*, May 23, 2006.
107. 引用自 Babington, "Immigration Bill Expected to Pass Senate This Week"。
108. Mike Madden, "Millions Spent Lobbying on Immigration in Last Congress," *Gannett News Service*, January 26, 2007.
109. 引用自 Reinhardt Krause, "Tech Firms Pushing for More H-1B Visas for Skilled Workers," *Investor's Business Daily*, April 11, 2007。
110. Eunice Moscoso, "Once Gung-Ho, Businesses See Flaws in Immigration Bill: Tech Sector Particularly Disturbed by Potential Changes in Visa Program," *Atlanta Journal-Constitution*, June 3, 2007.
111. Carolyn Lochhead, "Visa Plan Angers Silicon Valley," *SFGate*, June 7, 2007, www.sfgate.com/politics/article/VISA-PLAN-ANGERS-SILICON-VALLEY-Immigration-2588829.php.
112. Ana Avendano, interview, May 25, 2017.
113. Amanda Paulson, Faye Bowers, and Daniel Wood, "To Immigrants, US Reform Bill Is Unrealistic," *Christian Science Monitor*, May 21, 2007.
114. Quoted in Ryan Lizza, "Getting to Maybe," *New Yorker*, June 24, 2013, www.newyorker.com/magazine/2013/06/24/getting-to-maybe.
115. Shailagh Murray, "Careful Strategy Is Used to Derail Immigration Bill," *Washington Post*, June 8, 2007.
116. John Stanton and Jennifer Yachnin, "Reid Plots to Block Conservatives," *Roll Call*, June 18, 2007.
117. Robert Pear, "U.S. High-Tech Firms Stymied on Immigration for Skilled Workers," *New York Times*, June 25, 2007, www.nytimes.com/2007/06/25/technology/25iht-visas.4.6326165.html.
118. Daryl Buffenstein and Kevin Miner, interview.
119. Kathy Kiely, "Immigration Overhaul Crumbles in Senate Vote," *USA Today*, June 29, 2007.
120. Jonathan Weisman, "Immigration Bill Dies in Senate," *Washington Post*, June 29, 2007, www.washingtonpost.com/wp-dyn/content/article/2007/06/28/AR2007062800963.html.
121. Congressional aide, interview by author, May 24, 2017.
122. 引用自 Kiely, "Immigration Overhaul Crumbles in Senate Vote"。
123. Dana Milbank, "Jabs and All, the Ides of March Arrives Late," *Washington Post*, June 29, 2007.
124. Roy Beck, interview by author, April 3, 2015. 参见 Bruce Schreiner, "National Group Takes

Aim at McConnell on Immigration," *Associated Press*, June 27, 2007。

125. 引用自 Nicole Gaouette, "Immigration Bill Ignites a Grass-Roots Fire on the Right," *Los Angeles Times*, June 24, 2007, http://articles.latimes.com/2007/jun/24/nation/na-immig24。

126. Stuart Rothenberg, "Heeee's Back: The Fall and Rise of Sen. Trent Lott," *Roll Call*, May 22, 2006.

127. Milbank, "Jabs and All, the Ides of March Arrives Late."

128. Mitch McConnell (KY), "Immigration," *Congressional Record*, 110th Cong., 153, no. 106 (June 28, 2007): S8674.

129. Roy Beck, interview, April 3, 2015.

130. 引用自 Heather Greenfield, "Techies 'Disappointed' by Immigration Bill's Demise," *Technology Daily PM*, June 28, 2007。

131. 引用自 Robert Pear, "Little-Known Group Claims a Win on Immigration," *New York Times*, July 15, 2007.

132. 引用自 Gaouette, "Immigration Bill Ignites a Grass-Roots Fire on the Right"。

133. 引用自 Molly Ball, "Immigration Reformers Are Winning August," *The Atlantic*, August 21, 2013, www.theatlantic.com/politics/archive/2013/08/immigration-reformers-are-winning-august/278873/。

134. Nicholas Thompson, "Obama vs. McCain: The Wired.com Scorecard," *Wired*, October 12, 2008, www.wired.com/2008/10/obama-v-mccain/.

135. 引用自 Neil Munro, "IT Industry, Hispanics Team Up On Immigration," *National Journal*, April 9, 2010。

136. 引用自 Munro, "IT Industry, Hispanics Team Up On Immigration"。

137. 引用自 Munro, "IT Industry, Hispanics Team Up On Immigration"。

138. Terry Hartle, senior vice-president, and Steven Bloom, director for federal relations, American Council on Education, interview by author, September 8, 2015. 引自哈特尔。

139. Munro, "IT Industry, Hispanics Team Up On Immigration."

140. National Council of La Raza, *2011 Annual Report* (Washington, DC: National Council of La Raza, 2011), http://publications.nclr.org/handle/123456789/2; "Hispanic Business Magazine Includes 12 NCLR Affiliates Among Its Top 25 Nonprofits," *Targeted News Service*, June 9, 2011.

141. Mark Hugo Lopez, "The Hispanic Vote in the 2008 Election" (Washington, DC: Pew Research Center, November 5, 2008), www.pewhispanic.org/2008/11/05/the-hispanic-vote-in-the-2008-election/; Eric Schurenberg, "Why the Next Steve Jobs Could Be an Indian," *Mint*, October 28, 2011.

142. Munro, "IT Industry, Hispanics Team Up On Immigration."

143. "Sen. Chuck Grassley to Place Hold on Employment-Based Visa Bill," *NumbersUSA*, November 30, 2011, www.numbersusa.com/content/news/november-30-2011/sen-chuck-grassley-place-hold-employment-based-visa-bill.html.

144. David Bier, "High-Skilled Immigration Restrictions Are Economically Senseless," *Forbes*, July 22, 2012, www.forbes.com/sites/realspin/2012/07/22/high-skilled-immigration-restrictions-are-economically-senseless/; David Bier, "Why Does the Government Care

注 释

Where Immigrant Workers Were Born?" *Cato Institute*, January 18, 2017, www.cato.org/blog/why-does-government-care-where-immigrant-workers-were-born.
145. Former congressional aide, interview by author, June 9, 2017.
146. Laura Meckler, "Visas Could Aid Graduates," *Wall Street Journal*, October 22, 2011.
147. Bruce Morrison, interview. 莫里森当时代表 IEEE-USA。
148. Roy Beck, interview, April 3, 2015.
149. Chris Frates, "Why the Schumer–Smith Immigration Negotiations Broke Down," *The Atlantic*, September 20, 2012, www.theatlantic.com/politics/archive/2012/09/why-the-schumer-smith-immigration-negotiations-broke-down/428835/.
150. Suzy Khimm, "Why a Rare Bipartisan Consensus on Immigration Totally Fell Apart," *Washington Post*, September 21, 2012, www.washingtonpost.com/blogs/ezra-klein/wp/2012/09/21/why-a-rare-bipartisan-consensus-on-immigration-totally-fell-apart/.
151. Frates, "Why the Schumer–Smith Immigration Negotiations Broke Down."
152. Barack Obama, "Statement of Administration Policy: H.R. 6429—STEM Jobs Act of 2012," *American Presidency Project*, November 28, 2012, www.presidency.ucsb.edu/ws/?pid=102707.
153. Gregory Wallace and Deirdre Walsh, "House Passes Immigration Bill to Keep Science and Technology Students in U.S.," *CNN Wire*, November 30, 2012.
154. 引用自 Brian Fung, "Democrats' Dilemma on High-Skilled Immigration Reform," *National Journal*, March 6, 2013。
155. Ana Avendano, interview, February 21, 2015. 参见 Richard Trumka and Thomas J. Donohue, "Joint Statement of Shared Principles by U.S. Chamber of Commerce President and CEO Thomas J. Donohue and AFL-CIO President Richard Trumka," *AFL-CIO*, February 21, 2013, www.aflcio.org/Press-Room/Press-Releases/Joint-Statement-of-Shared-Principles-by-U.S.-Chamber-of-Commerce-President-and-CEO-Thomas-J.-Donohue-AFL-CIO-President-Richard-Trumka。
156. Lizza, "Getting to Maybe"; Jason Horowitz, "Marco Rubio Pushed for Immigration Reform with Conservative Media," *New York Times*, February 27, 2016, www.nytimes.com/2016/02/28/us/politics/marco-rubio-pushed-for-immigration-reform-with-conservative-media.html.
157. Center for Responsive Politics, "Lobbying Spending Database: Microsoft," *OpenSecrets.org*, 2015, www.opensecrets.org/lobby/clientsum.php?id=D000000115&year=2013.
158. Eric Lipton and Somini Sengupta, "Latest Product of Tech Firms: Immigrant Bill," *New York Times*, May 5, 2013.
159. Mark Zuckerberg, "Mark Zuckerberg: Immigrants Are the Key to a Knowledge Economy," *Washington Post*, April 10, 2013, www.washingtonpost.com/opinions/mark-zuckerberg-immigrants-are-the-key-to-a-knowledge-economy/2013/04/10/aba05554-a20b-11e2-82bc-511538ae90a4_story.html.
160. Border Security, Economic Opportunity, and Immigration Modernization Act of 2013, S. 744, 113th Cong. (2013), www.govtrack.us/congress/bills/113/s744.
161. Border Security, Economic Opportunity, and Immigration Modernization Act of 2013.

162. 最初的法案要求使用 H-1B 签证的公司首先在政府网站上宣传职位空缺 30 天，在雇用签证持有人之前向美国人提供优惠，并表明他们在招聘后三个月内没有解雇美国工人而去招聘来自海外的签证持有人。该法案还赋予劳工部在其制定后长达两年的审计和质疑公司招聘决策的权力。参见 Fredreka Schouten, "Tech Firms Would Skirt Hiring Restrictions Under Deal," *USA Today*, May 21, 2013; Lipton and Sengupta, "Latest Product of Tech Firms"。
163. Peter Walsten, Jia Lynn Yang, and Craig Timberg, "Facebook Flexes Political Muscle with Carve-Out in Immigration Bill," *Washington Post*, April 16, 2013.
164. Ana Avendano, interview, February 21, 2015.
165. Ana Avendano, personal communication, May 30, 2017.
166. Ronil Hira, testimony, *Hearing Before the Senate Judiciary Committee on the Border Security, Economic Opportunity, and Immigration Modernization Act, S.744*, 113th Cong. (April 22, 2013), 10; Paul Roy, "Impact of U.S. Senate Bill on Outsourcing," *Mondaq Business Briefing*, July 31, 2013.
167. Dhanya Ann Thoppil and Sean McLain, "Q&A: 'Parts of U.S. Visa Bill Discriminatory,'" *Wall Street Journal*, April 26, 2013. 2010 年，美国提高员工数达 50 名的公司的 H-IB 和 L-I 签证费用后，印度公司抱怨受到了歧视，这些公司中至少有 50% 依赖 HI-B 或 L-I 签证。
168. 引用自 Lipton and Sengupta, "Latest Product of Tech Firms"。
169. "Technology Leaders Urge U.S. Senate to Approve Comprehensive Immigration Reform Legislation," *Information Technology Industry Council*, June 20, 2013, www.itic.org/news-events/news-releases/technology-leaders-urge-u-s-senate-to-approve-comprehensive-immigration-reform-legislation.
170. American Council on Education, "Higher Education Associations Strongly Endorse Senate Immigration Reform Bill" (letter to the U.S. Senate), June 26, 2013, www.aau.edu/sites/default/files/AAU%20Files/Key%20Issues/Budget%20%26%20Appropriations/FY17/Endorsement-Letter-S-744_6-26-13.pdf.
171. Ball, "Immigration Reformers Are Winning August."
172. Zachary A. Goldfarb and Karen Tumulty, "IRS Admits Targeting Conservatives for Tax Scrutiny in 2012 Election," *Washington Post*, May 10, 2013, www.washingtonpost.com/business/economy/irs-admits-targeting-conservatives-for-tax-scrutiny-in-2012-election/2013/05/10/3b6a0ada-b987-11e2-92f3-f291801936b8_story.html.
173. Devin Burghart, *Special Report: The Status of the Tea Party Movement—Part Two* (Kansas, MO: Institute for Research and Education on Human Rights, 2014), www.irehr.org/2014/01/21/status-of-tea-party-by-the-numbers/.
174. Rebecca Kaplan, "How the Tea Party Came Around on Immigration," *National Journal*, March 21, 2013.
175. Jill Lawrence, "The Myth of Marco Rubio's Immigration Problem," *National Journal*, July 15, 2013.
176. Lawrence, "The Myth of Marco Rubio's Immigration Problem."
177. Linda Feldmann, "Is the Tea Party Running out of Steam?" *Christian Science Monitor*,

April 12, 2014.
178. Tea Party Patriots, "Senate Must Admit Full Costs of Immigration Bill Before Passing Another 'Train Wreck,' " *Tea Party Patriots*, May 6, 2013, www.teapartypatriots.org/all-issues/news/senate-must-admit-full-costs-of-immigration-bill-before-passing-another-train-wreck/.
179. Katherine Rosario, "Five Simple Signs the Senate Immigration Bill Is Bad News," *Heritage Action*, April 17, 2013, http://heritageaction.com/2013/04/5-simple-signs-the-senate-immigration-bill-is-bad-news/; David Nakamura, "Conservatives Split on Immigration Bill's Price Tag," *Washington Post*, May 7, 2013.
180. Daniel Horowitz, "Gang Immigration Bill (S.744) Is Comprehensively Flawed," *Madison Project*, May 1, 2013, http://madisonproject.com/2013/05/gang-immigration-bill-s-744-is-comprehensively-flawed/.
181. 引用自 Lawrence, "The Myth of Marco Rubio's Immigration Problem"。
182. Burghart and Zeskind, "Beyond FAIR," 23.
183. Roy Beck, interview, April 3, 2015.
184. Devin Burghart, "Mapping the Tea Party Caucus in the 112th Congress," *Institute for Research and Education on Human Rights*, March 17, 2011, https://irehr.org/issue-areas/tea-party-nationalism/tea-party-news-and-analysis/item/355-mapping-the-tea-party-caucus-in-the-112th-congress.
185. Laura Meckler, "Immigration-Bill Pressure Backfires: Overhaul Backers Target Majority Whip, but Tactic Provokes Response from Opponents," *Wall Street Journal*, December 25, 2013, www.wsj.com/articles/SB10001424052702304244904579276403694719232.
186. Quoted in Meckler, "Immigration-Bill Pressure Backfires."
187. Meckler, "Immigration-Bill Pressure Backfires."
188. Michael D. Shear and Ashley Parker, "Boehner Is Said to Back Change on Immigration," *New York Times*, January 1, 2014, www.nytimes.com/2014/01/02/us/politics/boehner-is-said-to-back-change-on-immigration.html.
189. Deirdre Shesgreen, "Immigration Reform Critics Blast Boehner's Remarks," *Gannett News Service*, April 25, 2014.
190. Roy Beck, interview, April 3, 2015.
191. Janet Hook, "Tea Party Faces Test of Its Clout in Primaries," *Wall Street Journal*, February 25, 2014.
192. Steven Rosenfeld, "The GOP's Vicious Internal War: Republican Establishment Trying to Exile Tea Partiers and Extremists," *AlterNet*, February 12, 2014, www.alternet.org/tea-party-and-right/gops-vicious-internal-war-republican-establishment-trying-exile-tea-partiers-and.
193. Craig Lindwarm, Director for Congressional and Governmental Affairs, Association for Public and Land Grant Universities, interview by author, September 11, 2015.
194. Scott Corley, executive director, Compete America, interview by author, May 18, 2017.
195. Jonathan Weisman, "Boehner Doubts Immigration Bill Will Pass in 2014," *New York Times*, February 6, 2014, www.nytimes.com/2014/02/07/us/politics/boehner-doubts-immigration-overhaul-will-pass-this-year.html.

196. Shear and Parker, "Boehner Is Said to Back Change on Immigration."
197. 引用自 Laura Meckler, "House Immigration Bills Are Still in the Mix," *Wall Street Journal*, April 18, 2014, www.wsj.com/articles/SB10001424052702304626304579508091839546088。
198. Shesgreen, "Immigration Reform Critics Blast Boehner's Remarks."
199. Gail Russell Chaddock, "Eric Cantor Upset Stuns GOP, Revives Tea Party," *Christian Science Monitor*, June 11, 2014, www.csmonitor.com/USA/Elections/2014/0611/Eric-Cantor-upset-stuns-GOP-revives-tea-party.
200. 例如，APLU 建议优先考虑向美国大学的毕业生分配 H-1B 签证。Craig Lindwarm, interview.
201. Obama administration White House official, interview by author, April 14, 2017.
202. Office of the Press Secretary, "Fact Sheet: Immigration Accountability Executive Action," *White House*, November 20, 2014, https://obamawhitehouse.archives.gov/the-press-office/2014/11/20/fact-sheet-immigration-accountability-executive-action.
203. Felicia Escobar Carrillo, special assistant to the president for immigration policy, 2014 to 2017, interviewed by anothor, May 18, 2017.
204. 引用自 Jessica Meyers, "Tech Companies See Few Big Gains in Obama's Executive Action," *Boston Globe*, November 24, 2014, www.bostonglobe.com/news/nation/2014/11/24/tech-companies-see-few-big-gains-obama-executive-action/dauDJujkOhe1qx5 ZQTScoM/story.html。
205. Chris Currie, "U.S. Public Overwhelmingly Opposed to H-1B Visa Expansion," *IEEE- USA*, September 16, 1998, www.ieeeusa.org/communications/releases/_private/1998/pr091698.html.
206. Jens Hainmueller and Michael J. Hiscox, "Attitudes Toward Highly Skilled and Low-Skilled Immigration: Evidence from a Survey Experiment," *American Political Science Review* 104, no. 1 (February 2010): 7.
207. Andrew Dugan, "Passing New Immigration Laws Is Important to Americans," Gallup. com, July 11, 2013, www.gallup.com/poll/163475/passing-new-immigration-laws-important-americans.aspx.

第 4 章　开放的大门：外国留学生

1. Organisation for Economic Co-operation and Development (OECD), *Education at a Glance 2014: OECD Indicators* (Paris: OECD, 2014), 344.
2. OECD, *Education at a Glance 2014*, 344.
3. Institute for International Education, "Top Twenty-Five Places of Origin of International Students, 2014/15 and 2015/16," *Open Doors Report on International Educational Exchange* (New York: Institute for International Education, 2016), www.iie.org/opendoors.
4. Todd M. Davis, *Open Doors 2000: Report on International Education Exchange* (New York: Institute for International Education, 2000), 8; Hey-Kyung Koh Chin, *Open Doors 2002: Report on International Educational Exchange* (New York: Institute for International Education, 2002), 8.

5. Patricia Chow and Rajika Bhandari, *Open Doors 2010: Report on International Educational Exchange* (New York: Institute for International Education, 2010), 5.
6. 除非另有说明，本章遵循美国国家科学基金会的做法，认为科学与工程领域包括物理科学（包括数学和计算机科学）、自然科学、社会科学和工程学。
7. Chad C. Haddal, *Foreign Students in the United States: Policies and Legislation* (Washington, DC: Congressional Research Service, 2008).
8. U.S. Department of State, "Nonimmigrant Visa Issuances by Visa Class and by Nationality," *Travel.State.Gov*, accessed September 9, 2016, https://travel.state.gov/content/visas/en/law-and-policy/statistics/non-immigrant-visas.html.
9. Paul Stephens, "International Students: Separate but Profitable," Washington Monthly, October 2013, www.washingtonmonthly.com/magazine/september_october_2013/features/international_students_separat046454.php?page=all.
10. Institute for International Education, *Open Doors Data: Fast Facts* (New York: Institute for International Education, 2014), www.iie.org/Research-and-Publications/Open-Doors/Data/Fast-Facts; Tamar Lewin, "Foreign Students Bring Cash, and Changes: U.S. Colleges Welcome Funds, but Some In-State Applicants Feel Left Out," *International Herald Tribune*, February 6, 2012.
11. National Science Foundation, *Science and Engineering Indicators 2016* (Arlington, VA: National Science Foundation, 2016), chapter 2, 71.
12. National Science Foundation, *Science and Engineering Indicators 2016*, chapter 2, appendix table 27.
13. National Science Foundation, *Science and Engineering Indicators 2016*, chapter 2, appendix table 27.
14. Gnanaraj Chellaraj, Keith E. Maskus, and Aaditya Mattoo, "The Contribution of International Graduate Students to US Innovation," *Review of International Economics* 16, no. 3 (August 2008): 444–62.
15. Eric T. Stuen, Ahmed Mushfiq Mobarak, and Keith E. Maskus, "Skilled Immigration and Innovation: Evidence from Enrolment Fluctuations in US Doctoral Programmes," *The Economic Journal* 122, no. 565 (2012): 1143–76.
16. National Science Foundation, "Table 53: Doctorate Recipients with Temporary Visas Intending to Stay in the United States After Doctorate Receipt, by Country of Citizen- ship: 2007–13," *Science and Engineering Doctorates*, December 2014, www.nsf.gov/statistics/sed/2013/data-tables.cfm.
17. Dick Startz, "Sealing the Border Could Block one of America's Crucial Exports: Education," *The Brookings Institution*, January 31, 2017, https://www.brookings.edu/blog/brown-center-chalkboard/2017/01/31/sealing-the-border-could-block-one-of-americas-crucial-exports-education/.
18. Harris Miller, president, Information Technology Association of America, 1995 to 2005, interview by author, July 1, 2015.
19. Terry Hartle, senior vice-president, and Steven Bloom, director for federal relations, American Council on Education, interview by author, Washington, DC, September 8, 2015.

这一点是哈特尔提出的。
20. Philip G. Altbach and Patti McGill Peterson, "Internationalize American Higher Education? Not Exactly," *Change* 30, no. 4 (1998): 39.
21. Altbach and McGill Peterson, "Internationalize American Higher Education?," 38.
22. Nicholas Confessore "Borderline Insanity," *Washingto Monthly*, May 2002, www.washingtonmonthly.com/features/2001/0205.confessore.html.
23. Michael S. Teitelbaum, *Falling Behind? Boom, Bust, and the Global Race for Scientific Talent* (Princeton, NJ: Princeton University Press, 2014), 112.
24. Robert Farley, "9/11 Hijackers and Student Visas," *Factcheck.org*, May 10, 2013, ww.factcheck.org/2013/05/911-hijackers-and-student-visas/.
25. 在"9·11"事件发生之前,申请人被告知他们申请成功。他们在佛罗里达州上的飞行学校在2002年3月收到了正式的批准函,这强调了美国移民系统的功能失调。参见 Mark Potter and Rich Philips, "Six Months after Sept. 11, Hijackers' Visa Approval Letters Received," *CNN*, March 13, 2002, http://edition.cnn.com/2002/US/03/12/inv.flight.school.visas/。
26. Thomas B. Edsall, "Attacks Alter Politics, Shift Focus of Immigration Debate," *Washington Post*, October 15, 2001.
27. Terry Hartle and Steven Bloom, interview.
28. "Senator Feinstein Urges Major Changes in U.S. Student Visa Program," *Advocacy and Public Policymaking*, September 27, 2001, http://lobby.la.psu.edu/_107th/119_Student_Visas_Security/Congressional_Statements/Senate/S_Feinstein_09272001.htm.
29. Terry Hartle and Steven Bloom, interview. 引自哈特尔。
30. Cindy Rodriguez, "Proposed Visa Ban Dropped," *Boston Globe*, November 23, 2001.
31. David Ward, "Letter to the Senate Judiciary Committee Regarding Feinstein Proposal on Student Visas," *American Association of Collegiate Registrars and Admissions Officers*, October 2, 2001, www.aacrao.org/advocacy/issues-advocacy/sevis.
32. Mark Sherman, "Feinstein Says Moratorium on Student Visas May Not Be Necessary," *Associated Press*, October 6, 2001.
33. Sherman, "Feinstein Says Moratorium on Student Visas May Not Be Necessary."
34. Rodriguez, "Proposed Visa Ban Dropped."
35. Sherman, "Feinstein Says Moratorium on Student Visas May Not Be Necessary."
36. Terry Hartle and Steven Bloom, interview. 参见 David Ward, "The Role of Technology in Preventing the Entry of Terrorists Into the United States," testimony, *Hearing Before the Subcommittee on Technology, Terrorism, and Government Information of the Senate Judiciary Committee*, 107th Cong. (October 12, 2001), 69。
37. Ward, "Letter to the Senate Judiciary Committee."
38. Cindy Rodriguez, "Congress Drops Plan to Bar Foreign Students," *Knight-Ridder Tribune Business News*, November 23, 2001.
39. Tucker Carlson and Bill Press, "Debating Immigration Policy," *Crossfire* (CNN, October 24, 2001).
40. Daniel Stein, president, Federation for American Immigration Reform, interview by author,

July 2, 2015.
41. Kevin Drew, "Terror Probe Reaches Nation's Campuses," *CNN*, October 25, 2001, http://edition.cnn.com/2001/LAW/10/24/inv.international.students/index.html.
42. Center for Immigration Studies, "Are Foreign Students Good for America?" (panel discussion transcript, Rayburn Building, House of Representatives, Washington, DC, June 25, 2002), www.cis.org/sites/cis.org/files/articles/2002/foreignstudents.html.
43. Terry Hartle and Steven Bloom, interview.
44. Stephen Yale-Loehr, Demetrios G. Papademetriou, and Betsy Cooper, *Secure Borders, Open Doors: Visa Procedures in the Post–September 11 Era* (Washington, DC: Migration Policy Institute, 2005), 176.
45. Yale-Loehr, Papademetriou, and Cooper, *Secure Borders, Open Doors*, 178.
46. Mark Clayton, "Academia Becomes Target for New Security Laws," *Christian Science Monitor*, September 24, 2002.
47. David Ward, "Dealing with Foreign Students and Scholars in an Age of Terrorism: Visa Backlogs and Tracking Systems," testimony, *Hearing Before the U.S. House of Representatives Committee on Science*, 108th Cong. (March 26, 2003), 23.
48. Caryle Murphy and Nurith C. Aizenman, "Foreign Students Navigate Labyrinth of New Laws: Slip-Ups Overlooked Before 9/11 Now Grounds for Deportation," *Washington Post*, June 9, 2003.
49. Yale-Loehr, Papademetriou, and Cooper, *Secure Borders, Open Doors*, 178.
50. 有关最后两句话，参见 Yale-Loehr, Papademetriou, and Cooper, *Secure Borders, Open Doors*, 177–78。
51. Lia Steakley, Debra K. Rubin, and Peter Reina, "After 9/11, Overseas Students Find Foreigners Need Not Apply: Visa Application Hurdles Start to Ease but Long-Term Impacts Loom," *Engineering News-Record*, December 6, 2004.
52. Andrew K. Collier, "Yale Chief Hits at US Student Visa Delays," *South China Morning Post*, November 14, 2003.
53. Murray Hiebert, "United States: The Cost of Security," *Far Eastern Economic Review*, November 28, 2002.
54. James Hattori, "Intel Plans for Future," *CNN*, September 14, 2002.
55. Martin Jischke, "Addressing the New Reality of Current Visa Policy on International Students and Researchers," testimony, *Hearing Before the U.S. Senate Committee on Foreign Relations*, 108th Cong. (October 6, 2004), 5–7, www.gpo.gov/fdsys/search/home.action.
56. Terry Hartle and Steven Bloom, interview.
57. Heather Stewart, counsel and director of immigration policy, NAFSA, interview by author, Washington, DC, September 11, 2015.
58. Terry Hartle and Steven Bloom, interview.
59. Heather Stewart, interview.
60. David Ward, "Dealing with Foreign Students and Scholars in an Age of Terrorism," 24.
61. Diana Jean Schemo, "Problems Slow Tracking of Students from Abroad," *New York Times*,

March 23, 2003.
62. Marlene Johnson, "Addressing the New Reality of Current Visa Policy on International Students and Researchers," testimony, *Hearing Before the U.S. Senate Committee on Foreign Relations*, 108th Cong. (October 6, 2004), 64, www.gpo.gov/fdsys/search/home.action.
63. Federation for American Immigration Reform, "Immigration Issues: Foreign Students," *Federation for American Immigration Reform*, May 2012, www.fairus.org/issue/foreign-students. FAIR 主席丹尼尔·斯坦因（Daniel Stein）后来回忆说，这一立场可能是在21世纪初期采取的。Daniel Stein, interview.
64. Roy Beck, president, NumbersUSA, interview by author, June 13, 2015.
65. George J. Borjas, "Rethinking Foreign Students," *National Review* 17 (June 17, 2002): 38–41. 博杰斯（Borjas）后来发表的研究发现，在一所特定大学的外国学生数量的增加与该大学研究生课程中的本土白人男性学生人数之间存在负相关关系，其中"挤出效应"在精英机构中最为强烈。George J. Borjas, "Do Foreign Students Crowd Out Native Students from Graduate Programs?" Working Paper No. 10349 (Cambridge, MA: National Bureau of Economic Research, 2004), www.nber.org/papers/w10349.
66. George J. Borjas, "An Evaluation of the Foreign Student Program," *Center for Immigration Studies* (Washington, DC: Center for Immigration Studies, June 1, 2002), http://cis.org/ForeignStudentProgram.
67. "Dealing with Foreign Students and Scholars in an Age of Terrorism: Visa Backlogs and Tracking Systems," *Hearing Before the U.S. House of Representatives Committee on Science*, 108th Cong. (March 26, 2003), www.gpo.gov/fdsys/search/home.action; "Addressing the New Reality of Current Visa Policy on International Students and Researchers," *Hearing Before the U.S. Senate Committee on Foreign Relations*, 108th Cong. (October 6, 2004), www.gpo.gov/fdsys/search/home.action.
68. U.S. Department of State, "Nonimmigrant Worldwide Issuance and Refusal Data by Visa Category," *Travel.State.Gov*, January 14, 2014, http://travel.state.gov/content/visas/english/law-and-policy/statistics/non-immigrant-visas.html.
69. U.S. General Accounting Office, *Improvements Needed to Reduce Time Taken to Adjudicate Visas for Science Students and Scholars* (Washington, DC: U.S. General Accounting Office, February 24, 2004), 2, www.gao.gov/products/GAO-04-443T.
70. U.S. Government Accountability Office, *Streamlined Visas Mantis Program Has Lowered Burden on Foreign Science Students and Scholars, but Further Refinements Needed* (Washington, DC: U.S. Government Accountability Office, February 18, 2005), 2, www.gao.gov/products/GAO-05-198.
71. U.S. Government Accountability Office, *Streamlined Visas Mantis Program Has Lowered Burden*, 7.
72. U.S. Government Accountability Office, *Challenges in Attracting International Students to the United States and Implications for Global Competitiveness* (Washington, DC: U.S. Government Accountability Office, June 29, 2007), 13, www.gao.gov/products/GAO-07-1047T.

73. Marlene Johnson, "Addressing the New Reality of Current Visa Policy on International Students and Researchers," 64.
74. U.S. Government Accountability Office, *Performance of Foreign Student and Exchange Visitor Information System Continues to Improve, but Issues Remain* (Washington, DC: U.S. Government Accountability Office, March 17, 2005), 2, www.gao.gov/products/GAO-05-440T.
75. Bureau of Industry and Security, U.S. Department of Commerce, "Revision and Clarification of Deemed Export Related Regulatory Requirements," *Federal Register*, March 28, 2005.
76. 美国法规认为一项技术的"出口"包括将其发布给美国境内的外国公民。因此，如果在特定情况下控制技术，则必须在发布之前颁发许可证。
77. Toby Smith, Association of American Universities, and Robert Hardy, Council on Governmental Relations, interview by author, May 23, 2017. 感谢史密斯和哈代向我提供了这些信件的复印件。
78. Danielle Belopotosky, "Policy Change On 'Deemed Exports' Is Widely Panned," *Technology Daily PM*, August 19, 2005.
79. Bureau of Industry and Security, U.S. Department of Commerce, "Revisions and Clarification of Deemed Export Related Regulatory Requirements," *Federal Register*, May 31, 2006, 30840.
80. Robert Hardy, "Commerce Withdraws ANPR on Deemed Exports," May 31, 2006. 感谢哈代提供这一备忘录的复印件。
81. 例如，2010—2014年，出口许可证申请总数每年从633到1 450不等。绝大多数（92%）的申请获得批准，7%的申请未经采取行动而被退回，不到1%的申请被拒绝。Bureau of Industry and Security, US. Department of Commerce, response to *Freedom of Information Act request*, tracking number BIS 15-136, February 11, 2016.
82. Terry Hartle and Steven Bloom, interview.
83. U.S. Department of State, "Nonimmigrant Worldwide Issuance and Refusal Data by Visa Category."
84. Jeff Allum, "Findings from the 2014 CGS International Graduate Admissions Survey—Phase II: Final Applications and Initial Offers of Admission" (Washington, DC: Council of Graduate Schools, 2014), 5.
85. Karin Fischer, "State Department Promises Speedier Visa Review," *Chronicle of Higher Education*, June 12, 2009.
86. Times Higher Education, "World University Rankings 2014–2015," 2014, *Times Higher Education*, www.timeshighereducation.co.uk/world-university-rankings/2014-15/world-ranking.
87. Joseph Carroll, "American Public Opinion About Immigration," *Gallup.com*, July 26, 2005, www.gallup.com/poll/14785/Immigration.aspx.

第5章 基本开放：全球研发活动

1. 关于CFIUS的更多信息，参见James K. Jackson, *The Committee on Foreign Investment*

in the United States (CFIUS) (Washington, DC: Congressional Research Service, 2014)。
2. Harris Miller, president, Information Technology Association of America, 1995 to 2005, interviewed by author, July 1, 2015.
3. Robert T. Kudrle and Davis B. Bobrow, "U.S. Policy Toward Foreign Direct Investment," *World Politics* 34, no. 3 (April 1982): 367.
4. Andrew D. Gross and Michael S. Schadewald, "Prospects for U.S. Corporate Tax Reform," *The CPA Journal* 82, no. 1 (January 1, 2012).
5. Gross and Schadewald, "Prospects for U.S. Corporate Tax Reform."
6. "U.S. Led Effort Reaches 'Major Breakthrough' to Expand Information Technology Agreement," *Office of the United States Trade Representative*, July 2015, https://ustr.gov/about-us/policy-offices/press-office/press-releases/2015/july/us-led-effort-reaches-%E2%80%98major.
7. 例如，参见 recommendations in Daniel Marschall and Laura Clawson, *Sending Jobs Overseas: The Cost to America's Economy and Working Families* (Washington, DC: Working America and the AFL-CIO, 2010)。
8. Hugo Meijer, *Trading with the Enemy: The Making of US Export Control Policy Toward the People's Republic of China* (Oxford: Oxford University Press, 2016), 165–97.
9. 对民用和军用仍然控制的技术是辐射强化的微处理器，因为它们经常用于武器系统。
10. Christopher A. Padilla, vice-president, government and regulatory affairs, IBM, interviewed by author, March 25, 2016. 帕迪拉还指出，当出口管制成为问题时，IBM 已经提前与美国官员就特定技术，特定的最终用户，以解决任何潜在的问题进行了讨论。
11. Bill Greenwalt, "We Haven't Won Yet on Export Control Reforms," *Breaking Defense*, November 21, 2013, http://breakingdefense.com/2013/11/we-havent-won-yet-on-export-control-reforms/; Doug Cameron and Julian E. Barnes, "Pentagon Criticizes Contractors' R&D," *Wall Street Journal*, November 21, 2014.
12. Andrew B. Kennedy, "Unequal Partners: U.S. Collaboration with China and India in Research and Development," *Political Science Quarterly* 132, no. 1 (2017), 71.
13. Kennedy, "Unequal Partners," 72.
14. 引用自 Steve Lohr, "New Economy: Offshore Jobs in Technology; Opportunity or a Threat?" *New York Times*, December 22, 2003, www.nytimes.com/2003/12/22/business/new-economy-offshore-jobs-in-technology-opportunity-or-a-threat.html。
15. 引用自 Steve Lohr, "Many New Causes for Old Problem of Jobs Lost Abroad," *New York Times*, February 15, 2004。
16. Ron Hira, "Implications of Offshore Outsourcing" (Paper presented at the Globalization, Employment, and Economic Development Workshop, Sloan Workshop Series in Industry Studies, Rockport, MA, January 3, 2004), 4–5.
17. Alec Gallup and Frank Newport, *The Gallup Poll: Public Opinion 2004* (Lanham, MD: Rowman and Littlefield, 2006), 110.
18. Joseph I. Lieberman, *Offshore Outsourcing and America's Competitive Edge: Losing Out in the High Technology R&D and Services Sectors* (Washington, DC: Office of Senator Joseph I. Lieberman, May 11, 2004), 5.

19. Lieberman, "Offshore Outsourcing and America's Competitive Edge," 16.
20. William Reinsch, "What Is to Be Done on Trade?" *Stimson Spotlight*, June 7, 2016, www.stimson.org/content/what-be-done-trade. 赖因施（Reinsch）于2001—2016年担任国家对外贸易委员会（NFTC）主席，当时他还是中美经济与安全审查委员会的成员。在加入NFTC之前，赖因施曾担任美国商务部出口管理副秘书长和国会的立法助理。
21. Jonathan Weisman, "Bush, Adviser Assailed for Stance on 'Offshoring' Jobs," *Washington Post*, February 11, 2004.
22. Alan S. Blinder, "Offshoring: The Next Industrial Revolution?" *Foreign Affairs* 85, no. 2 (2006): 113–28.
23. J. Bradford Jensen, *Global Trade in Services: Fear, Facts, and Offshoring* (Washington, DC: Peterson Institute for International Economics, 2011).
24. Gary Clyde Hufbauer, Theodore H. Moran, and Lindsay Oldenski, *Outward Foreign Direct Investment and US Exports, Jobs, and R&D: Implications for US Policy* (Washington, DC: Peterson Institute for International Economics, 2013).
25. "IEEE Advocates Limits on Offshore Outsourcing," *Information Week*, March 15, 2004, www.informationweek.com/ieee-advocates-limits-on-offshore-outsourcing/d/d-id/1023812.
26. Melissa Block, "Analysis: Industry Groups Fight Anti-outsourcing Legislation," *National Public Radio: All Things Considered*, March 5, 2004.
27. Michael Schroeder, "Business Coalition Battles Outsourcing Backlash," *Wall Street Journal*, March 1, 2004, www.wsj.com/articles/SB107809268846542227.
28. Schroeder, "Business Coalition Battles Outsourcing Backlash."
29. Block, "Analysis: Industry Groups Fight Anti-outsourcing Legislation."
30. Ben Worthen, "Regulations: What to Worry About," *CIO*, June 15, 2004.
31. American Federation of Labor and Congress of Industrial Organizations (AFL-CIO), "Summary of Activities Regarding Off-Shore Outsourcing, June 2003–May 2004," *Department for Professiona Employees, AFL-CIO*, 2004, http://dpeaflcio.org/archives/legislative-reports-2/summary-of-activities-regarding-off-shore-outsourcing-june-2003-may-2004/.
32. 特例是允许在美国境外进行的工作。参见Wilson Dizard, "New Law Will Curb Offshoring of Federal IT Work," *Government Computer News*, February 23, 2004。
33. Harris Miller, interview.
34. 引用自Shumita Sharma, "US Offshore Outsourcing Ban Sparks Fears of Similar Laws," *Dow Jones International Newswires*, January 30, 2004。
35. Harris Miller, interview.
36. AFL-CIO, "Summary of Activities Regarding Off-Shore Outsourcing."
37. Martin Vaughan and Susan Davis, "Senate Ends Corporate Tax Debate for Now, OKs Outsourcing Deal," *Congress Daily*, March 5, 2004.
38. Lori Simpson, *Engineering Aspects of Offshore Outsourcing* (Alexandria, VA: National Society of Professional Engineers, August 6, 2004), 3, www.wise-intern.org/journal/2004/wise2004-lorisimpsonfinalpaper.pdf.
39. 虽然多德的原始法案允许总统认证的契约的国家安全例外，但这些变化使得机构负责人有广泛的权力来确定哪些契约是出于国家安全的目的。此外，新的语言使得这些限制取决于商务部的年度认证，即限制所造成的美国失业人数不超过他们保留的工作岗位数量。最后，新语言豁免了国防部和国土安全部，情报机构以及能源部的国家安全计划。参见 Vaughan and Davis, "Senate Ends Corporate Tax Debate for Now, OKs Outsourcing Deal"。

40. Jobs and Trade Network, "Jobs and Trade Network to Hold Press Luncheon with U.S. Sen. Dodd: National Fair Trade Group to Advocate Against Outsourcing Policies," *Economic Policy Institute*, February 20, 2004.

41. Brian Tumulty, "Small Manufacturers Aim Buy American Challenge at U.S. Job Losses," *Gannett News Service*, October 31, 2003, http://global.factiva.com/redir/default.aspx?P=sa&an=GNS0000020040107dzav000j7&cat=a&ep=ASE.

42. Ed Frauenheim, "Tech Professionals Group Wary of Offshoring," *CNET News*, March 18, 2004.

43. Harris Miller, interview.

44. Harris Miller, interview.

45. Keith Koffler, "Business Coalition Rewrites Lexicon for Jobs 'Outsourcing,'" *Congress Daily*, March 2, 2004.

46. Gail Repsher Emery, "Industry Fights Dodd Legislation," *Newsbytes News Network*, April 15, 2004.

47. Repsher Emery, "Industry Fights Dodd Legislation."

48. Mary Dalrymple, "Senate Passes Corporate Tax Bill," *Associated Press*, May 12, 2004.

49. "US's Grassley— 'Difficult' to Get Quick Action on Tax Bill," *Market News International*, June 22, 2004.

50. Jonathan Weisman and Mark Kaufman, "Tax-Cut Bill Draws White House Doubts: Corporate Provisions Go Beyond 'Core Objective,' Treasury Secretary Says," *Washington Post*, October 5, 2004.

51. Paul Almeida, president, AFL-CIO Department for Professional Employees, interview by author, August 21, 2015.

52. AFL-CIO, "Outsourcing America," *AFL-CIO*, March 11, 2004, www.aflcio.org/About/Exec-Council/EC-Statements/Outsourcing-America.

53. "Kerry Tax Plan Proposes to Slow Loss of US Jobs Overseas," *Dow Jones International News*, March 26, 2004.

54. David J. Lynch, "Does Tax Code Encourage U.S. Companies to Cut Jobs at Home? Presidential Candidates Target Corporate Tax Breaks for Offshoring," *USA Today*, March 21, 2008.

55. Barack Obama, "Remarks of President Barack Obama: Address to Joint Session of Congress," *Whitehouse.gov*, February 24, 2009, www.whitehouse.gov/the-press-office/remarks-president-barack-obama-address-joint-session-congress.

56. "Obama Lowers Temperature Against Outsourcing," *Economic Times*, March 28, 2009.

57. Office of the Press Secretary, "Leveling the Playing Field: Curbing Tax Havens and Removing Tax Incentives for Shifting Jobs Overseas," *U.S. Department of the Treasury Press Center*, May 4, 2009, www.treasury.gov/press-center/press-releases/Pages/tg119.aspx.

注 释

58. Jackie Calmes and Edmund Andrews, "Obama Seeks to Curb Foreign Tax Havens," *New York Times*, May 4, 2009, www.nytimes.com/2009/05/05/business/05tax.html?pagewanted=all&_r=1&.
59. Kate Ackley, "Offshore Accounts Present a Taxing Situation," *Roll Call*, May 6, 2009; "Bond, Thune Spearhead Efforts to Gut Foreign Tax Provisions from Bill," *Inside U.S. Trade*, June 18, 2010.
60. Neil King and Elizabeth Williamson, "Business Fends Off Tax Hit: Obama Adminis- tration Shelves Plan to Change How U.S. Treats Overseas Profits," *Wall Street Journal*, October 13, 2009.
61. King and Williamson, "Business Fends Off Tax Hit."
62. Obama administration White House official, interview by author, April 14, 2017.
63. Obama administration White House official, interview.
64. John D. McKinnon, "Plan Would Raise Taxes on Businesses," *Wall Street Journal*, February 2, 2010, www.wsj.com/articles/SB10001424052748704107204575039073372259004.
65. Shailagh Murray, "In Senate and on Trail, Democrats Target Jobs Moving Abroad," *Washington Post*, June 9, 2010.
66. Richard Trumka, "Statement by AFL-CIO President Richard Trumka on the Promoting American Jobs and Closing Tax Loopholes Act," *AFL-CIO*, May 24, 2010, http://ftp.workingamerica.org/Press-Room/Press-Releases/Statement-by-AFL-CIO-President-Richard-Trumka-on-t14.
67. 引用自 Murray, "In Senate and on Trail, Democrats Target Jobs Moving Abroad"。
68. "Bond, Thune Spearhead Efforts to Gut Foreign Tax Provisions from Bill."
69. Peter Schroeder, "Extender Efforts Hit Roadblock as Senate Tables Tax Package," *Bond Buyer*, June 28, 2010.
70. "Amendments Submitted and Proposed," *Congressional Record*, 111th Cong. 156, no. 115 (August 2, 2010): S6586–93.
71. Martin Vaughan, "Businesses Split Over Tax Credits," *Wall Street Journal*, August 4, 2010.
72. "The Eternal 'Emergency,'" *Wall Street Journal*, August 6, 2010.
73. FAA Air Transportation Modernization and Safety Improvement Act of 2010, H.R. 1586, 111th Cong. (2010), www.govtrack.us/congress/bills/111/hr1586.
74. Ronald Brownstein, "Back to Basics," *National Journal*, September 9, 2010.
75. Creating American Jobs and Ending Offshoring Act of 2010, S.3816, 111th Cong. (2010), www.govtrack.us/congress/bills/111/s3816.
76. Philip J. Bond, "Opposition to S.3816," September 27, 2010, www.techamerica.org/content/wp-content/uploads/2010/09/9-27-10_S3816.pdf.
77. Jennifer Liberto and Dana Bash, "Bill to Hike Taxes on Overseas Jobs Fails Senate Test Vote," *CNN*, September 28, 2010, http://money.cnn.com/2010/09/28/news/economy/Outsource_jobs_bill_dead/.
78. Richard Trumka, "Statement by AFL-CIO President Richard Trumka on Creating American Jobs and Ending Offshoring Act," *AFL-CIO*, September 28, 2010, www.aflcio.org/Press-Room/Press-Releases/Statement-by-AFL-CIO-President-Richard-Trumka-on-C8.

79. Melanie Trottman, "Web Tool Could Help Boost Union Voter Turnout," *Wall Street Journal*, October 7, 2010.
80. Marschall and Clawson, "Sending Jobs Overseas: The Cost to America's Economy and Working Families," 22.
81. Daniel Marschall, legislative and policy specialist for workforce issues, AFL-CIO, interview by author, December 18, 2014. 这些是马歇尔的个人观点，不是作为 AFL-CIO 的发言人发表讲话。
82. Patrick Thibodeau, interview by author, September 8, 2015. 作为《计算机世界》（Computerworld）驻华盛顿记者锡伯杜已报道离岸外包问题十多年。
83. Bring Jobs Home Act of 2011/12, S.3364, 112th Cong. (2011/12), www.congress.gov/bill/112th-congress/senate-bill/3364.
84. Bring Jobs Home Act of 2013/14, S.2569, 113th Cong. (2013/14), www.congress.gov/bill/112th-congress/senate-bill/2569.
85. National Foundation for American Policy, *NFAP Policy Brief: Anti-outsourcing Efforts Down but Not Out* (Arlington, VA: National Foundation for American Policy, April 2007), 2, 4, www.nfap.com/pdf/0407OutsourcingBrief.pdf.
86. Greg Schneider, "Anxious About Outsourcing: States Try to Stop U.S. Firms from Sending High-Tech Work Overseas," *Washington Post*, January 31, 2004.
87. 引用自 Carolyn Duffy Marsan, "A Political Hot Potato: Legislatures Juggle Offshore Outsourcing Regulations," *Network World*, July 5, 2004。
88. 引用自 Block, "Analysis: Industry Groups Fight Anti-outsourcing Legislation"。
89. National Foundation for American Policy, "Anti-Outsourcing Efforts Down but Not Out," 2–3.
90. Michael Schroeder, "States' Efforts to Curb Outsourcing Stymied: Business Groups Take the Lead in Weakening Attempts to Limit Work from Moving Abroad," *Wall Street Journal*, April 16, 2004.
91. 引用自 Schroeder, "States' Efforts to Curb Outsourcing Stymied"。
92. Harris Miller, interview.
93. 如果在美国境内无法提供服务或者法律的适用会违反联邦政府的任何拨款、资金或财政援助的条款，法律允许豁免。参见 Service Contract Requirements for the Performance of Service Contracts Within the United States, Pub. L. No. 2005, c. 92 (New Jersey, 2005), www.njleg.state.nj.us/bills/BillView.asp。
94. Michael Schroeder, "States Fight Exodus of Jobs: Lawmakers, Unions Seek to Block Outsourcing Overseas," *Wall Street Journal*, June 3, 2003.
95. Bill Tucker, "Job Creation Stalls: Interview with Commerce Secretary Don Evans," *Lou Dobbs Tonight* (CNN, January 9, 2004).
96. Schroeder, "States Fight Exodus of Jobs."
97. Schneider, "Anxious About Outsourcing."
98. 引用自 Schneider, "Anxious About Outsourcing"。
99. James E. McGreevey, *The Confession* (New York: Harper Collins, 2006), 223.
100. 引用自 "McGreevey Edict Restricts Outsourcing by Agencies," *Congress Daily*, September

13, 2004。
101. Shirley Turner, New Jersey state senator, interview by author, September 11, 2015.
102. David Kocienieski, "For Trenton's Lame Duck, the Question Is, 'How Lame?,'" *New York Times*, September 12, 2004.
103. "McGreevey Edict Restricts Outsourcing by Agencies."
104. 引用自 Josh Gohlke, "Cipel Was No Security Risk, McGreevey Says: Governor Speaks of Former Aide by Name for First Time," *Record*, September 10, 2004.
105. Shirley Turner, interview.
106. Shirley Turner, interview.
107. "New Jersey Governor Quits, Comes Out as Gay," *CNN*, August 13, 2004, http://edition.cnn.com/2004/ALLPOLITICS/08/12/mcgreevey.nj/.
108. LexisNexis State Net database, accessed August 14, 2015.
109. Patrick Thibodeau, "Ohio Bans Offshoring as It Gives Tax Relief to Outsourcing Firm," *Computerworld*, September 7, 2010, www.computerworld.com/article/2515465/it-outsourcing/ohio-bans-offshoring-as-it-gives-tax-relief-to-outsourcing-firm.html.
110. Factiva 数据库中包含"离岸外包"一词或"外包"一词以及"国家"和"法案"的美国文章数量在 2004 年达到 3 441 篇，并且此后每年下降到不到 2 000（除了 2010 年和 2012 年的上升，总数分别为 2 117 和 2 504）。

总　结　创新全球化

1. Robert O. Keohane, "The Old IPE and the New," *Review of International Political Economy* 16, no. 1 (2009): 34.
2. Edward D. Mansfield and Diana C. Mutz, "US Versus Them: Mass Attitudes Toward Offshore Outsourcing," *World Politics* 65, no. 4 (2013): 571–608.
3. Brenton D. Peterson, Sonal S. Pandya, and David Leblang, "Doctors with Borders: Occupational Licensing as an Implicit Barrier to High Skill Migration," *Public Choice* 160, no. 1–2 (July 2014): 45–63; Neil Malhotra, Yotam Margalit, and Cecilia Hyunjung Mo, "Economic Explanations for Opposition to Immigration: Distinguishing Between Prevalence and Conditional Impact," *American Journal of Political Science* 57, no. 2 (April 2013): 391–410; Giovanni Facchini and Anna Maria Mayda, "Individual Attitudes Towards Skilled Migration: An Empirical Analysis Across Countries," *The World Economy* 35, no. 2 (2012): 183–96; Jens Hainmueller and Michael J. Hiscox, "Attitudes Toward Highly Skilled and Low-Skilled Immigration: Evidence from a Survey Experiment," *American Political Science Review* 104, no. 1 (February 2010): 61–84; Kenneth F. Scheve and Matthew Jon Slaughter, *Globalization and the Perceptions of American Workers* (Washington, DC: Peterson Institute, 2001).
4. Peterson, Pandya, and Leblang, "Doctors with Borders."
5. Margaret E. Peters, "Trade, Foreign Direct Investment, and Immigration Policy Making in the United States," *International Organization* 68, no. 4 (2014): 811–44.

6. Ayelet Shachar, "Talent Matters: Immigration Policy-Setting as a Competitive Scramble Among Jurisdictions," in *Wanted and Welcome? Policies for Highly Skilled Immigrants in Comparative Perspective*, ed. Triadafilos Triadafilopoulos (New York: Springer, 2013), 91.
7. William Aspray, Frank Mayadas, and Moshe Vardi, "Globalization and Offshoring of Software: A Report of the ACM Job Migration Task Force" (New York: Association for Computing Machinery, 2006), 52, www.acm.org/globalizationreport.
8. 例如，参见 Martin Ruhs, *The Price of Rights: Regulating International Labor Migration* (Princeton, NJ: Princeton University Press, 2013)。加里·弗里曼似乎也倾向于这种观点，至少在欧洲国家方面是如此。参见 Gary P. Freeman, "National Models, Policy Types, and the Politics of Immigration in Liberal Democracies," *West European Politics* 29, no. 2 (March 1, 2006): 237–38。
9. Shachar, "Talent Matters"; Christiane Kuptsch and Eng Fong Pang, "Introduction," in *Competing for Global Talent*, ed. Christiane Kuptsch and Eng Fong Pang (Geneva: International Labor Office, 2006), 1–8; James F. Hollifield, "The Emerging Migration State," *International Migration Review* 38, no. 3 (2004): 191.
10. Georg Menz, *The Political Economy of Managed Migration: Nonstate Actors, Europeanization, and the Politics of Designing Migration Policies* (Oxford: Oxford University Press, 2008); Lucie Cerna, "The Varieties of High-Skilled Immigration Policies: Coalitions and Policy Outputs in Advanced Industrial Countries," *Journal of European Public Policy* 16, no. 1 (January 2009): 144–61; Alexander A. Caviedes, *Prying Open Fortress Europe: The Turn to Sectoral Labor Migration* (Lanham, MD: Lexington Books, 2010); Lucie Cerna, "Attracting High-Skilled Immigrants: Policies in Comparative Perspective," *International Migration* 52, no. 3 (June 2014): 69–84.
11. Chris F. Wright, "Why Do States Adopt Liberal Immigration Policies? The Policymaking Dynamics of Skilled Visa Reform in Australia," *Journal of Ethnic and Migration Studies* 41, no. 2 (January 28, 2015): 306–28.
12. Hollifield, "The Emerging Migration State."
13. Linsu Kim, *Imitation to Innovation: The Dynamics of Korea's Technological Learning* (Cambridge, MA: Harvard Business Press, 1997); Sean O'Riain, *The Politics of High Tech Growth: Developmental Network States in the Global Economy* (Cambridge: Cambridge University Press, 2004); Dan Breznitz, *Innovation and the State* (New Haven, CT: Yale University Press, 2007); Dieter Ernst, *A New Geography of Knowledge in the Electronics Industry? Asia's Role in Global Innovation Networks* (Honolulu, HI: East-West Center, 2009); Joseph Wong, *Betting on Biotech: Innovation and the Limits of Asia's Developmental State* (New York: Cornell University Press, 2011); Sung-Young Kim, "Transitioning from Fast-Follower to Innovator: The Institutional Foundations of the Korean Telecommunications Sector," *Review of International Political Economy* 19, no. 1 (February 2012): 140–68.
14. Andrew B. Kennedy, "Slouching Tiger, Roaring Dragon: Comparing India and China as Late Innovators," *Review of International Political Economy* 23, no. 2 (2016): 1–28.
15. 这一有关发展中国家的技术民族主义和技术全球主义的文献呈现了这种趋势的部分例

外，但这一研究有地域限制，主要集中在东亚，且更关注技术发展，而不是特别关注创新。对于此文献的评论，参见 Andrew B. Kennedy, "China's Search for Renewable Energy: Pragmatic Techno-Nationalism," *Asian Survey* 53, no. 5 (2013): 911–13。

16. Mancur Olson, *The Rise and Decline of Nations: Economic Growth, Stagflation, and Social Rigidities* (New Haven, CT: Yale University Press, 1982), 217.
17. Espen Moe, *Governance, Growth and Global Leadership: The Role of the State in Technological Progress, 1750–2000* (Hampshire, UK: Ashgate, 2013); Mark Zachary Taylor, *The Politics of Innovation: Why Some Countries Are Better Than Others at Science and Technology* (Oxford: Oxford University Press, 2016).
18. Michael G. Finn, "Stay Rates of Foreign Doctorate Recipients from U.S. Universities, 2001" (Oak Ridge, TN: Oak Ridge Institute for Science and Education, November 2003), 7, http://orise.orau.gov/files/sep/stay-rates-foreign-doctorate-recipients-2001.pdf.
19. Testimony of Bruce Morrison, *Hearing Before the Committee on the Judiciary of the United States House of Representatives Subcommittee on Immigration Policy and Enforcement*, March 5, 2013, 4.
20. Vivek Wadhwa, *The Immigrant Exodus: Why America Is Losing the Global Race to Capture Entrepreneurial Talent* (Philadelphia: Wharton Digital, 2012), 49.
21. "Four Ways to Tackle H-1B Visa Reform," *IEEE Spectrum*, April 19, 2017.
22. David Bier, "No One Knows How Long Legal Immigrants Will Have to Wait," *Cato Institute*, July 28, 2016, www.cato.org/blog/no-one-knows-how-long-legal-immigrants-will-have-wait.
23. Andrew B. Kennedy, "Unequal Partners: U.S. Collaboration with China and India in Research and Development," *Political Science Quarterly* 132, no. 1 (2017): 63–86.
24. Lee Branstetter, Guangwei Lee, and Francisco Veloso, "The Rise of International Coinvention," in *The Changing Frontier: Rethinking Science and Innovation Policy*, ed. Adam B. Jaffe and Benjamin F. Jones (Chicago: University of Chicago Press, 2015), 140, 159.
25. 这一发现归因于几个因素，包括对当地人才的竞争加剧、外国公司保护知识产权的努力、外国和当地公司能力之间的差距，以及外国公司在本国进行核心研发的趋势。参见 Xiaolan Fu and Yundan Gong, "Indigenous and Foreign Innovation Efforts and Drivers of Technological Upgrading: Evidence from China," *World Develop- ment* 39, no. 7 (July 2011): 1213–25。
26. Xiaohong Quan, "Knowledge Diffusion from MNC R&D Labs in Developing Countries: Evidence from Interaction Between MNC R&D Labs and Local Universities in Beijing," *International Journal of Technology Management* 51, no. 2 (2010): 364–86.
27. Anabel Marin and Subash Sasidharan, "Heterogeneous MNC Subsidiaries and Technological Spillovers: Explaining Positive and Negative Effects in India," *Research Policy* 39, no. 9 (November 2010): 1227–41.
28. Kennedy, "Slouching Tiger, Roaring Dragon."
29. Mark Foulon and Christopher A. Padilla, "In Pursuit of Security and Prosperity: Technology Controls for a New Era," *Washington Quarterly* 30, no. 2 (2007): 88.

30. Mark Foulon, former acting undersecretary of Commerce for Industry and Security, interviewed by anthor, July 21, 2015.
31. Christopher A. Padilla, vice-president, Government and Regulatory Affairs, IBM, interview by author, March 25, 2016.
32. 总体来讲，政府与私营部门之间信息共享的潜在障碍是私营部门担心无意中披露政府执法官员可能认为违反美国出口管制规定的行为。为了实现更多的信息共享，美国政府必须找到一种方法，在不放弃出口管制的总体承诺的情况下向公司保证这方面的安全。William Reinsch, President, National Foreign Trade Council, interviewed by author, February 3, 2016.
33. Vernon M. Briggs, *Immigration and American Unionism* (Ithaca, NY: Cornell University Press, 2001); Aristide Zolberg, *A Nation by Design: Immigration Policy in the Fashioning of America* (Cambridge, MA: Harvard University Press, 2006); Daniel J. Tichenor, *Dividing Lines: The Politics of Immigration Control in America* (Princeton, NJ: Princeton University Press, 2002); Peters, "Trade, Foreign Direct Investment, and Immigration Policy Making in the United States."
34. Jennifer Steinhauer, Jonathan Martin, and David M. Herszenhorn, "Paul Ryan Calls Donald Trump's Attack on Judge 'Racist,' but Still Backs Him," *New York Times*, June 7, 2016,www.nytimes.com/2016/06/08/us/politics/paul-ryan-donald-trump-gonzalo-curiel.html.
35. Seth Fiegerman, "Silicon Valley Throws Big Money at Clinton and Virtually Nothing at Trump," *CNN*, August 23, 2016, http://money.cnn.com/2016/08/23/technology/hillary-clinton-tech-fundraisers/.
36. Jessica Meyers, "Tech Companies See Few Big Gains in Obama's Executive Action," *Boston Globe*, November 24, 2014, www.bostonglobe.com/news/nation/2014/11/24/tech-companies-see-few-big-gains-obama-executive-action/dauDJujkOhe1qx5ZQTScoM/story.html.
37. Todd Frankel and Tracy Jan, "Trump's New Travel Ban Raises the Same Silicon Valley Objections," *Washington Post*, March 6, 2017, www.washingtonpost.com/news/the-switch/wp/2017/03/06/trumps-new-travel-ban-raises-the-same-silicon-valley-objections/.
38. Rebecca Dickson, "Trump Officials Clamp Down on Worker Visas," *The Hill*, April 6, 2017, http://thehill.com/business-a-lobbying/business-a-lobbying/327507-trump-officials-clamp-down-on-worker-visas.
39. Tony Romm, "How Silicon Valley Is Trying to Topple Trump—Beginning with a Special Election in Montana," *Recode*, May 25, 2017, www.recode.net/2017/5/25/15686802/silicon-valley-trump-montana-tech-for-campaigns.
40. Donald J. Trump, "Presidential Executive Order on Buy American and Hire American," White House, April 18, 2017, www.whitehouse.gov/the-press-office/2017/04/18/presidential-executive-order-buy-american-and-hire-american.
41. Joshua Brustein, "The Secret Way Silicon Valley Uses the H-1B Program," Bloomberg, June 6, 2017, www.bloomberg.com/news/articles/2017-06-06/silicon-valley-s-h-1b-secret.
42. Kate Kelly, Rachel Abrams, and Alan Rappeport, "Trump Is Said to Abandon Contentious

Border Tax on Imports," New York Times, April 25, 2017, www.nytimes.com/2017/04/25/us/politics/orrin-hatch-trump-tax-cuts-deficit-economy.html.
43. "Briefing by Secretary of the Treasury Steven Mnuchin and Director of the National Economic Council Gary Cohn," White House, April 26, 2017, www.whitehouse.gov/the-press-office/2017/04/26/briefing-secretary-treasury-steven-mnuchin-and-director-national.
44. Information Technology Industry Council, "ITI on Trump Tax Reform Principles," Information Technology Industry Council, April 26, 2017, www.itic.org/news-events/news-releases/iti-on-trump-tax-reform-principles; Tony Romm, "Finally, Silicon Valley and Donald Trump Agree on Something: Taxes," Recode, April 26, 2017, www.recode.net/2017/4/26/15437330/silicon-valley-tech-donald-trump-agree-tax-repatriation-reform.
45. Joseph G. Paul and Frank Caruso, "One of Trump's Biggest Plans to Stimulate the Economy Won't Be Great for Most Americans," Business Insider, June 1, 2017, www.business insider.com.au/alliancebernstein-on-trump-tax-plan-2017-5?r=US&IR=T.

参考文献

Abate, Tom, and Jon Swartz. "Eleventh-Hour Victory for Tech: Visa Increase, R&D Tax Measure in Budget Bill." *San Francisco Chronicle*, October 16, 1998. www.sfgate.com/business/article/11th-Hour-Victory-For-Tech-Visa-increase-R-D-2984825.php.

"About SMART." *Singapore–MIT Alliance for Research and Technology*, 2013. http://smart.mit.edu/about-smart/about-smart.html.

Ackley, Kate. "Offshore Accounts Present a Taxing Situation." *Roll Call*, May 6, 2009.

"Address by House Speaker J. Dennis Hastert: Reflections on Role of Speaker in Modern Day House of Representatives." *U.S. Newswire*, November 12, 2003.

"Addressing the New Reality of Current Visa Policy on International Students and Researchers." *Hearing Before the U.S. Senate Committee on Foreign Relations*. 108th Cong., October 6, 2004. www.gpo.gov/fdsys/search/home.action.

Albanesius, Chloe. "Outsourcing Controversy Influences Debate on H-1B Visas." *Technology Daily*, May 6, 2004.

Alden, Edward. "Emigrants to US Face Long Wait for Green Card." *Financial Times*, October 12, 2005.

Alden, Edward, and Stephanie Kirchgaessner. "Universities in Fury at Plan to Curb 'Chinese Espionage.'" *Financial Times*, November 25, 2005.

Allum, Jeff. "Findings from the 2014 CGS International Graduate Admissions Survey—Phase II: Final Applications and Initial Offers of Admission." Washington, DC: Council of Graduate Schools, 2014.

Altbach, Philip G., and Jane Knight. "The Internationalization of Higher Education: Motivations and Realities." *Journal of Studies in International Education* 11, no. 3–4 (2007): 290–305.

Altbach, Philip G., and Patti McGill Peterson. "Internationalize American Higher Education? Not Exactly." *Change* 30, no. 4 (1998): 36–39.

"Amendments Submitted and Proposed." *Congressional Record*. 111th Cong. 156, no. 115, August 2, 2010.

American Competitiveness in the Twenty-First Century Act of 2000. S.2045. 106th Cong., 2000. www.gpo.gov/fdsys/pkg/BILLS-106s2045enr/pdf/BILLS-106s2045enr.pdf.

American Council on Education. "Higher Education Associations Strongly Endorse Senate Immigration Reform Bill." Letter to the U.S. Senate, June 26, 2013. https://www.aau.edu/sites/default/files/AAU%20Files/Key%20Issues/Budget%20%26%20Appropriations/FY17/Endorsement-Letter-S-744_6-26-13.pdf.

American Enterprise Institute. "China Global Investment Tracker." *AEI*, April 30, 2017. www.aei.org/china-global-investment-tracker/.

American Federation of Labor and Congress of Industrial Organizations (AFL-CIO). "Immigration." *AFL-CIO*, February 16, 2000. www.aflcio.org/About/Exec-Council/EC-Statements/Immigration2.

——. "Outsourcing America." *AFL-CIO*, March 11, 2004. www.aflcio.org/About/Exec-Council/EC-Statements/Outsourcing-America.

——. "Summary of Activities Regarding Off-Shore Outsourcing, June 2003–May 2004." *Department for Professional Employees, AFL-CIO*, 2004. http://dpeaflcio.org/archives/legislative-reports-2/summary-of-activities-regarding-off-shore-outsourcing-june-2003-may-2004/.

American Immigration Lawyers Association. "Analysis of the American Competitiveness in the Twenty-First Century Act." *Shusterman.com*. Accessed March 2, 2016. http://shusterman.com/h1b-analysisofac21.html.

"Analysis: Look at the Controversy Over H-1B Visas." *National Public Radio: Talk of the Nation*, September 26, 2000.

Archibugi, Daniele, and Simona Iammarino. "The Globalization of Technological Innovation: Definition and Evidence." *Review of International Political Economy* 9, no. 1 (Spring 2002): 98–122.

Aronson, Jonathan D. "International Intellectual Property Rights in a Networked World." In *Power, Interdependence, and Nonstate Actors in World Politics*, edited by Helen V. Milner and Andrew Moravcsik, 185–203. Princeton, NJ: Princeton University Press, 2011.

Arslan, Cansin, Jean-Christophe Dumont, Zovanga Kone, Yasser Moullan, Caglar Ozden, Christopher Parsons, and Theodora Xenogiani. *A New Profile of Migrants in the Aftermath of the Recent Economic Crisis*. OECD Social, Employment and Migration Working Paper No. 160 2014. www.oecd.org/els/mig/WP160.pdf.

Asheim, Bjørn T., and Meric S. Gertler. "The Geography of Innovation: Regional Innovation Systems." In *The Oxford Handbook of Innovation*, edited by Jan Fagerberg, David C. Mowery, and Richard R. Nelson, 291–317. Oxford: Oxford University Press, 2005.

Asian Development Bank. *Counting the Cost: Financing Asian Higher Education for Inclusive Growth*. Manila: Asian Development Bank, 2012.

Aspray, William, Frank Mayadas, and Moshe Vardi. "Globalization and Offshoring of Software: A Report of the ACM Job Migration Task Force." New York: Association for Computing Machinery, 2006. www.acm.org/globalizationreport.

Australian Government Department of Education. "International Student Enrolments by Nationality in 2013," April 2014. https://internationaleducation.gov.au/research/research-snapshots/pages/default.aspx.

Australian Government Department of Education and Training. "International Students Studying

Science, Technology, Engineering and Mathematics (STEM) in Australian Higher Education Institutions." *Research Snapshots*, October 2015. https://internationaleducation.gov.au/research/Research-Snapshots/Documents/STEM%202014.pdf.

Babington, Charles. "Immigration Bill Expected to Pass Senate This Week: Hastert May Block Version That Divides House GOP." *Washington Post*, May 23, 2006.

Ball, Molly. "Immigration Reformers Are Winning August." *Atlantic*, August 21, 2013. www.theatlantic.com/politics/archive/2013/08/immigration-reformers-are-winning-august/278873/.

——. "The Little Group Behind the Big Fight to Stop Immigration Reform." *Atlantic*, August 1, 2013. www.theatlantic.com/politics/archive/2013/08/the-little-group-behind-the-big-fight-to-stop-immigration-reform/278252/.

Baumgartner, Frank R., Jeffrey M. Berry, Marie Hojnacki, Beth L. Leech, and David C. Kimball. *Lobbying and Policy Change: Who Wins, Who Loses, and Why*. Chicago: University of Chicago Press, 2009.Baumgartner, Frank R., and Beth L. Leech. *Basic Interests: The Importance of Groups in Politics and in Political Science*. Princeton, NJ: Princeton University Press, 1998.

Belopotosky, Danielle. "Efforts to Change Visa Law for Skilled Workers Gains Steam." Technology Daily, October 1, 2004.

——. "Lobbyists Push Congress for Action on H-1B Visas." *Technology Daily*, November 16, 2004.

——. "Policy Change On 'Deemed Exports' Is Widely Panned." *Technology Daily PM*, August 19, 2005.

Bernstein, Nina. "In the Streets, Suddenly, an Immigrant Groundswell." *New York Times*, March 27, 2006.

Berry, Jeffrey M. *The New Liberalism: The Rising Power of Citizen Groups*. Washington, DC: Brookings Institution, 1999.

Bier, David. "High-Skilled Immigration Restrictions Are Economically Senseless." *Forbes*, July 22, 2012. www.forbes.com/sites/realspin/2012/07/22/high-skilled-immigration-restrictions-are-economically-senseless/.

——. "No One Knows How Long Legal Immigrants Will Have to Wait." *Cato Institute*, July 28, 2016. www.cato.org/blog/no-one-knows-how-long-legal-immigrants-will-have-wait.

——. "Why Does the Government Care Where Immigrant Workers Were Born?" *Cato Institute*, January 18, 2017. www.cato.org/blog/why-does-government-care-where-immigrant-workers-were-born.

Blinder, Alan S. "Offshoring: The Next Industrial Revolution?" *Foreign Affairs* 85, no. 2 (2006): 113–28.

Block, Melissa. "Analysis: Industry Groups Fight Anti-outsourcing Legislation." *National Public Radio: All Things Considered*, March 5, 2004.

Bloom, Nicholas, Raffaella Sadun, and John Van Reenen. "Americans Do IT Better: US Multinationals and the Productivity Miracle." *The American Economic Review* 102, no. 1 (2012): 167–201.

Bond, Philip J. "Opposition to S.3816." *TechAmerica*, September 27, 2010. www.techamerica.org/content/wp-content/uploads/2010/09/9-27-10_S3816.pdf.

"Bond, Thune Spearhead Efforts to Gut Foreign Tax Provisions from Bill." *Inside U.S. Trade*, June 18, 2010.

Border Security, Economic Opportunity, and Immigration Modernization Act of 2013. S. 744. 113th Cong., 2013. www.govtrack.us/congress/bills/113/s744.

Borjas, George J. "An Evaluation of the Foreign Student Program." Washington, DC: Center for Immigration Studies, June 2002. http://cis.org/ForeignStudentProgram.

———. *Immigration Economics*. Cambridge, MA: Harvard University Press, 2014.

———. "Rethinking Foreign Students." *National Review* 17 (June 17, 2002): 38–41.

Borroz, Tony. "Chevrolet's Mouse that Roared." *Wired*, August 22, 2011. www.wired.com/2011/08/chevrolets-mouse-that-roared/.

Boyd, Monica. "Recruiting High Skill Labour in North America: Policies, Outcomes and Futures." *International Migration* 52, no. 3 (June 2014): 40–54.

Brandt, Loren, and Eric Thun. "The Fight for the Middle: Upgrading, Competition, and Industrial Development in China." *World Development* 38, no. 11 (November 2010): 1555–74.

Branigin, William. "Visa Deal for Computer Programmers Angers Labor Groups." *Washington Post*, September 27, 1998.

Branstetter, Lee, Guangwei Lee, and Francisco Veloso. "The Rise of International Coinvention." In *The Changing Frontier: Rethinking Science and Innovation Policy*, edited by Adam B. Jaffe and Benjamin F. Jones, 135–68. Chicago: University of Chicago Press, 2015.

Breznitz, Dan. *Innovation and the State*. New Haven, CT: Yale University Press, 2007.

Breznitz, Dan, and Michael Murphree. *Run of the Red Queen: Government, Innovation, Globalization, and Economic Growth in China*. New Haven, CT: Yale University Press, 2011.

"Briefing by Secretary of the Treasury Steven Mnuchin and Director of the National Economic Council Gary Cohn." *The White House*, April 26, 2017. www.whitehouse.gov/the-press-office/2017/04/26/briefing-secretary-treasury-steven-mnuchin-and-director-national.

Briggs, Vernon M. *Immigration and American Unionism*. Ithaca, NY: Cornell University Press, 2001.

Bring Jobs Home Act of 2011/12. S.3364. 112th Cong., 2011/12. www.congress.gov/bill/112th-congress/senate-bill/3364.

Bring Jobs Home Act of 2013/14, S.2569, 113th Cong., 2013/14. www.congress.gov/bill/112th-congress/senate-bill/2569.

Brooks, Stephen G. *Producing Security: Multinational Corporations, Globalization, and the Changing Calculus of Conflict*. Princeton, NJ: Princeton University Press, 2005.

Brownstein, Ronald. "Back to Basics." *National Journal*, September 9, 2010.

Bruche, Gert. "The Emergence of China and India as New Competitors in MNCs' Innovation Networks." *Competition & Change* 13, no. 3 (2009): 267–88.

Brustein, Joshua. "The Secret Way Silicon Valley Uses the H-1B Program." *Bloomberg*, June 6, 2017. www.bloomberg.com/news/articles/2017-06-06/silicon-valley-s-h-1b-secret.

Buderi, Robert, and Gregory T. Huang. *Guanxi (The Art of Relationships): Microsoft, China, and Bill Gates' Plan to Win the Road Ahead*. London: Random House, 2006.

Bureau of Economic Analysis. "Foreign Direct Investment in the U.S., Majority-Owned Bank and

Nonbank U.S. Affiliates, Research and Development Expenditures for 2013." *International Data: Direct Investment and Multinational Enterprises*, 2016. www.bea.gov/iTable/index_MNC.cfm.

———. "U.S. Direct Investment Abroad, All Majority-Owned Foreign Affiliates, Research and Development Expenditures for 2013." *International Data: Direct Investment and Multinational Enterprises*, 2016. www.bea.gov/iTable/index_MNC.cfm.

Bureau of Industry and Security. "Revision and Clarification of Deemed Export Related Regulatory Requirements." *Federal Register*, March 28, 2005.

———. "Revisions and Clarification of Deemed Export Relate Regulatory Requirements." Federal Register, May 31, 2006.

Burghart, Devin. "Mapping the Tea Party Caucus in the 112th Congress." Institute for Research and Education on Human Rights, March 17, 2011. https://irehr.org/issue-areas/tea-party-nationalism/tea-party-news-and-analysis/item/355-mapping-the-tea-party-caucus-in-the-112th-congress.

———. "Special Report: The Status of the Tea Party Movement—Part Two." Institute for Research and Education on Human Rights, January 21, 2014. www.irehr.org/2014/01/21/status-of-tea-party-by-the-numbers/.

Burghart, Devin, and Leonard Zeskind. "Beyond FAIR: The Decline of the Established Anti-immigration Organizations and the Rise of Tea Party Nativism." Kansas City, MO: Institute for Research and Education on Human Rights, 2012. www.irehr.org/issue-areas/tea-party-nationalism/beyond-fair-report.

Calmes, Jackie, and Edmund Andrews. "Obama Seeks to Curb Foreign Tax Havens." *New York Times*, May 4, 2009. www.nytimes.com/2009/05/05/business/05tax.html?pagewanted=all&_r=1&.

Cameron, Doug, and Julian E. Barnes. "Pentagon Criticizes Contractors' R&D." *Wall Street Journal*, November 21, 2014.

Cameron, Doug, and Alistair Barr. "Google Snubs Robotics Rivals, Pentagon." *Wall Street Journal*, March 5, 2015. www.wsj.com/articles/google-snubs-robotics-rivals-pentagon-1425580734.

Cao, Cong, Ning Li, Xia Li, and Li Liu. "Reforming China's S&T System." *Science* 341, no. 6145 (2013): 460–62.

Carlson, Tucker, and Bill Press. "Debating Immigration Policy." *Crossfire*. CNN, October 24, 2001.

Carroll, Joseph. "American Public Opinion About Immigration." *Gallup.com*, July 26, 2005. www.gallup.com/poll/14785/Immigration.aspx.

Caviedes, Alexander A. Prying Open Fortress Europe: The Turn to Sectoral Labor Migration. Lanham, MD: Lexington, 2010.

Center for Immigration Studies. "Are Foreign Students Good for America?" Panel discussion transcript. Rayburn Building, House of Representatives, Washington, DC, June 25, 2002. www.cis.org/sites/cis.org/files/articles/2002/foreignstudents.html.

Center for Responsive Politics. "Interest Groups." *OpenSecrets.org*. Accessed March 16, 2017. www.opensecrets.org/industries/.

———. "Lobbying Spending Database." *OpenSecrets.org*. Accessed March 3, 2017. www.opensecrets.org/lobby/.

———. "Lobbying Spending Database—Microsoft." *OpenSecrets.org*, 2015. www.opensecrets.org/lobby/clientsum.php?id=D000000115&year=2013.

Cerna, Lucie. "Attracting High-Skilled Immigrants: Policies in Comparative Perspective." *International Migration* 52, no. 3 (June 2014): 69–84.

———. "The EU Blue Card: Preferences, Policies, and Negotiations between Member States." *Migration Studies* 2, no. 1 (March 1, 2014): 73–96.

———. "The Varieties of High-Skilled Immigration Policies: Coalitions and Policy Outputs in Advanced Industrial Countries." *Journal of European Public Policy* 16, no. 1 (January 2009): 144–61.

Chaddock, Gail Russell. "Eric Cantor Upset Stuns GOP, Revives Tea Party." *Christian Science Monitor*, June 11, 2014. www.csmonitor.com/USA/Elections/2014/0611/Eric-Cantor-upset-stuns-GOP-revives-tea-party.

Chakravorty, Sanjoy, Devesh Kapur, and Nirvikar Singh. *The Other One Percent: Indians in America*. Oxford: Oxford University Press, 2016.

Chase, Kerry A. "Moving Hollywood Abroad: Divided Labor Markets and the New Politics of Trade in Services." *International Organization* 62, no. 4 (2008): 653–87.

Chellaraj, Gnanaraj, Keith E. Maskus, and Aaditya Mattoo. "The Contribution of International Graduate Students to US Innovation." *Review of International Economics* 16, no. 3 (August 2008): 444–62.

Chen, Weihua. "US Immigration Reform a Challenge for China." *China Daily*, February 8, 2013. http://europe.chinadaily.com.cn/opinion/2013-02/08/content_16216633.htm.

Chendakera, Nair. "U.S., India Move to Boost Cooperation in R&D." *Electronic Engineering Times*, March 27, 2000.

Cheng, Ruowei. "Woguo Liushi Dingjian Rencai Shu Ju Shijie Shouwei [China's Loss of Top Talent Is Greatest in the World]." *Renmin Ribao [People's Daily]*, June 6, 2013. http://finance.people.com.cn/n/2013/0606/c1004-21754321.html.

Cheung, Tai Ming, and Bates Gill. "Trade Versus Security: How Countries Balance Technology Transfers with China." *Journal of East Asian Studies* 13, no. 3 (2013): 443–56.

Chin, Hey-Kyung Koh. Open Doors 2002: Report on International Educational Exchange. New York. Institute for International Education, 2002.

"China Encourages More VC Funding, Promises Foreign Firms Equal Treatment." *Reuters*, September 1, 2016. www.reuters.com/article/us-china-economy-idUSKCN1175BT.

China Scholarship Council. "2012 Nian Guojia Liuxue Jijin Zizhu Chuguo Liuxue Renyuan Xuanpai Jianzhang [Briefing on the Selection of Awardees for Study Abroad Financial Support in 2012]," November 1, 2011. http://v.csc.edu.cn/Chuguo/739b1b8c118441e5bb211c388563f7da.shtml.

———. "2015 Nian Guojia Gongpai Chuguo Liuxue Xuanpai Jihua Queding [Government Deter- mines Plan for Study Abroad Awards in 2015]." Beijing: Chinese Education Online and Best Choice for Education, October 30, 2014. www.csc.edu.cn/News/2acf973ba1a84ca69f53

86a574771906.shtml.

———. "2017 Nian Guojia Liuxue Jijin Zizhu Chuguo Liuxue Renyuan Xuanpai Jianzhang [Briefing on the Selection of Awardees for Study Abroad Financial Support in 2017]," December 12, 2016. www.csc.edu.cn/article/709.

"China to Overtake US as New Frontier for Global R&D." *People's Daily Online*, January 27, 2014. http://english.peopledaily.com.cn/98649/8523078.html.

Chiswick, Barry R., and Timothy Hatton. "International Migration and the Integration of Labor Markets." In *Globalization in Historical Perspective*, edited by Michael D. Bordo, Alan M. Taylor, and Jeffrey G. Williamson, 65–119. Chicago: University of Chicago Press, 2003.

Chow, Patricia, and Rajika Bhandari. *Open Doors 2010: Report on International Educational Exchange*. New York: Institute for International Education, 2010.

Clayton, Mark. "Academia Becomes Target for New Security Laws." *Christian Science Monitor*, September 24, 2002.

Collier, Andrew K. "Yale Chief Hits at US Student Visa Delays." *South China Morning Post*, November 14, 2003.

Communist Party of China. "Zhonggong Zhongyang Guanyu Jianli Shehuizhuyi Shichang Jingji Tizhi Ruogan Wenti de Jueding [Chinese Communist Party Decision Regarding Several Questions in Building a Socialist Market Economy System]." *Zhongguo Gongchandang Xinwen Wang*, November 14, 1993. http://cpc.people.com.cn/GB/64162/134902/8092314.html.

"Compete America." *Technology Daily PM*, October 4, 2005.

Comprehensive Immigration Reform Act of 2006. S.2611. 109th Cong., 2006. www.congress.gov/bill/109th-congress/senate-bill/2611.

Confessore, Nicholas. "Borderline Insanity." *Washington Monthly*, May 2002. www.washingtonmonthly.com/features/2001/0205.confessore.html.

Copeland, Dale C. Economic Interdependence and War. Princeton, NJ: Princeton University Press, 2014.

———. "Economic Interdependence and War: A Theory of Trade Expectations." *International Security* 20, no. 4 (1996): 5–41.

Costa, Daniel. "Little-Known Temporary Visas for Foreign Tech Workers Depress Wages." *The Hill*, November 11, 2014. http://thehill.com/blogs/pundits-blog/technology/223607-little-known-temporary-visas-for-foreign-tech-workers-depress.

Costlow, Terry. "Senate Set to Vote This Week on Visa-Cap Bill: High Noon Approaches for H-1B Friends, Foes." *Electronic Engineering Times*, October 2, 2000.

Coutin, Susan Bibler. *Nations of Emigrants: Shifting Boundaries of Citizenship in El Salvador and the United States*. Ithaca, NY: Cornell University Press, 2007.

Creating American Jobs and Ending Offshoring Act of 2010. S.3816. 111th Cong., 2010. www.govtrack.us/congress/bills/111/s3816.

Crouzet, François. *The Victorian Economy*. London: Methuen, 1982.

Currie, Chris. "U.S. Public Overwhelmingly Opposed to H-1B Visa Expansion." *IEEE-USA*, September 16, 1998. www.ieeeusa.org/communications/releases/_private/1998/pr091698.html.

Dalrymple, Mary. "Senate Passes Corporate Tax Bill." *Associated Press*, May 12, 2004.

Davis, Christina L., and Sophie Meunier. "Business as Usual? Economic Responses to Political Tensions." *American Journal of Political Science* 55, no. 3 (July 2011): 628–46.
Davis, Todd M. *Open Doors 2000: Report on International Education Exchange*. New York: Institute for International Education, 2000.
"Dealing with Foreign Students and Scholars in an Age of Terrorism: Visa Backlogs and Tracking Systems." *Hearing Before the U.S. House of Representatives Committee on Science*. 108th Cong., March 26, 2003. www.gpo.gov/fdsys/search/home.action.
Deng, Xiaoping. "Gist of Speeches Made in Wuchang, Shenzhen, Zhuhai and Shanghai (From January 18 to February 21, 1992)." Beijing Review, February 7, 1994.
Destler, I. M. American Trade Politics. New York: Columbia University Press, 2005.
Dickson, Rebecca. "Trump Officials Clamp Down on Worker Visas." *The Hill*, April 6, 2017. http://thehill.com/business-a-lobbying/business-a-lobbying/327507-trump-officials-clamp-down-on-worker-visas.
"Dishiyipi Qianren Jihua Qingnian Rencai, Chuangye Rencai Ruxuan Mingdan [Name List for the Eleventh Batch of Awardees Under the Thousand Youth Talents and Startup Talents Plan]." *Qianren Jihua Wang*, May 13, 2015. http://1000plan.org/qrjh/article/61716.
Dizard, Wilson. "New Law Will Curb Offshoring of Federal IT Work." *Government Computer News*, February 23, 2004.
Docquier, Frédéric, Olivier Lohest, and Abdeslam Marfouk. "Brain Drain in Developing Countries." *The World* Bank Economic Review 21, no. 2 (January 1, 2007): 193–218.
Dossani, Rafiq, and Martin Kenney. "Creating an Environment for Venture Capital in India." World Development 30, no. 2 (2002): 227–53.
Drew, Kevin. "Terror Probe Reaches Nation's Campuses." *CNN*, October 25, 2001. http://edition.cnn.com/2001/LAW/10/24/inv.international.students/index.html.
Drezner, Daniel. "State Structure, Technological Leadership and the Maintenance of Hegemony." *Review of International Studies* 27, no. 1 (2001): 3–25.
Dugan, Andrew. "Passing New Immigration Laws Is Important to Americans." *Gallup.com*, July 11, 2013. www.gallup.com/poll/163475/passing-new-immigration-laws-important-americans.aspx.
Dür, Andreas, Patrick Bernhagen, and David Marshall. "Interest Group Success in the European Union: When (and Why) Does Business Lose?" *Comparative Political Studies* 48, no. 8 (2015): 951–83.
Dür, Andreas, and Gemma Mateo. "Public Opinion and Interest Group Influence: How Citizen Groups Derailed the Anti-counterfeiting Trade Agreement." *Journal of European Public Policy* 21, no. 8 (2014): 1199–1217.
Edsall, Thomas B. "Attacks Alter Politics, Shift Focus of Immigration Debate." *Washington Post*, October 15, 2001.
Elmer-DeWitt, Philip. "Apple as the Goose That Laid the Golden Eggs. Five of Them." *Fortune*, November 25, 2013. http://fortune.com/2013/11/25/apple-as-the-goose-that-laid-the-golden-eggs-five-of-them/.
Emery, Gail Repsher. "Industry Fights Dodd Legislation." *Newsbytes News Network*, April 15,

2004.

Englesberg, Paul. "Reversing China's Brain Drain: The Study-Abroad Policy, 1978–1993." In *Great Policies: Strategic Innovations in Asia and the Pacific Basin*, edited by John Dickey Montgomery and Dennis A. Rondinelli, 99–122. Westport, CT: Praeger, 1995.Ernst and Young. Globalizing Venture Capital: Global Venture Capital Insights and Trends Report, 2012. www. ey.com/Publication/vwLUAssets/Globalizing_venture_capital_VC_insights_and_trends_report_CY0227/$FILE/Globalizing%20venture%20capital_VC%20insights%20and%20trends%20report_CY0227.pdf.

Ernst, Dieter. *A New Geography of Knowledge in the Electronics Industry? Asia's Role in Global Innovation Networks*. Honolulu, HI: East-West Center, 2009.

——. *Innovation Offshoring: Exploring Asia's Emerging Role in Global Innovation Networks*. East-West Center Special Report No. 10 (July 2006). "The Eternal 'Emergency.'" Wall Street Journal, August 6, 2010.

European Commission. "The 2016 EU Industrial R&D Investment Scoreboard." E*conomics of Industrial Research and Innovation*. Accessed March 13, 2017. http://iri.jrc.ec.europa.eu/score board16.html.

Ewell, Miranda. "Clinton Opposes Higher Visa Cap; Focus on 'Home-Grown' Talent, Commerce Chief Says." *San Jose Mercury News*, January 13, 1998.

FAA Air Transportation Modernization and Safety Improvement Act of 2010. H.R. 1586. 111th Cong. (2010). www.govtrack.us/congress/bills/111/hr1586.

Facchini, Giovanni, and Anna Maria Mayda. "Individual Attitudes Towards Skilled Migration: An Empirical Analysis Across Countries." *The World Economy* 35, no. 2 (2012): 183–96.

Facchini, Giovanni, Anna Maria Mayda, and Prachi Mishra. "Do Interest Groups Affect US Immigration Policy?" *Journal of International Economics* 85, no. 1 (September 2011): 114–28.

Fagerberg, Jan. "Innovation: A Guide to the Literature." In *The Oxford Handbook of Innovation*, edited by Jan Fagerberg, David C. Mowery, and Richard R. Nelson, 1–26. Oxford: Oxford University Press, 2005.

Fagerberg, Jan, David Mowery, and Richard R. Nelson, eds. *The Oxford Handbook of Innovation*. Oxford: Oxford University Press, 2006.

"FAIR Statement on the Pioneer Fund." *PR Newswire*, March 4, 1998.

Farley, Robert. "9/11 Hijackers and Student Visas." *Factcheck.org*, May 10, 2013. www.factcheck. org/2013/05/911-hijackers-and-student-visas/.

Fearon, James D. "Rationalist Explanations for War." *International Organization* 49, no. 3 (1995): 379–414.

Federation for American Immigration Reform. "Immigration Issues: Foreign Students," May 2012. www.fairus.org/issue/foreign-students.

Feldmann, Linda. "Is the Tea Party Running Out of Steam?" *Christian Science Monitor*, April 12, 2014.

Fiegerman, Seth. "Silicon Valley Throws Big Money at Clinton and Virtually Nothing at Trump." *CNN*, August 23, 2016. http://money.cnn.com/2016/08/23/technology/hillary-clinton-tech-

fundraisers/.
Fine, Janice, and Daniel J. Tichenor. "An Enduring Dilemma: Immigration and Organized Labor in Western Europe and the United States." In *The Oxford Handbook of the Politics of International Migration*, edited by Marc Rosenblum and Daniel J. Tichenor, 532–72. Oxford: Oxford University Press, 2012.
Finn, Michael G. "Stay Rates of Foreign Doctorate Recipients from U.S. Universities, 2001." Oak Ridge, TN: Oak Ridge Institute for Science and Education, November 2003. http:// orise. orau.gov/files/sep/stay-rates-foreign-doctorate-recipients-2001.pdf.
———. "Stay Rates of Foreign Doctorate Recipients from U.S. Universities, 2011." Oak Ridge, TN: Oak Ridge Institute for Science and Education, January 2014. http://orise.orau.gov/science-education/difference/stay-rates-impact.aspx.
Fischer, Karin. "State Department Promises Speedier Visa Review." Chronicle of Higher Education, June 12, 2009.
Fitzgerald, David. "Inside th Sending State: The Politics of Mexican Emigration Control." International Migration Review 40, no. 2 (2006): 259–93.
Fletcher, Michael. "Bush Immigration Plan Meets GOP Opposition: Lawmakers Resist Temporary-Worker Proposal." *Washington Post*, January 2, 2005.
Foreign Broadcast Information Service. "Foreign Schooling Policy Remains Unchanged." *FBIS-CHI-88-224*, November 14, 1988.
"Fortune 500." *Fortune*, 2015. http://fortune.com/fortune500/.
"Fortune 500: 1955 Ful List." *Fortune*, 2015. http://archive.fortune.com/magazines/fortune/fortune500_archive/full/1955/.
Foulon, Mark, and Christopher A. Padilla. "In Pursuit of Security and Prosperity: Technology Controls for a New Era." *Washington Quarterly* 30, no. 2 (2007): 83–90.
"Four Ways to Tackle H-1B Visa Reform." *IEEE Spectrum*, April 19, 2017.
Frankel, Todd, and Tracy Jan. "Trump's New Travel Ban Raises the Same Silicon Valley Objections." Washington Post, March 6, 2017. www.washingtonpost.com/news/the-switch/wp/2017/03/06/trumps-new-travel-ban-raises-the-same-silicon-valley-objections/.
Fraser, Steve. "The Hollowing Out of America." *The Nation*, December 3, 2012. www.thenation.com/article/171563/hollowing-out-america#.
Frates, Chris. "Why the Schumer–Smith Immigration Negotiations Broke Down." *Atlantic*, September 20, 2012. www.theatlantic.com/politics/archive/2012/09/why-the-schumer-smith-immigration-negotiations-broke-down/428835/.
Frauenheim, Ed. "Tech Professionals Group Wary of Offshoring." *CNET News*, March 18, 2004.
Freeman, Christopher. *Technology, Policy, and Economic Performance: Lessons from Japan*. London: Pinter, 1987.
Freeman, Gary P. "National Models, Policy Types, and the Politics of Immigration in Liberal Democracies." *West European Politics* 29, no. 2 (March 1, 2006): 227–47.
Freeman, Gary P., and David K. Hill. "Disaggregating Immigration Policy: The Politics of Skilled Labor Recruitment in the US." *Knowledge, Technology & Policy* 19, no. 3 (2006): 7–26.
Friedel, Robert, and Paul B. Israel. *Edison's Electric Light: The Art of Invention*. Baltimore, MD:

Johns Hopkins University Press, 2010.

Fu, Xiaolan, and Yundan Gong. "Indigenous and Foreign Innovation Efforts and Drivers of Technological Upgrading: Evidence from China." *World Development* 39, no. 7 (July 2011): 1213–25.Fu, Xiaolan, and Hongru Xiong. "Open Innovation in China: Policies and Practices." Journal of Science and Technology Policy in China 2, no. 3 (2011): 196–218.

Fuller, Douglas B. *Paper Tigers, Hidden Dragons: Firms and the Political Economy of China's Technological Development*. Oxford: Oxford University Press, 2016.

Fung, Brian. "Democrats' Dilemma on High-Skilled Immigration Reform." *National Journal*, March 6, 2013.

Gaillard, Jacques, and Anne-Marie Gaillard. "Introduction: The International Mobility of Brains—Exodus or Circulation?" *Science, Technology & Society* 2, no. 2 (1997): 195–228.

Gallup, Alec, and Frank Newport. The Gallup Poll: Public Opinion 2004. Lanham, MD: Rowman& Littlefield, 2006.

Gamboa, Suzanne. "Senate Vote Sidetracks Immigration Compromise." *Associated Press*, April 7, 2006.

Gandhi, Rajiv. "Keep Pace with Technology." Indian National Congress, December 19, 1985. www.inc.in/resources/speeches/315-Keep-Pace-with-Technology.

———. "Revamping the Educational System." Indian National Congress, August 29, 1985. www.inc.in/resources/speeches/345-Revamping-the-Educational-System.

Gansler, Jacques S., and William Lucyshyn. *Commercial-Off-the-Shelf (COTS): Doing It Right*. College Park: University of Maryland Center for Public Policy and Private Enterprise, 2008. www.dtic.mil/dtic/tr/fulltext/u2/a494143.pdf.

Gaouette, Nicole. "Immigration Bill Ignites a Grass-Roots Fire on the Right." *Los Angeles Times*, June 24, 2007. http://articles.latimes.com/2007/jun/24/nation/na-immig24.

"General Electric Research Lab History." *Edison Tech Center*, 2015. www.edisontechcenter.org/GEresearchLab.html.

George, Alexander, and Andrew Bennett. *Case Studies and Theory Development in the Social Sciences*. Cambridge, MA: MIT Press, 2005.

Gilens, Martin, and Benjamin I. Page. "Testing Theories of American Politics: Elites, Interest Groups, and Average Citizens." *Perspectives on Politics* 12, no. 3 (2014): 564–81.

Gilpin, Robert. *Global Political Economy: Understanding the International Economic Order*. Princeton, NJ: Princeton University Press, 2001.

———. *U.S. Power and the Multinational Corporation: The Political Economy of Foreign Direct Investment*. New York: Basic Books, 1975.

———. *War and Change in World Politics*. Cambridge: Cambridge University Press, 1983.

Glanz, William. "High-Tech Lobbyist Counts Washington Successes." *Knight-Ridder Tribune Business News*, October 14, 2000.

"G.M. Earnings in ' 55 Go Over Billion Mark." *Chicago Tribune*, February 3, 1956.

Godwin, R. Kenneth. *One Billion Dollars of Influence: The Direct Marketing of Politics*. Chatham, NJ: Chatham House, 1988.

Gohlke, Josh. "Cipel Was No Security Risk, McGreevey Says: Governor Speaks of Former Aide by Name for First Time." *The Record*, September 10, 2004.

Goldfarb, Zachary A., and Karen Tumulty. "IRS Admits Targeting Conservatives for Tax Scrutiny in 2012 Election." *Washington Post*, May 10, 2013. www.washingtonpost.com/business/economy/ irs-admits-targeting-conservatives-for-tax-scrutiny-in-2012-election/2013/05/10/3b6a0ada-b987-11e2-92f3-f291801936b8_story.html.

Goldstein, Judith. *Ideas, Interests, and American Trade Policy*. Ithaca, NY: Cornell University Press, 1993.

"Gonggu Fazhan Zui Guangfan de Aiguo Tongyi Zhanxian Wei Shixian Zhongguo Meng Tigong Guangfan Liliang Zhichi [Consolidate and Develop the Most Wide-Ranging Patriotic United Front to Provide Extensive Supporting Strength to the Chinese Dream]." *Renmin Ribao [People's Daily]*, May 21, 2015. http://paper.people.com.cn/rmrb/html/2015-05/21/nw. D110000renmrb_20150521_2-01.htm.

Government of India. Emigration Act of 1983. Pub. L. No. 31 (1983). http://moia.gov.in/write readdata/pdf/emig_act.pdf.

——. Passports Act of 1967. Pub. L. No. 15 (1967). http://passportindia.gov.in/AppOnlineProject/ pdf/passports_act.pdf.

Government of India Department of Science and Technology. *Science, Technology and Innovation Policy 2013*. New Delhi: Ministry of Science and Technology, 2013. www.dst.gov.in/sti-policy-eng.pdf.

Greenfield, Heather. "Techies 'Disappointed' by Immigration Bill's Demise." *Technology Daily PM*, June 28, 2007.

Greenwalt, Bill. "We Haven't Won Yet on Export Control Reforms." *Breaking Defense*, November 21, 2013. http://breakingdefense.com/2013/11/we-havent-won-yet-on-export-control-reforms/.

Grieco, Joseph M. "Anarchy and the Limits of Cooperation: A Realist Critique of the Newest Liberal Institutionalism." In *Neorealism and Neoliberalism: The Contemporary Debate*, 116–40. New York: Columbia University Press, 1993.

Gross, Andrew D., and Michael S. Schadewald. "Prospects for U.S. Corporate Tax Reform." *The CPA Journal* 82, no. 1 (January 1, 2012).

"Guancha: Zhongguo Gaoduan Rencai Liushi Lu Jugao Buxia [Observation: The Rate of China's High-End Brain Drain Remains High]." *Zhongguo Jiaoyu Bao [China Education Daily]*, January 20, 2014. http://edu.sina.com.cn/a/2014-01-20/1148238838.shtml.

"Guanyu Gongbu Dishier Pi Guojia Qianren Jihua Qingnian Rencai, Chuanye Rencai Ruxuan Renyuan Mingdan de Gonggao [Proclamation Announcing the Twelfth Batch of Awardees for the Thousand Youth Talents and Start-up Talents Plan]." *Qianren Jihua Wang*, March 14, 2016. http://1000plan.org/qrjh/article/61716.

"Guanyu Gongbu Dishisan Pi Guojia Qianren Jihua Qingnian Xiangmu Chuangye Rencai Xiangmu Ruxuan Renyuan Mingdan de Gonggao [Announcement of the Thirteenth Batch of Awardees for the Youth and Startup Talent Programs of the National Thousand Talents Plan]." *Qianren Jihua Wang*, May 11, 2017. http://1000plan.org/qrjh/article/69239.

"Guanyu Gongbu Diyipi Qingnian Qianren Jihua Yinjin Rencai Mingdan de Gonggao [Proclamation Announcing the First Batch of Names for the Thousand Youth Talents Plan to Attract Talent]." *Qianren Jihua Wang*, November 11, 2011.

Guo, Di, and Kun Jiang. "Venture Capital Investment and the Performance of Entrepreneurial Firms: Evidence from China." *Journal of Corporate Finance* 22 (2013): 375–95.

Guojia Jiaowei Shehui Kexue Yanjiu yu Yishu Jiaoyusi, Guojia Jiaowei Sixiang Zhengzhi Gongzuosi, and Beijing Shiwei Gaodeng Xuexiao Gongzuo Weiyuanhui. *Wushitian de Huigu Yu Fansi [Looking Back and Reflecting on Fifty Days]*. Beijing: Gaodeng Jiaoyu Chubanshe, 1989.

"Guruduth Banavar." *LinkedIn*, accessed February 11, 2016. www.linkedin.com/in/banavar.

Haddal, Chad C. *Foreign Students in the United States: Policies and Legislation*. Washington, DC: Congressional Research Service, 2008.

Haggard, Stephan. "The Institutional Foundations of Hegemony: Explaining the Reciprocal Trade Agreements Act of 1934." *International Organization* 42, no. 1 (1988): 91–119.

Hahm, Jung S. "American Competitiveness and Workforce Improvement Act of 1998: Balancing Economic and Labor Interests Under the New H-1B Visa Program." *Cornell Law Review* 85 (1999): 1673–1701.

Hainmueller, Jens, and Michael J. Hiscox. "Attitudes Toward Highly Skilled and Low-Skilled Immigration: Evidence from a Survey Experiment." *American Political Science Review* 104, no. 1 (February 2010): 61.

Hannas, William C., James Mulvenon, and Anna B. Puglisi. *Chinese Industrial Espionage: Technology Acquisition and Military Modernization*. New York: Routledge, 2013.

Hart, David. "High-Tech Learns to Play the Washington Game, or the Political Education of Bill Gates and Other Nerds." In *Interest Group Politics*, edited by Allan J. Cigler and Burdett Loomis. 6th ed. Washington, DC: CQ, 2002.

——. "New Economy, Old Politics: The Evolving Role of the High-Technology Industry in Washington, D.C." In *Governance amid Bigger, Better Markets*, edited by Joseph S. Nye and John D. Donahue, 235–65. Washington, DC: Brookings Institution, 2004.

——. "Red, White, and 'Big Blue': IBM and the Business–Government Interface in the United States, 1956–2000." *Enterprise and Society* 8, no. 1 (2007): 1–34.

Hart, David M. "'Business' Is Not an Interest Group: On the Study of Companies in American National Politics." *Annual Review of Political Science* 7 (2004): 47–69.

——. "Political Representation in Concentrated Industries: Revisiting the 'Olsonian Hypothesis.'" *Business and Politics* 5, no. 3 (2003): 261–86.

——. "Understanding Immigration in a National Systems of Innovation Framework." *Science & Public Policy* 34, no. 1 (2007): 45–53.

Hattori, James. "Intel Plans for Future." CNN, September 14, 2002.

Hawthorne, Lesleyanne. "The Growing Global Demand for Students as Skilled Migrants." Washington, DC: Migration Policy Institute, 2008. www.migrationpolicy.org/sites/default/files/publications/intlstudents_0.pdf.

Heath, Jena. "Congressman Switches Focus to High-Tech: Republican, New to Area, Softens Immigration Stance, Trumpets Tech." *Austin American-Statesman*, July 7, 2002.

Helpman, Elhanan. *The Mystery of Economic Growth*. Cambridge, MA: Harvard University Press,

2004.

Hempel, Jessi. "DOD Head Ashton Carter Enlists Silicon Valley to Transform the Military." *Wired*, November 18, 2015. www.wired.com/2015/11/secretary-of-defense-ashton-carter/.

Henderson, Richard M., and Kim B. Clark. "Architectural Innovation: The Reconfiguration of Existing Product Technologies and the Failure of Established Firms." *Administrative Science Quarterly* 35, no. 1 (March 1990): 9–30.

Heppenheimer, T. A. *Turbulent Skies: The History of Commercial Aviation*. New York: Wiley, 1995.

Hicks, Raymond, Helen V. Milner, and Dustin Tingley. "Trade Policy, Economic Interests, and Party Politics in a Developing Country: The Political Economy of CAFTA-DR." *Interna- tional Studies Quarterly* 58, no. 1 (March 2014): 106–17.Hiebert, Murray. "United States: The Cost of Security." *The Far Eastern Economic Review*, November 28, 2002.

Higgins, John K. "Proposed 2016 Federal Budget Plumps IT Spending by $2B." *E-Commerce Times*, March 11, 2015. www.ecommercetimes.com/story/81805.html.

High Level Committee on the Indian Diaspora. "The Indian Diaspora." New Delhi: Ministry of External Affairs, 2001. http://indiandiaspora.nic.in/contents.htm.

Hira, Ron. "Implications of Offshore Outsourcing." Paper presented at the Globalization, Employment, and Economic Development Workshop. Sloan Workshop Series in Industry Studies, Rockport, MA, January 3, 2004.

Hira, Ronil. Testimony. *Hearing Before the Senate Judiciary Committee on the Border Security, Economic Opportunity, and Immigration Modernization Act, S.744*. 113th Cong. (April 22, 2013).

———. "New Data Show How Firms Like Infosys and Tata Abuse the H-1B Program." *Economic Policy Institute*, February 19, 2015. www.epi.org/blog/new-data-infosys-tata-abuse-h-1b-program/.

———. "U.S. Immigration Regulations and India's Information Technology Industry." *Technological Forecasting and Social Change* 71, no. 8 (October 2004): 837–54. "Hispanic Business Magazine Includes Twelve NCLR Affiliates Among Its Top Twenty-Five Nonprofit." *Targeted News Service*, June 9, 2011.

Hollifield, James F. "The Emerging Migration State." International Migration Review 38, no. 3 (2004): 885–912.

Holyoke, Thomas T. "The Interest Group Effect on Citizen Contact with Congress." *Party Politics* 19, no. 6 (November 1, 2013): 925–44.

Hook, Janet. "Tea Party Faces Test of Its Clout in Primaries." *Wall Street Journal*, February 25, 2014. Horowitz, Daniel. "Gang Immigration Bill (S.744) Is Comprehensively Flawed." *Madison Project*. May 1, 2013. http://madisonproject.com/2013/05/gang-immigration-bill-s-744-is-comprehensively-flawed/.

Horowitz, Jason. "Marco Rubio Pushed for Immigration Reform with Conservative Media." *New York Times*, February 27, 2016. www.nytimes.com/2016/02/28/us/politics/marco-rubio-pushed-for-immigration-reform-with-conservative-media.html.

Horowitz, Michael C. *The Diffusion of Military Power: Causes and Consequences for International Politics*. Princeton, NJ: Princeton University Press, 2010.

Hounshell, David A., and John Kenly Smith. *Science and Corporate Strategy: Du Pont R&D, 1902–1980*. Cambridge: Cambridge University Press, 1988.

"House Dems, AFL-CIO Discuss H-1B Visas." *Congress Daily*, March 14, 2000.

Hufbauer, Gary Clyde, Theodore H. Moran, and Lindsay Oldenski. *Outward Foreign Direct Investment and US Exports, Jobs, and R&D: Implications for US Policy*. Washington, DC: Peterson Institute for International Economics, 2013.

Hughes, Llewelyn. *Globalizing Oil: Firms and Oil Market Governance in France, Japan, and the United States*. New York: Cambridge University Press, 2014.

Humphery-Jenner, Mark, and Jo-Ann Suchard. "Foreign Venture Capitalists and the Internationalization of Entrepreneurial Companies: Evidence from China." *Journal of International Business Studies* 44, no. 6 (2013): 607–21.

IBM. "IBM Research: Global Labs." *IBM*, accessed April 3, 2015. www.research.ibm.com/labs/.

"IEEE Advocates Limits on Offshore Outsourcing." *Information Week*, March 15, 2004. www.informationweek.com/ieee-advocates-limits-on-offshore-outsourcing/d/d-id/1023812.

Ikenberry, G. John. *After Victory: Institutions, Strategic Restraint, and the Rebuilding of Order after Major Wars*. Princeton, NJ: Princeton University Press, 2001.

Ikenberry, G. John, David A. Lake, and Michael Mastanduno. "Introduction: Approaches to Explaining American Foreign Economic Policy." In *The State and American Foreign Economic Policy*, edited by G. John Ikenberry and David A. Lake. Ithaca, NY: Cornell University Press, 1988. "India May Drag US to WTO for Hiking H-1B Visa Fee." *Times of India*, August 17, 2010. http://timesofindia.indiatimes.com/business/india-business/India-may-drag-US-to-WTO-for-hiking-H-1B-visa-fee/articleshow/6325497.cms.

Information Technology Industry Council. "ITI on Trump Tax Reform Principles," *Information Technology Industry Council*, April 26, 2017. www.itic.org/news-events/news-releases/iti-on-trump-tax-reform-principles.

Institute for International Education. "International Student Totals by Place of Origin, 2013/14–2014/15." *Open Doors Report on International Educational Exchange*, 2015. www.iie.org/Research-and-Publications/Open-Doors/Data/International-Students/All-Places-of-Origin/2013-15.

——. "Open Doors Data: Fast Facts." *Institute for International Education*, 2014. www.iie.org/Research-and-Publications/Open-Doors/Data/Fast-Facts.

——. "Top Twenty-Five Places of Origin of International Students, 2014/15 and 2015/16." *Open Doors Report on International Educational Exchange*. New York: Institute for International Education, 2016. www.iie.org/opendoors.

Institute for Regional Studies. "Silicon Valley Index 2017." *Silicon Valley Indicators*, February 2017. http://jointventure.org/images/stories/pdf/index2017.pdf.

"Intel China Research Center." *Intel*. Accessed May 6, 2014. www.intel.com/cd/corporate/icrc/apac/eng/about/167066.htm.

Jackson, James K. *The Committee on Foreign Investment in the United States (CFIUS)*. Washington, DC: Congressional Research Service, 2014.

Jacobsen, Annie. *Operation Paperclip: The Secret Intelligence Program That Brought Nazi*

Scientists to America. New York: Little, Brown, 2014.

Janardhanan, Arun. "US Move to Lure Science Grads Worries India." *Times of India—Chennai Edition*, February 4, 2013.

Jaruzelski, Barry, Volker Staack, and Aritomo Shinozaki. "2016 Global Innovation 1000 Study." *PwC*. Accessed March 15, 2017. www.strategyand.pwc.com/innovation1000.

———. "Software-as-a-Catalyst." *Strategy+Business*, October 25, 2016. www.strategy-business.com/feature/Software-as-a-Catalyst?gko=7a1ae.

Jensen, J. Bradford. *Global Trade in Services: Fear, Facts, and Offshoring*. Washington, DC: Peterson Institute for International Economics, 2011.

Jeronimides, H. Rosemary. "The H-1B Visa Category: A Tug of War." *Georgetown Immigration Law Journal* 7 (1993): 367–91.

Jischke, Martin. "Addressing the New Reality of Current Visa Policy on International Students and Researchers." Testimony. *Hearing Before the U.S. Senate Committee on Foreign Relations*. 108th Cong. (October 6, 2004). www.gpo.gov/fdsys/search/home.action.

Jobs and Trade Network. "Jobs and Trade Network to Hold Press Luncheon with U.S. Sen. Dodd: National Fair Trade Group to Advocate Against Outsourcing Policies," February 20, 2004. http://epi.3cdn.net/664ff3156937cef731_oom6bxahk.pdf.

John, Sujit. "Cisco Needs to Align with Indian Government's Goals." *Times of India*, July 2, 2014. John, Sujit, and Shilpa Phadnis. "For MNCs, India Still an R&D Hub and It's Growing." *Times of India*, March 2, 2017. http://timesofindia.indiatimes.com/city/bengaluru/for-mncs-india-still-an-rd-hub-and-its-growing/articleshow/57421665.cms.

Johnson, Marlene. Testimony. "Addressing the New Reality of Current Visa Policy on International Students and Researchers." *Hearing Before the U.S. Senate Committee on Foreign Relations*. 108th Cong. (October 6, 2004). www.gpo.gov/fdsys/search/home.action.

Kaar, Robbert van het, and Marianne Grünell. "Industrial Relations in the Information and Communications Technology Sector." *Eurofound*, August 27, 2001. www.eurofound.europa.eu/observatories/eurwork/comparative-information/industrial-relations-in-the-information-and-communications-technology-sector.

Kamieniecki, Sheldon. *Corporate America and Environmental Policy: How Often Does Business Get Its Way?* Stanford, CA: Stanford University Press, 2006.

Kaplan, Rebecca. "How the Tea Party Came Around on Immigration." *National Journal*, March 21, 2013.

Kapur, Devesh. *Diaspora, Development, and Democracy: The Domestic Impact of International Migration from India*. Princeton, NJ: Princeton University Press, 2010.

———. "Indian Higher Education." In *American Universities in a Global Market*, edited by Charles T. Clotfelter, 305–34. Chicago: University of Chicago Press, 2010.

Kelly, Kate, Rachel Abrams, and Alan Rappeport. "Trump Is Said to Abandon Contentious Border Tax on Imports." *New York Times*, April 25, 2017. www.nytimes.com/2017/04/25/us/politics/orrin-hatch-trump-tax-cuts-deficit-economy.html.

Kennedy, Andrew B. "China's Search for Renewable Energy: Pragmatic Techno-Nationalism." *Asian Survey* 53, no. 5 (2013): 909–30.

———. "India's Nuclear Odyssey: Implicit Umbrellas, Diplomatic Disappointments, and the Bomb." *International Security* 36, no. 2 (2011): 120–53.

———. *The International Ambitions of Mao and Nehru: National Efficacy Beliefs and the Making of Foreign Policy*. New York: Cambridge University Press, 2012.

———. "Powerhouses or Pretenders? Debating China's and India's Emergence as Technological Powers." *The Pacific Review* 28, no. 2 (2015): 281–302.

———. "Slouching Tiger, Roaring Dragon: Comparing India and China as Late Innovators." Review of International Political Economy 23, no. 2 (2016): 1–28.

———. "Unequal Partners: U.S. Collaboration with China and India in Research and Development." Political Science Quarterly 132, no. 1 (2017).

Kennedy, Paul. The Rise and Fall of the Great Powers. New York: Vintage, 1987.

Keohane, Robert O. "The Old IPE and the New." Review of Inter*national Political Economy* 16, no. 1 (2009): 34–46.

"Kerry Tax Plan Proposes to Slow Loss of US Jobs Overseas." *Dow Jones International News*, March 26, 2004.

Kessler, Glen, and Kevin Sullivan. "Powell Cautious About Immigration Changes." *Washington Post*, November 10, 2004.

Khadria, Binod. "Brain Drain, Brain Gain, India." In *The Encyclopedia of Global Human Migrtion*, edited by Immanuel Ness, 743–49. New York: Wiley-Blackwell, 2013.

Khimm, Suzy. "Why a Rare Bipartisan Consensus on Immigration Totally Fell Apart." *Washington Post*, September 21, 2012. www.washingtonpost.com/blogs/ezra-klein/wp/2012/09/21/why-a-rare-bipartisan-consensus-on-immigration-totally-fell-apart/.

Kiely, Kathy. "Immigration Overhaul Crumbles in Senate Vote." *USA Today*, June 29, 2007.

Kim, Dong Jung. "Cutting Off Your Nose? A Reigning Power's Commercial Containment of a Military Challenger." Ph.D. diss., University of Chicago, 2015.

———. "Trading with the Enemy? The Futility of US Commercial Countermeasures Against the Chinese Challenge." *Pacific Review*, November 2, 2016, 1–20.

Kim, In Song. "Political Cleavages Within Industry: Firm Level Lobbying for Trade Liberalization." *American Political Science Review* 111 (2017): 1–20.

Kim, Linsu. *Imitation to Innovation: The Dynamics of Korea's Technological Learning*. Cambridge, MA: Harvard Business Press, 1997.

Kim, Sung-Young. "Transitioning from Fast-Follower to Innovator: The Institutional Foundations of the Korean Telecommunications Sector." *Review of International Political Economy* 19, no. 1 (February 2012): 140–68.

Kimball, David C., Frank R. Baumgartner, Jeffrey M. Berry, Marie Hojnacki, Beth L. Leech, and Bryce Summary. "Who Cares About the Lobbying Agenda?" *Interest Groups & Advocacy* 1, no. 1 (May 2012): 5–25.

Kindleberger, Charles Poor. *The World in Depression, 1929–1939*. Berkeley: University of California Press, 1973.

King, Neil, and Elizabeth Williamson. "Business Fends Off Tax Hit: Obama Administration Shelves Plan to Change How U.S. Treats Overseas Profits." *Wall Street Journal*, October 13,

2009.

Kocieniski, David. "For Trenton's Lame Duck, the Question Is, 'How Lame?'" *New York Times*, September 12, 2004.

Koehn, Peter H. "Developments in Transnational Research Linkages: Evidence from US Higher-Education Activity." *Journal of New Approaches in Educational Research* 3, no. 2 (2014): 52–58.

Koffler, Keith. "Business Coalition Rewrites Lexicon for Jobs 'Outsourcing.'" *Congress Daily*, March 2, 2004.

Kollman, Ken. *Outside Lobbying: Public Opinion and Interest Group Strategies*. Princeton, NJ: Princeton University Press, 1998.

KPMG and CB Insights. *Venture Pulse 2016*. New York: CB Insights, April 13, 2016. https://www.cbinsights.com/research-venture-capital-Q1-2016.

Krasner, Stephen D. "State Power and the Structure of International Trade." *World Politics* 28, no. 3 (1976): 317–47.

Krause, Reinhardt. "Tech Firms Pushing for More H-1B Visas for Skilled Workers." *Investor's Business Daily*, April 11, 2007.

Kudrle, Robert T., and Davis B. Bobrow. "U.S. Policy Toward Foreign Direct Investment." *World Politics* 34, no. 3 (April 1982): 353–79.

Kumar, Nirmalya, and Phanish Puranam. *India Inside: The Emerging Innovation Challenge to the West*. Cambridge, MA: Harvard Business Press, 2012.

Kuptsch, Christiane, and Eng Fong Pang. "Introduction." In *Competing for Global Talent*, edited by Christiane Kuptsch and Eng Fong Pang, 1–8. Geneva: International Labor Office, 2006.

Lake, David A. "Leadership, Hegemony, and the International Economy: Naked Emperor or Tattered Monarch with Potential?" *International Studies Quarterly* 37, no. 4 (December 1993): 459.

——. "Open Economy Politics: A Critical Review." *The Review of International Organizations* 4, no. 3 (September 2009): 219–44.

Lampton, David M. *A Relationship Restored: Trends in U.S.–China Educational Exchanges, 1978–1984*. Washington, DC: National Academies Press, 1986.

Landes, David S. *The Unbound Prometheus: Technological Change and Industrial Development in Western Europe from 1750 to the Present*. Cambridge: Cambridge University Press, 2003.

Lane, Jason, and Kevin Kinser. "Is Today's University the New Multinational Corporation?" *The Conversation*, June 5, 2015. http://theconversation.com/is-todays-university-the-new-multinational-corporation-40681.

Lawrence, Jill. "The Myth of Marco Rubio's Immigration Problem." *National Journal*, July 15, 2013.

Lazonick, William. *Sustainable Prosperity in the New Economy? Business Organization and High-Tech Employment in the United States*. Kalamazoo, MI: W. E. Upjohn Institute, 2009.

Leibovich, Mark. "High Tech Is King of the Hill." *Washington Post*, October 16, 1998.

Lewin, Tamar. "Foreign Students Bring Cash, and Changes: U.S. Colleges Welcome Funds, but Some In-State Applicants Feel Left Out." *International Herald Tribune*, February 6, 2012.

Liberto, Jennifer, and Dana Bash. "Bill to Hike Taxes on Overseas Jobs Fails Senate Test Vote."

CNN, September 28, 2010. http://money.cnn.com/2010/09/28/news/economy/Outsource_jobs_bill_dead/.

Lieberman, Joseph I. *Offshore Outsourcing and America's Competitive Edge: Losing Out in the High Technology R&D and Services Sectors*. Washington, DC: Office of Senator Joseph I. Lieberman, May 11, 2004.

Lipton, Eric, and Somini Sengupta. "Latest Product of Tech Firms: Immigrant Bill." *New York Times*, May 5, 2013.

Lissardy, Gerardo. "Leading Hispanic Group Joins Immigrant-Rights Coalition." *EFE News Service*, May 12, 2006.

Liu, Charlotte, Nick Campbell, Ed Gerstner, Amy Lin, Piao Li, Stephen Pincock, Chandler Gibbons, et al. "Turning Point: Chinese Science in Transition." Shanghai: Nature Publishing Group, November 2015. www.nature.com/press_releases/turning_point.pdf.

Liu, Hong, and Els van Dongen. "China's Diaspora Policies as a New Mode of Transnational Governance." *Journal of Contemporary China* 25, no. 102 (2016): 1–17.

Lizza, Ryan. "Getting to Maybe." *New Yorker*, June 24, 2013. www.newyorker.com/magazine/2013/06/24/getting-to-maybe.

Lochhead, Carolyn. "Bill to Boost Tech Visas Sails Through Congress." *San Francisco Chronicle*, October 4, 2000. www.sfgate.com/news/article/Bill-to-Boost-Tech-Visas-Sails-Through-Congress-2735682.php.

———. "Visa Plan Angers Silicon Valley." *SFGate*, June 7, 2007. www.sfgate.com/politics/article/VISA-PLAN-ANGERS-SILICON-VALLEY-Immigration-2588829.php.

Lohr, Steve. "Many New Causes for Old Problem of Jobs Lost Abroad." *New York Times*, February 15, 2004.

———. "New Economy; Offshore Jobs in Technology: Opportunity or a Threat?" *New York Times*, December 22, 2003. www.nytimes.com/2003/12/22/business/new-economy-offshore-jobs-in-technology-opportunity-or-a-threat.html.

Lopez, Mark Hugo. "The Hispanic Vote in the 2008 Election." *Pew Research Center*, November 5, 2008. www.pewhispanic.org/2008/11/05/the-hispanic-vote-in-the-2008-election/.

"Lott Wants Agreement with Dems on H-1B Visa Measure." *Congress Daily*, September 14, 2000.

Lucas, Louise. "US Concerns Grow Over Chinese Chip Expansion." Financial Times, January 16, 2017. www.ft.com/content/fb2e4454-c36e-11e6-9bca-2b93a6856354.

Ludden, Jennifer. "Strange Bedfellows Join Forces for Immigration Reform." *National Public Radio: All Things Considered*, January 19, 2006.

Lundvall, Bengt-Åke. *National Systems of Innovation: Toward a Theory of Innovation and Interactive Learning*. London: Pinter, 1992.

Lynch, David J. "Does Tax Code Encourage U.S. Companies to Cut Jobs at Home? Presidential Candidates Target Corporate Tax Breaks for Offshoring." USA Today, March 21, 2008.

Ma, Chi. "Famous Science Projects Face Axe in Funding Overhaul." China Daily, January 8, 2015. www.chinadaily.com.cn/china/2015-01/08/content_19275863.htm.

Madden, Mike. "Millions Spent Lobbying on Immigration in Last Congress." *Gannett News*

Service, January 26, 2007.

Malhotra, Neil, Yotam Margalit, and Cecilia Hyunjung Mo. "Economic Explanations for Opposition to Immigration: Distinguishing Between Prevalence and Conditional Impact." American Journal of Political Science 57, no. 2 (April 2013): 391–410.

Mansfield, Edward D., and Diana C. Mutz. "US Versus Them: Mass Attitudes Toward Offshore Outsourcing." *World Politics* 65, no. 4 (2013): 571–608.

Mansfield, Edward D., and Brian Pollins. "Interdependence and Conflict: An Introduction." In *Economic Interdependence and International Conflict: New Perspectives on an Enduring Debate*, edited by Edward D. Mansfield and Brian Pollins. Ann Arbor: University of Michigan Press, 2003.

Marin, Anabel, and Subash Sasidharan. "Heterogeneous MN Subsidiaries and Technological Spillovers: Explaining Positive and Negative Effects in India." *Research Policy* 39, no. 9 (November 2010): 1227–41.

Marro, Nick. "Foreign Company R&D: In China, for China." *China Business Review*, June 1, 2015.

Marsan, Carolyn Duffy. "A Political Hot Potato: Legislatures Juggle Offshore Outsourcing Regulations." *Network World*, July 5, 2004.

Marschall, Daniel, and Laura Clawson. *Sending Jobs Overseas: The Cost to America's Economy and Working Families*. Washington, DC: Working America and the AFL-CIO, 2010.

Mastanduno, Michael. *Economic Containment: CoCom and the Politics of East–West Trade*. Ithaca, NY: Cornell University Press, 1992.

Matloff, Norman. "On the Need for Reform of the H-1B Non-immigrant Work Visa in Computer-Related Occupations." University of Michigan Journal of Law Reform 36, no. 4 (Fall 2003): 815–914.

McConnell, Mitch. (KY). "Immigration." *Congressional Record*, 110th Cong., 153, no. 106 (June 28, 2007): S8674.

"McGreevey Edict Restricts Outsourcing by Agencies." *Congress Daily*, September 13, 2004.

McGreevey, James E. *The Confession*. New York: Harper Collins, 2006.

McKinnon, John D. "Plan Would Raise Taxes on Businesses." *Wall Street Journal*, February 2, 2010. www.wsj.com/articles/SB10001424052748704107204575039073372259004.

Mearsheimer, John J. *The Tragedy of Great Power Politics*. New York: W. W. Norton, 2001.

Meckler, Laura. "House Immigration Bills Are Still in the Mix." *Wall Street Journal*, April 18, 2014. www.wsj.com/articles/SB10001424052702304626304579508091839546088.

——. "Immigration-Bill Pressure Backfires; Overhaul Backers Target Majority Whip, but Tactic Provokes Response from Opponents." *Wall Street Journal*, December 25, 2013. www.wsj.com/articles/SB10001424052702304244904579276403694719232.

——. "Visas Could Aid Graduates." *Wall Street Journal*, October 22, 2011.

Meijer, Hugo. *Trading with the Enemy: The Making of US Export Control Policy Toward the People's Republic of China*. Oxford: Oxford University Press, 2016.

Menz, Georg. *The Political Economy of Managed Migration: Nonstate Actors, Europeanization, and the Politics of Designing Migration Policies*. Oxford: Oxford University Press, 2008.

Meyers, Jessica. "Tech Companies See Few Big Gains in Obama's Executive Action." *Boston Globe*, November 24, 2014. www.bostonglobe.com/news/nation/2014/11/24/tech-companies-see-few-big-gains-obama-executive-action/dauDJujkOhe1qx5ZQTScoM/story.html.

Milbank, Dana. "Jabs and All, the Ides of March Arrives Late." *Washington Post*, June 29, 2007.

Miller, Matthew. "Spy Scandal Weighs on U.S. Tech Firms in China, Cisco Takes Hit." Reuters. November 14, 2013. www.reuters.com/article/2013/11/14/us-china-cisco-idUSBRE9AD0J420131114.

Milner, Helen V. *Resisting Protectionism: Global Industries and the Politics of International Trade*.

Princeton, NJ: Princeton University Press, 1988.

Milner, Helen, and David B. Yoffie. "Between Free Trade and Protectionism: Strategic Trade Policy and a Theory of Corporate Trade Demands." *International Organization* 43, no. 2 (Spring 1989): 239–72.

Milton, Laurie P. "An Identity Perspective on the Propensity of High-Tech Talent to Unionize." Journal of Labor Research 24, no. 1 (2003): 31–53.

Mitchell, Brian. "Frist's Border Control-Only Bill Spurs Broad Immigration Deals." Investor's Business Daily, March 20, 2006.

Modelski, George, and William R. Thompson. *Leading Sectors and World Powers: The Coevolution of Global Politics and Economics*. Columbia, SC: University of South Carolina Press, 1996.

Modi, Narendra. "Modi Speaks in San Jose: The Indian Prime Minister in His Own Words." SiliconValleyOneWorld, September 27, 2015. www.siliconvalleyoneworld.com/2015/09/30/modi-speaks-in-san-jose-the-indian-prime-minister-in-his-own-words/.

——. "PM's Address to the Nation from the Ramparts of the Red Fort on the Sixty-Eighth Independence Day," August 15, 2014. http://pmindia.gov.in/en/news_updates/text-of-pms-address-in-hindi-to-the-nation-from-the-ramparts-of-the-red-fort-on-the-68th-independence-day/.

——. "PM's Speech to 104th Session of the Indian Science Congress, Tirupati (Full Text)." *Microfinance Monitor*, January 3, 2017. www.microfinancemonitor.com/pms-speech-to-104th-session-of-the-indian-science-congress-tirupati-full-text/43799.

——. "Text of PM Shri Narendra Modi's Address at the 102nd Indian Science Congress." *Official Website of Narendra Modi*, January 3, 2015. www.narendramodi.in/text-of-pm-shri-narendra-modis-address-at-the-102nd-indian-science-congress.

Moe, Espen. *Governance, Growth and Global Leadership: The Role of the State in Technological Progress, 1750–2000*. Hampshire, UK: Ashgate, 2013.

——. "Mancur Olson and Structural Economic Change: Vested Interests and the Industrial Rise and Fall of the Great Powers." *Review of International Political Economy* 16, no. 2 (June 26, 2009): 202–30.

Mokyr, Joel. *The Lever of Riches: Technological Creativity and Economic Progress*. New York: Oxford University Press, 1990.

Moravcsik, Andrew. "Liberal Theories of International Law." In *Interdisciplinary Perspectives on International Law and International Relations: The State of the Art*, edited by Jeffrey L. Dunoff and Mark A. Pollack, 83–118. Cambridge: Cambridge University Press, 2013.

——. "Taking Preferences Seriously: A Liberal Theory of International Politics." *International Organization* 51, no. 4 (1997): 513–53.

Morrison, Bruce. Testimony. *Hearing Before the Committee on the Judiciary of the United States House of Representatives Subcommittee on Immigration Policy and Enforcement.* 113th Cong. (March 5, 2013).

Morrison, James Ashley. "Before Hegemony: Adam Smith, American Independence, and the Origins of the First Era of Globalization." *International Organization* 66, no. 3 (2012): 395–428.

Moscoso, Eunice. "Once Gung-Ho, Businesses See Flaws in Immigration Bill: Tech Sector Particularly Disturbed by Potential Changes in Visa Program." *The Atlanta Journal-Constitution*, June 3, 2007.

Moser, Petra, Alessandra Voena, and Fabian Waldinger. "German Jewish Émigrés and US Invention." *The American Economic Review* 104, no. 10 (2014): 3222–55.

Mowery, David C., and Nathan Rosenberg. "The U.S. National Innovation System." In *National Innovation Systems: A Comparative Analysis*, edited by Richard R. Nelson, 29–75. Oxford: Oxford University Press, 1993.

Mowery, David. C., and Bhaven N. Sampat, "Universities in National Innovation Systems." In *The Oxford Handbook of Innovation*, edited by Jan Fagerberg, David Mowery, and Richard R. Nelson. Oxford: Oxford University Press, 2006.

Mrinalini, N., Pradosh Nath, and G. D. Sandhya. "Foreign Direct Investment in R&D in India." *Current Science* 105, no. 6 (September 2013): 767–73.

Mueller, Dennis C. "First-Mover Advantages and Path Dependence." *International Journal of Industrial Organization* 15, no. 6 (October 1997): 827–50.

Mufson, Steven. "Once a Recession Remedy, GM's Empire Falls." *Washington Post*, June 2, 2009.

Mukem, Anne C. "Firebrand Tancredo Puts Policy Over Party Line." *Denver Post*, November 27, 2005.

Munoz, Sara Schaefer. "Firms Push to Expand Visa Program." Wall Street Journal, March 11, 2004.

Munro, Neil. "IT Industry, Hispanics Team Up On Immigration." National Journal, April 9, 2010.

Murmann, Johann Peter, and Ralph Landau. "On the Making of Competitive Advantage: The Development of the Chemical Industry in Britain and Germany Since 1850." In Chemicals and Long-Term Economic Growth: Insights from the Chemical Industry, edited by Ashish Arora, Ralph Landau, and Nathan Rosenberg, 27–70. New York: Wiley, 1998.

Murphy, Caryle, and Nurith C. Aizenman. "Foreign Students Navigate Labyrinth of New Laws: Slip-Ups Overlooked Before 9/11 Now Grounds for Deportation." *Washington Post*, June 9, 2003.

Murphy, Colum, and Lilian Lin. "For China's Jobseekers, Multinational Companies Lose Their Magic." *Wall Street Journal*, April 3, 2014. http://blogs.wsj.com/chinarealtime/2014/04/03/for-chinas-jobseekers-multinational-companies-lose-their-magic/?mod=chinablog.

Murray, Michael A. "Defining the Higher Education Lobby." *The Journal of Higher Education* 47, no. 1 (January 1976): 79–92.

Murray, Shailagh. "Careful Strategy Is Used to Derail Immigration Bill." *Washington Post*, June 8, 2007.

———. "In Senate and on Trail, Democrats Target Jobs Moving Abroad." *Washington Post*, June 9, 2010.

Nakamura, David. "Conservatives Split on Immigration Bill's Price Tag." *Washington Post*, May 7, 2013.

Narula, Rajneesh, and Antonello Zanfei. "Globalization of Innovation: The Role of Multinational Enterprises." In *The Oxford Handbook of Innovation*, edited by Jan Fagerberg, David C. Mowery, and Richard R. Nelson, 318–45. Oxford: Oxford University Press, 2005.

National Council of La Raza. 2011 Annual Report. Washington, DC: National Council of La Raza, 2011. http://publications.nclr.org/handle/123456789/2.

National Foundation for American Policy. *NFAP Policy Brief: Anti-outsourcing Efforts Down but Not Out*. Arlington, VA: National Foundation for American Policy, April 2007. www.nfap.com/pdf/0407OutsourcingBrief.pdf.

National Science Foundation. *Science and Engineering Indicators 2004*. Arlington, VA: National Science Foundation, 2004.

———. *Science and Engineering Indicators 2012*. Arlington, VA: National Science Foundation, 2012.

———. *Science and Engineering Indicators 2014*. Arlington, VA: National Science Foundation, 2014.

———. *Science and Engineering Indicators 2016*. Arlington, VA: National Science Foundation, 2016.

———. "Table 53: Doctorate Recipients with Temporary Visas Intending to Stay in the United States After Doctorate Receipt, by Country of Citizenship: 2007–13." *Science and Engineering Doctorates*, December 2014. www.nsf.gov/statistics/sed/2013/data-tables.cfm.

Naujoks, Daniel. *Migration, Citizenship, and Development: Diasporic Membership Policies and Overseas Indians in the United States*. New Delhi: Oxford University Press, 2013.

"Navigating China's Tech Jungle." *Business Times*, September 1, 2012.

Nelson, David, and Susan Webb Yackee. "Lobbying Coalitions and Government Policy Change: An Analysis of Federal Agency Rulemaking." *The Journal of Politics* 74, no. 2 (2012): 339–53.

Nelson, Richard R., ed. *National Innovation Systems: A Comparative Analysis*. Oxford: Oxford University Press, 1993.

"New Jersey Governor Quits, Comes Out as Gay." *CNN*, August 13, 2004. http://edition.cnn.com/2004/ALLPOLITICS/08/12/mcgreevey.nj/.

"NumbersUSA Activists Squash Amnesty in Senate: Senate Rejects Cloture on Amnesty Bill 46–53." *PR Newswire*, June 28, 2007.

"Obama Assures Modi on Concerns Over H-1B Visa Issue." *Times of India*, January 26, 2015. http://timesofindia.indiatimes.com/india/Obama-assures-Modi-on-concerns-over-H-1B-visa-issue/articleshow/46022377.cms.

Obama, Barack. "Remarks of President Barack Obama: Address to Joint Session of Congress." *Whitehouse.gov*, February 24, 2009. www.whitehouse.gov/the-press-office/remarks-president-barack-obama-address-joint-session-congress.

———. "Statement of Administration Policy: H.R. 6429—STEM Jobs Act of 2012." *American Presidency Project*, November 28, 2012. www.presidency.ucsb.edu/ws/?pid=102707.

"Obama Lowers Temperature Against Outsourcing." *Economic Times*, March 28, 2009.

O'Connor, Patrick. "Anti-immigration Group Up Against Unusual Coalition." *The Hill*, February 28, 2006.

Office of the Press Secretary. "Fact Sheet: Immigration Accountability Executive Action." *White House*, November 20, 2014. https://obamawhitehouse.archives.gov/the-press-office/2014/11/20/fact-sheet-immigration-accountability-executive-action.

———. "Leveling the Playing Field: Curbing Tax Havens and Removing Tax Incentives for Shift- ing Jobs Overseas." *White House*. Accessed March 26, 2015. https://www.whitehouse.gov/node/2739.

Olson, Elizabeth. "Congress Raises Limit on Skilled-Work Visas." *International Herald Tribune*, November 24, 2004.

Olson, Mancur. *The Rise and Decline of Nations: Economic Growth, Stagflation, and Social Rigidities*. New Haven, CT: Yale University Press, 1982.

"One Year of Startup India: Report Card." *TechCircle*, January 16, 2017.

Organisation for Economic Co-operation and Development (OECD). *Education at a Glance 2014: OECD Indicators*. Paris: OECD, 2014.

———. *The Measurement of Scientific and Technological Activities (Oslo Manual)*. Paris: OECD, 1997.

———. "Population." *OECD.Stat*, March 23, 2016. http://stats.oecd.org/Index.aspx?DatasetCode=POP_FIVE_HIST.

O'Riain, Sean. *The Politics of High Tech Growth: Developmental Network States in the Global Economy*. Cambridge: Cambridge University Press, 2004.

"ORISE Workforce Studies Infographics—StayRates." *Oak Ridge Institute for Science and Education*, March 31, 2017. https://public.tableau.com/views/ORISEWorkforceStudiesInfographics-StayRates-mobilefriendly/5-YearStayRates?%3Aembed=y&%3AshowVizHome=no&%3Adisplay_count=y&%3Adisplay_static_image=y&%3AbootstrapWhenNotified=true.

Orleans, Leo A. "China's Changing Attitude Toward the Brain Drain and Policy Toward Returning Students." *China Exchange News* 17, no. 2 (1989): 2–5.

Papademetriou, Demetrios G., and Stephen Yale-Loehr. "Balancing Interests: Rethinking U.S. Selection of Skilled Immigrants." Washington, DC: Carnegie Endowment for International Peace, 1996.

Park, Haeyoun. "How Outsourcing Companies Are Gaming the Visa System." *New York Times*, November 10, 2015.

Paul, Joseph G., and Frank Caruso. "One of Trump's Biggest Plans to Stimulate the Economy Won't Be Great for Most Americans." *Business Insider*, June 1, 2017. www.businessinsider.com.au/alliancebernstein-on-trump-tax-plan-2017-5?r=US&IR=T.

Paulson, Amanda, Faye Bowers, and Daniel Wood. "To Immigrants, US Reform Bill Is Unrealistic." *Christian Science Monitor*, May 21, 2007.

Pavitt, Keith. "Innovation Processes." In *The Oxford Handbook of Innovation*, edited by Jan Fagerberg, David Mowery, and Richard R. Nelson. Oxford: Oxford University Press, 2006.

Pear, Robert. "Clinton Asks Congress to Raise the Limit on Visas for Skilled Workers." *New York Times*, May 12, 2000.

——. "Little-Known Group Claims a Win on Immigration." *New York Times*, July 15, 2007.

——. "U.S. High-Tech Firms Stymied on Immigration for Skilled Workers." *New York Times*, June 25, 2007. www.nytimes.com/2007/06/25/technology/25iht-visas.4.6326165.html.

Peters, Margaret E. "Trade, Foreign Direct Investment, and Immigration Policy Making in the United States." *International Organization* 68, no. 4 (2014): 811–44.

Peterson, Brenton D., Sonal S. Pandya, and David Leblang. "Doctors with Borders: Occupational Licensing as an Implicit Barrier to High Skill Migration." *Public Choice* 160, no. 1–2 (July 2014): 45–63.

Phillips, Kate. "Business Lobbyists Call for Action on Immigration." *New York Times*, April 15, 2006. www.nytimes.com/2006/04/15/us/15lobby.html.

Pietrucha, Bill. "Labor Challenges High Tech Job Shortage Claims." *Newsbytes News Network*, March 19, 1998.

"PM for Reverse Brain Drain of Scientists." *Economic Times*, January 4, 2011. http://articles.economictimes.indiatimes.com/2011-01-04/news/28424740_1_scientists-of-indian-origin-talent-pool-98th-indian-science.

Posner, Michael. "Groups Jockey for Position on Possible Boost in H-1B Visas." *Congress Daily*, November 17, 2004.

Potter, Mark, and Rich Philips. "Six Months after Sept. 11, Hijackers' Visa Approval Letters Received." *CNN*, March 13, 2002. http://edition.cnn.com/2002/US/03/12/inv.flight.school.visas/.

Powell, Colin. "Remarks at the Elliott School of International Affairs." Speech at George Washington University, Washington, DC, September 5, 2003. https://2001-2009.state.gov/secretary/former/powell/remarks/2003/23836.htm.

"Qianren Jihua [Thousand Talents Plan]." Qianren Jihua Wang, 2016. www.1000plan.org/qrjh/section/2.

Qin, Fei. "Global Talent, Local Careers: Circular Migration of Top Indian Engineers and Professionals." *Research Policy* 44, no. 2 (2015): 405–20.

Qualcomm. *Qualcomm Annual Report 2016*. San Diego, CA: Qualcomm, 2016. http://investor.qualcomm.com/annuals-proxies.cfm.

Quan, Xiaohong. "Knowledge Diffusion from MNC R&D Labs in Developing Countries: Evidence from Interaction Between MNC R&D Labs and Local Universities in Beijing." *International Journal of Technology Management* 51, no. 2 (2010): 364–86.

Rao, Nirupama. "America Needs More High-Skilled Worker Visas." *USA Today*, April 14, 2013. www.usatoday.com/story/opinion/2013/04/14/india-trade-technology-column/2075159/.

Ravenhill, John. "The Economics-Security Nexus in the Asia-Pacific region." In *Security Politics in the Asia-Pacific: A Regional-Global Nexus?*, edited by William Tow, 188-207. New York: Cambridge University Press, 2009.

——. "US Economic Relations with East Asia: From Hegemony to Complex Interdependence?"

In *Bush and Asia: America's Evolving Relations with East Asia*, edited by Mark Beeson, 42-63. London: Routledge, 2006.

"RBI Eases Norms for Foreign Investment in Startups." TechCircle, October 21, 2016.

"R&D Technology Center China." GE Lighting Asia Pacific. Accessed April 16, 2014. www.gereveal.ca/LightingWeb/apac/resources/world-of-ge-lighting/research-and-development/china-technology-centre.jsp.

Reinsch, William. "What Is to Be Done on Trade?" *Stimson Spotlight*, June 7, 2016. www.stimson.org/content/what-be-done-trade.

"Rep. Tancredo Slams Senate's Compromise on Amnesty." *U.S. Fed News*, May 11, 2006.

"Research and Development." *General Electric*, 2017. www.ge.com/in/about-us/research-and-development.

Reuveny, Rafael, and William R. Thompson. *Growth, Trade, and Systemic Leadership*. Ann Arbor: University of Michigan Press, 2009.

Robbins, Liz. "New U.S. Rule Extends Stay for Some Foreign Graduates." *New York Times*, March 9, 2016. www.nytimes.com/2016/03/09/nyregion/new-us-rule-extends-stay-for-some-foreign-graduates.html.

Rodriguez, Cindy. "Congress Drops Plan to Bar Foreign Students." *Knight-Ridder Tribune Business News*, November 23, 2001.

——. "Foreign Workers Bill Approved." *Boston Globe*, October 4, 2000.

——. "Proposed Visa Ban Dropped." *Boston Globe*, November 23, 2001.

Romer, Paul M. "Endogenous Technological Change." Journal of Political Economy 98, no. 5 (1990): S71–S102.

Romm, Tony. "Apple Takes Washington." Politico, August 27, 2015. http://politi.co/1Px6AWo.

——. "Finally, Silicon Valley and Donald Trump Agree on Something: Taxes." Recode, April 26, 2017. www.recode.net/2017/4/26/15437330/silicon-valley-tech-donald-trump-agree-tax-repatriation-reform.

——. "How Silicon Valley Is Trying to Topple Trump—Beginning with a Special Election in Montana." *Recode*, May 25, 2017. www.recode.net/2017/5/25/15686802/silicon-valley-trump-montana-tech-for-campaigns.

Rosario, Katherine. "Five Simple Signs the Senate Immigration Bill Is Bad News," April 17, 2013. http://heritageaction.com/2013/04/5-simple-signs-the-senate-immigration-bill-is-bad-news/. Rosenbaum, Jessica F. "Exploiting Dreams: H-1B Visa Fraud, Its Effects, and Potential Solutions." University of Pennsylvania Journal of Business Law 13, no. 3 (2010): 797–816.

Rosenfeld, Steven. "The GOP's Vicious Internal War: Republican Establishment Trying to Exile Tea Partiers and Extremists." *AlterNet*, February 12, 2014. www.alternet.org/tea-party-and-right/gops-vicious-internal-war-republican-establishment-trying-exile-te-partiers-and.

Rothenberg, Stuart. "Heeee's Back: The Fall and Rise of Sen. Trent Lott." *Roll Call*, May 22, 2006.

Roy, Paul. "Impact of U.S. Senate Bill on Outsourcing." *Mondaq Business Briefing*, July 31, 2013. Rubinstein, Ellis. "China's Leader Commits to Global Science and Scientific Exchange." *Science*, October 6, 2000. www.sciencemag.org/careers/2000/10/chinas-leader-commits-global-science-and-scientific-exchange.

Ruhs, Martin. *The Price of Rights: Regulating International Labor Migration.* Princeton, NJ: Princeton University Press, 2013.

Ruiz, Neil G., Jill H. Wilson, and Shyamali Choudhury. "The Search for Skills: Demand for H-1B Immigrant Workers in U.S. Metropolitan Areas." Washington, DC: Brookings Institu- tion, 2012.

Rulon, Richard. "Competing for Foreign Talent." *Legal Intelligencer*, December 15, 2004.

"Ruxuan Zhongguo Qianren Jihua Waizhuan Xiangmu de Zhuanjia Da 381 Ming [Three Hundred Eighty-One Individuals Selected for China's Thousand Talents Foreign Experts Program]." *Kexue Wang [Science Net]*, April 15, 2017. http://news.sciencenet.cn/htmlnews/2017/4/373557.shtm.

Sabato, Larry. *PAC Power: Inside the World of Political Action Committees.* New York: Norton, 1984.

——. *Paying for Elections: The Campaign Finance Thicket.* New York: Priority, 1989.

Saxenian, AnnaLee. *The New Argonauts: Regional Advantage in a Global Economy.* Cambridge, MA: Harvard University Press, 2006.

Sazabo, Joan. "Opening Doors for Immigrants." Nation's Business, August 1, 1989.

Schemo, Diana Jean. "Problems Slow Tracking of Students from Abroad." *New York Times*, March 23, 2003.

Scheve, Kenneth F., and Matthew Jon Slaughter. *Globalization and the Perceptions of American Workers.* Washington, DC: Peterson Institute, 2001.

Schilling, Melissa. "Technology Shocks, Technological Collaboration, and Innovation Out- comes." *Organization Science* 26, no. 3 (May–June 2015): 668–86.

——. "Understanding the Alliance Data." *Strategic Management Journal* 30, no. 3 (2009): 233– 60. Schneider, Greg. "Anxious About Outsourcing; States Try to Stop U.S. Firms from Sending High-Tech Work Overseas." *Washington Post*, January 31, 2004.

Schouten, Fredreka. "Tech Firms Would Skirt Hiring Restrictions Under Deal." *USA Today*, May 21, 2013.

Schreiner, Bruce. "National Group Takes Aim at McConnell on Immigration." *Associated Press*, June 27, 2007.

Schroeder, Michael. "Business Coalition Battles Outsourcing Backlash." *Wall Street Journal*, March 1, 2004. www.wsj.com/articles/SB107809268846542227.

——. "States' Efforts to Curb Outsourcing Stymied: Business Groups Take the Lead in Weakening Attempts to Limit Work from Moving Abroad." *Wall Street Journal*, April 16, 2004.

——. "States Fight Exodus of Jobs: Lawmakers, Unions Seek to Block Outsourcing Overseas." *Wall Street Journal*, June 3, 2003.

Schroeder, Peter. "Extender Efforts Hit Roadblock as Senate Tables Tax Package." *Bond Buyer*, June 28, 2010.

Schröter, Harm G., and Anthony S. Travis. "An Issue of Different Mentalities: National Approaches to the Development of the Chemical Industry in Britain and Germany Before 1914." In *The Chemical Industry in Europe, 1850–1914*, edited by Ernst Homburg, Anthony S. Travis, and Harm G. Schröter, 95–120. Dordrecht, Netherlands: Kluwer, 1998.

Schumpeter, Joseph A. *Business Cycles: A Theoretical, Historical, and Statistical Analysis of the Capitalist Process*. New York: McGraw-Hill, 1939.

Schurenberg, Eric. "Why the Next Steve Jobs Could Be an Indian." *Mint*, October 28, 2011.

Schwaag-Serger, Sylvia. "Foreign Corporate R&D in China: Trends and Policy Issues." In *The New Asian Innovation Dynamics: China and India in Perspective*, edited by Govindan Parayil and Anthony P. D'Costa, 50–78. New York: Palgrave MacMillan, 2009.

Sell, Susan K. *Private Power, Public Law: The Globalization of Intellectual Property Rights*. Cam- bridge: Cambridge University Press, 2003.

Sen, Amiti. "India to Ask US for More H-1B Visas." *Economic Times*, October 19, 2009.

"Sen. Chuck Grassley to Place Hold on Employment-Based Visa Bill." *NumbersUSA*, November 30, 2011. www.numbersusa.com/content/news/november-30-2011/sen-chuck-grassley-place-hold-employment-based-visa-bill.html.

"Senator Feinstein Urges Major Changes in U.S. Student Visa Program." *Advocacy and Public Policymaking*, September 27, 2001. http://lobby.la.psu.edu/_107th/119_Student_Visas_Security/Congressional_Statements/Senate/S_Feinstein_09272001.htm.

"Senator Kerry Delivers Democratic Hispanic Radio Address." U.S. Fed News, April 1, 2006.

Service Contract Requirements for the Performance of Service Contracts Within the United States. Pub. L. No. 2005, c. 92 (New Jersey, 2005). www.njleg.state.nj.us/bills/BillView.asp.

Shachar, Ayelet. "Talent Matters: Immigration Policy-Setting as a Competitive Scramble Among Jurisdictions." In Wanted and Welcome? Policies for Highly Skilled Immigrants in Comparative Perspective, edited by Triadafilos Triadafilopoulos, 85–104. New York: Springer, 2013.

Shackelford, Brandon, and John Jankowski. "Information and Communications Technology Industries Account for $133 Billion of Business R&D Performance in the United States in 2013." *National Center for Science and Engineering Statistics*, April 2016. www.nsf.gov/statistics/2016/nsf16309/nsf16309.pdf.

Sharma, Dinesh C. *The Long Revolution: The Birth and Growth of India's IT Industry*. Noida: Harper Collins, 2009.

Sharma, Shumita. "US Offshore Outsourcing Ban Sparks Fears of Similar Laws." *Dow Jones International Newswires*, January 30, 2004.

Shear, Michael D., and Ashley Parker. "Boehner Is Said to Back Change on Immigration." *New York Times*, January 1, 2014. www.nytimes.com/2014/01/02/us/politics/boehner-is-said-to-back-change-on-immigration.html.

Sherman, Mark. "Feinstein Says Moratorium on Student Visas Ma Not Be Necessary." *Associated Press*, October 6, 2001.

Shesgreen, Deirdre. "Immigration Reform Critics Blast Boehner's Remarks." *Gannett News Service*, April 25, 2014.

Shi, Heping. "Beijing's China Card." *Harper's Magazine*, September 1990.

Shiver, Jube. "Alliance Fights Boost in Visas for Tech Workers." *Los Angeles Times*, August 5, 2000. http://articles.latimes.com/2000/aug/05/business/fi-64994.

Simmons, Joel W. *The Politics of Technological Progress*. Cambridge: Cambridge University Press, 2016. Simon, Denis Fred, and Cong Cao. *China's Emerging Technological Edge: Assessing the Role of High-End Talent*. New York: Cambridge University Press, 2009.

Simons, John. "Impasse on Bill to Boost Visas Persists Between Firms, U.S." *Wall Street Journal*, August 6, 1998.

Simpson, Lori. *Engineering Aspects of Offshore Outsourcing*. Alexandria, VA: National Society of Professional Engineers, August 6, 2004. www.wise-intern.org/journal/2004/wise2004-lorisimpsonfinalpaper.pdf.

Singh, J., and V. V. Krishna. "Trends in Brain Drain, Gain and Circulation: Indian Experience of Knowledge Workers." *Science Technology & Society* 20, no. 3 (November 1, 2015): 300–21.

Smith, Mark A. *American Business and Political Power: Public Opinion, Elections, and Democracy*. Chicago: University of Chicago Press, 2000.

——. "The Mobilization and Influence of Business Interests." In *The Oxford Handbook of American Political Parties and Interest Groups*, edited by L. Sandy Maisel and Jeffrey M. Berry, 451–67. Oxford: Oxford University Press, 2010.

Solon, Olivia. "US Tech Firms Bypassing Pentagon to Protect Deals with China, Strategist Says." *The Guardian*, March 2, 2016. www.theguardian.com/technology/2016/mar/02/us-tech-firms-pentagon-national-security-china-deals.

Southern Poverty Law Center. "John Tanton Is the Mastermind Behind the Organized Anti-immigration Movement." *Intelligence Report*, no. 106 (Summer 2002). www. splcenter.org/get-informed/intelligence-report/browse-all-issues/2002/summer/the-puppeteer?page=0,3.

Stanton, John, and Jennifer Yachnin. "Reid Plots to Block Conservatives." *Roll Call*, June 18, 2007. Startz, Dick. "Sealing the Border Could Block One of America's Crucial Exports: Education." *The Brookings Institution* (January 31, 2017). www.brookings.edu/blog/brown-center-chalkboard/2017/01/31/sealing-the-border-could-block-one-of-americas-crucial-exports-education/.

State Council of the People's Republic of China. "Guojia Zhongchangqi Kexue He Jishu Fazhan Guihua Gangyao (2006–2020 Nian) [National Medium- and Long-Term Program for Science and Technology Development (2006–2020)]," *Zhongguo Zhengfu Menhu Wangzhan [Chinese Government Gateway Website]*, February 9, 2006. www.gov.cn/jrzg/2006-02/09/content_183787.htm.

——. "Guomin Jingji He Shehui Fazhan Dishierge Wunian Guihua Gangyao (Quan Wen) [Compendium of the Twelfth Five-Year Plan for Development of the National Economy and Society (Full Text)]," *Zhongguo Zhengfu Menhu Wangzhan [Chinese Government Gateway Website]*, March 16, 2011. www.gov.cn/2011lh/content_1825838.htm.

——. "Guowuyuan Guanyu Jiakuai Peiyu He Fazhan Zhanluexing Xinxing Chanye de Jueding [State Council Decision on Accelerating the Cultivation and Development of Strategic Emerging Industries]," *Zhongguo Zhengfu Menhu Wangzhan [Chinese Government Gateway Website]*, October 10, 2010. www.gov.cn/zwgk/2010-10/18/content_1724848.htm.

Steakley, Lia, Debra K. Rubin, and Peter Reina. "After 9/11, Overseas Students Find Foreigners Need Not Apply: Visa Application Hurdles Start to Ease but Long-Term Impacts Loom." *Engineering News-Record*, December 6, 2004.

Steinfeld, Edward S. *Playing Our Game: Why China's Rise Doesn't Threaten the West*. New York:

Oxford University Press, 2010.

Steinhauer, Jennifer, Jonathan Martin, and David M. Herszenhorn. "Paul Ryan Calls Donald Trump's Attack on Judge 'Racist,' but Still Backs Him." *New York Times*, June 7, 2016. www.nytimes.com/2016/06/08/us/politics/paul-ryan-donald-trump-gonzalo-curiel.html.

Stephens, Paul. "International Students: Separate but Profitable." *Washington Monthly*, October 2013. www.washingtonmonthly.com/magazine/september_october_2013/features/international_students_separat046454.php?page=all.

Stokes, Bruce. "India's Paradox." *National Journal*, April 7, 2007.

Stuen, Eric T., Ahmed Mushfiq Mobarak, and Keith E. Maskus. "Skilled Immigration and Innovation: Evidence from Enrolment Fluctuations in US Doctoral Programmes." *The Economic Journal* 122, no. 565 (2012): 1143–76.

Swarns, Rachel L. "Senate, in Bipartisan Act, Passes an Immigration Bill." *New York Times*, May 26, 2006. www.nytimes.com/2006/05/26/washington/26immig.html.

Taylor, Mark Zachary. *The Politics of Innovation: Why Some Countries Are Better Than Others at Science and Technology*. Oxford: Oxford University Press, 2016.Tea Party Patriots. "Senate Must Admit Full Costs of Immigration Bill Before Passing Another 'Train Wreck.'" *Tea Party Patriots*, May 6, 2013. www.teapartypatriots.org/all-issues/news/senate-must-admit-full-costs-of-immigration-bill-before-passing-another-train-wreck/. "Technology Leaders Urge U.S. Senat to Approve Comprehensive Immigration Reform Legislation." *Information Technology Industry Council*, June 20, 2013. www.itic.org/news-events/news-releases/technology-leaders-urge-u-s-senate-to-approve-comprehensive-immigration-reform-legislation.

Teitelbaum, Michael S. *Falling Behind? Boom, Bust, and the Global Race for Scientific Talent*. Princeton, NJ: Princeton University Press, 2014.

Tellis, Ashley J., Janice Bially, Christopher Layne, Melissa McPherson, and Jerry M. Sollinger. *Measuring National Power in the Post-Industrial Age*. Santa Monica, CA: RAND, 2000.

Thibodeau, Patrick. "Ohio Bans Offshoring as It Gives Tax Relief to Outsourcing Firm." *Computerworld*, September 7, 2010. www.computerworld.com/article/2515465/it-outsourcing/ohio-bans-offshoring-as-it-gives-tax-relief-to-outsourcing-firm.html.

Thompson, Nicholas. "Obama vs. McCain: The Wired.com Scorecard." *Wired*, October 12, 2008. www.wired.com/2008/10/obama-v-mccain/.

Thompson, William R. "Long Waves, Technological Innovation, and Relative Decline." *International Organization* 44, no. 2 (1990): 201–33.

———. "Systemic Leadership, Evolutionary Processes, and International Relations Theory: The Unipolarity Question." *International Studies Review* 8, no. 1 (2006): 1–22.

Thomson Reuters. SDC Platinum Database. 2015. Access via subscription only.

Thoppil, Dhanya Ann, and Sean McLain. "Q&A: 'Parts of U.S. Visa Bill Discriminatory.'" *Wall Street Journal*, April 26, 2013.

Tichenor, Daniel J. *Dividing Lines: The Politics of Immigration Control in America*. Princeton, NJ: Princeton University Press, 2002.

Times Higher Education. "World University Rankings 2014–2015." *Times Higher Education*,

2014. www.timeshighereducation.co.uk/world-university-rankings/2014-15/world-ranking.

Tingley, Dustin H. "The Dark Side of the Future: An Experimental Test of Commitment Problems in Bargaining." *International Studies Quarterly* 55, no. 2 (June 2011): 521–44.

Trottman, Melanie. "Web Tool Could Help Boost Union Voter Turnout." *Wall Street Journal Online*, October 7, 2010.

Trumka, Richard. "Statement by AFL-CIO President Richard Trumka on Creating American Jobs and Ending Offshoring Act." *AFL-CIO*, September 28, 2010. www.aflcio.org/Press-Room/Press-Releases/Statement-by-AFL-CIO-President-Richard-Trumka-on-C8.

——. "Statement by AFL-CIO President Richard Trumka on the Promoting American Jobs and Closing Tax Loopholes Act." *AFL-CIO*, May 24, 2010. http://ftp.workingamerica.org/ Press-Room/Press-Releases/Statement-by-AFL-CIO-President-Richard-Trumka-on-t14.

Trumka, Richard, and Thomas J. Donohue. "Joint Statement of Shared Principles by U.S. Chamber of Commerce President and CEO Thomas J. Donohue and AFL-CIO President Richard Trumka." *AFL-CIO*, February 21, 2013. www.aflcio.org/Press-Room/Press-Releases/Joint-Statement-of-Shared-Principles-by-U.S.-Chamber-of-Commerce-President-and-CEO-Thomas-J.-Donohue-AFL-CIO-President-Richard-Trumka.

Trump, Donald J. "Presidential Executive Order on Buy American and Hire American." *White House*, April 18, 2017. www.whitehouse.gov/the-press-office/2017/04/18/presidential-executive-order-buy-american-and-hire-american.

Tucker, Bill. "Job Creation Stalls; Interview with Commerce Secretary Don Evans." *Lou Dobbs Tonight*. CNN, January 9, 2004.

Tumulty, Brian. "Small Manufacturers Aim Buy American Challenge at U.S. Job Losses." *Gannett News Service*, October 31, 2003. http://global.factiva.com/redir/default.aspx?P=sa& an=GNS0000020040107dzav000j7&cat=a&ep=ASE.

United Nations Educational, Scientific and Cultural Organization (UNESCO). "Education Data." *UIS.Stat*, 2014. www.uis.unesco.org/datacentre/pages/default.aspx.

——. "Global Flow of Tertiary-Level Students." *UIS.Stat*. Accessed December 10, 2014. www.uis.unesco.org/EDUCATION/Pages/international-student-flow-viz.aspx.

U.S. Citizenship and Immigration Services. *Characteristics of H-1B Specialty Occupation Workers: Fiscal Year 2015*. Washington, DC: U.S. Department of Homeland Security, 2016.

U.S. Department of Labor. "Fact Sheet 62: What Are 'Exempt' H-1B Nonimmigrants?" *Wage and Hour Division*, July 2008. www.dol.gov/whd/regs/compliance/FactSheet62/whdfs62Q.pdf.

U.S. Department of State. "Nonimmigrant Visa Issuances by Visa Class and by Nationality." *Travel.State.Gov*, 2016. http://travel.state.gov/content/visas/english/law-and-policy/statistics /non-immigrant-visas.html.

——. "Nonimmigrant Worldwide Issuance and Refusal Data by Visa Category." *Travel.State. Gov*, January 14, 2014. http://travel.state.gov/content/visas/english/law-and-policy/statistics/non-immigrant-visas.html.

U.S. General Accounting Office. *Assessment of the Department of Commerce's Report on Workforce Demand and Supply*. Washington, DC: U.S. General Accounting Office, 1998. http://gao.gov/assets/230/225415.pdf.

——. *Immigration and the Labor Market: Nonimmigrant Alien Workers in the United States*. Washington, DC: U.S. General Accounting Office, 1992. www.gao.gov/assets/160/151654.pdf.

——. *Improvements Needed to Reduce Time Taken to Adjudicate Visas for Science Students and Scholars*. Washington, DC: U.S. General Accounting Office, 2004. www.gao.gov/index.html.

U.S. Government Accountability Office. *Challenges in Attracting International Students to the United States and Implications for Global Competitiveness*. Washington, DC: U.S. Government Accountability Office, 2007. www.gao.gov/index.html.

——. *Performance of Foreign Student and Exchange Visitor Information System Continues to Improve, but Issues Remain*. Washington, DC: U.S. Government Accountability Office, 2005.

——. *Streamlined Visas Mantis Program Has Lowered Burden on Foreign Science Students and Scholars, but Further Refinements Needed*. Washington, DC: U.S. Government Accountability Office, 2005.

U.S. Immigration and Naturalization Service. *Report on Characteristics of Specialty Occupation Workers (H-1B): Fiscal Year 2000*. Washington, DC: U.S. Immigration and Naturalization Service, 2002. "U.S. Led Effort Reaches 'Major Breakthrough' to Expand Information Technology Agree- ment." *Office of the United States Trade Representative*, July 2015. https://ustr.gov/about-us/policy-offices/press-office/press-releases/2015/july/us-led-effort-reaches-%E2%80%98major.

"US's Grassley— 'Difficult' to Get Quick Action on Tax Bill." *Market News International*, June 22, 2004.

"Vajpayee Calls for Reversing Brain Drain, Cutting Red Tape." *Hindu Business Line*, January 4, 2003. www.thehindubusinessline.com/bline/2003/01/04/stories/2003010402410500.htm.

Valbrun, Marjorie, and Scott Thurm. "Foreign Workers Will Soon Get Fewer U.S. Visas." *Wall Street Journal*, October 1, 2003.

VandeHei, Jim, and Zachary A. Goldfarb. "Immigration Deal at Risk as House GOP Looks to Voters." *Washington Post*, May 28, 2006.

Vaughan, Martin. "Businesses Split Over Tax Credits." *Wall Street Journal*, August 4, 2010.

Vaughan, Martin, and Susan Davis. "Senate Ends Corporate Tax Debate for Now, Oks Outsourcing Deal." *Congress Daily*, March 5, 2004.

Vogel, David. *Fluctuating Fortunes: The Political Power of Business in America*. New York: Basic Books, 1989.

Wadhwa, Vivek. *The Immigrant Exodus: Why America Is Losing the Global Race to Capture Entrepreneurial Talent*. Philadelphia: Wharton Digital Press, 2012.

Wadhwa, Vivek, AnnaLee Saxenian, Richard B. Freeman, and Alex Salkever. *Losing the World's Best and Brightest: America's New Immigrant Entrepreneurs, Part V*. Kansas City, MO: Ewing Marion Kauffman Foundation, March 2009.

Wallace, Gregory, and Deirdre Walsh. "House Passes Immigration Bill to Keep Science and Technology Students in U.S." *CNN Wire*, November 30, 2012.

Walsten, Peter, Jia Lynn Yang, and Craig Timberg. "Facebook Flexes Political Muscle with Carve-Out in Immigration Bill." *Washington Post*, April 16, 2013.

Wang, Huiyao. *Rencai Zhanzheng [Talent War]*. Beijing: China CITIC, 2009.

Wang, Huiyao, David Zweig, and Xiaohua Lin. "Returnee Entrepreneurs: Impact on China's

Globalization Process." *Journal of Contemporary China* 20, no. 70 (June 2011): 413–31.

Wang, Jian, Lan Xue, and Zheng Liang. "Multinational R&D in China: From Home-Country-Basedto Host-Country-Based." *Innovation: Management, Policy & Practice* 14, no. 2 (June 2012): 192–202.

Ward, David. "Letter to the Senate Judiciary Committee Regarding Feinstein Proposal on Student Visas." *American Association of Collegiate Registrars and Admissions Officers*, October 2, 2001. www.aacrao.org/advocacy/issues-advocacy/sevis.

Ward, David. Testimony. "Dealing with Foreign Students and Scholars in an Age of Terrorism: Visa Backlogs and Tracking Systems." *Hearing Before the U.S. House of Representatives Committee on Science*. 108th Cong., March 26, 2003.

——. "The Role of Technology in Preventing the Entry of Terrorists into the United States." *Hearing Before the Subcommittee on Technology, Terrorism, and Government Information of the Senate Judiciary Committee*. 107th Cong., October 12, 2001.

Wasem, Ruth Ellen. *Immigration: Legislative Issues on Nonimmigrant Professional Specialty (H-1B) Workers*. Washington, DC: Congressional Research Service, 2004.

——. *Immigration: Legislative Issues on Nonimmigrant Professional Specialty (H-1B) Workers*. Washington, DC: Congressional Research Service, 2007.

Washington Higher Education Secretariat. "About WHES." *Washington Higher Education Secretariat*. Accessed February 3, 2016. www.whes.org/index.html.

Wei, Yu, and Zhaojun Sun. "China: Building an Innovation Talent Program System and Facing Global Competition in a Knowledge Economy." *Academic Executive Brief*, 2012. http://academicexecutives.elsevier.com/articles/china-building-innovation-talent-program-system-and-facing-global-competition-knowledge.

Weisman, Jonathan. "Boehner Doubts Immigration Bill Will Pass in 2014." *New York Times*, February 6, 2014. www.nytimes.com/2014/02/07/us/politics/boehner-doubts-immigration-overhaul-will-pass-this-year.html.

——. "Bush, Adviser Assailed for Stance on 'Offshoring' Jobs." *Washington Post*, February 11, 2004.

——. "Immigration Bill Dies in Senate." *Washington Post*, June 29, 2007. www.washingtonpost.com/wp-dyn/content/article/2007/06/28/AR2007062800963.html.

Weisman, Jonathan, and Mark Kaufman. "Tax-Cut Bill Draws White House Doubts: Corporate Provisions Go Beyond 'Core Objective,' Treasury Secretary Says." *Washington Post*, October 5, 2004.

Weisman, Jonathan, and Jim VandeHei. "Immigration Bill Lobbying Focuses on House Leaders: With Senate in Hand, Bush May Face a Skeptical GOP Base." Washington Post, May 1, 2006.

Weiss, Linda. America Inc.? Innovation and Enterprise in the National Security State. Ithaca, NY: Cornell University Press, 2014.

Wong, Carolyn. Lobbying for Inclusion: Rights Politics and the Making of Immigration Policy. Stanford, CA: Stanford University Press, 2006.

Wong, Joseph. Betting on Biotech: Innovation and the Limits of Asia's Developmental State. New York: Cornell University Press, 2011.

World Bank Migration and Remittances Team. *Migration and Remittances: Recent Developments and Outlook*. Migration and Development Brief No. 23 (October 6, 2014). http://siteresources.worldbank.org/INTPROSPECTS/Resources/334934-1288990760745/MigrationandDevelopmentBrief23.pdf.

Worthen, Ben. "Regulations: What to Worry About." *CIO*, June 15, 2004.

Wright, Chris F. "Why Do States Adopt Liberal Immigration Policies? The Policymaking Dynamics of Skilled Visa Reform in Australia." *Journal of Ethnic and Migration Studies* 41, no. 2 (January 28, 2015): 306–28.

Wright, John R. *Interest Groups and Congress: Lobbying, Contributions and Influence*. Boston: Allyn and Bacon, 1996.

Yale-Loehr, Stephen, Demetrios G. Papademetriou, and Betsy Cooper. *Secure Borders, Open Doors: Visa Procedures in the Post–September 11 Era*. Washington, DC: Migration Policy Institute, 2005.

Ye, Min. *Diasporas and Foreign Direct Investment in China and India*. New York: Cambridge University Press, 2014.

Zengerle, Jason. "Silicon Smoothies." *New Republic*, June 8, 1998.

Zhao, Minyuan. "Conducting R&D in Countries with Weak Intellectual Property Rights Protection." *Management Science* 52, no. 8 (August 2006): 1185–99.

Zolberg, Aristide. *A Nation by Design: Immigration Policy in the Fashioning of America*. Cambridge, MA: Harvard University Press, 2006.

Zuckerberg, Mark. "Mark Zuckerberg: Immigrants Are the Key to a Knowledge Economy." *Washington Post*, April 10, 2013. www.washingtonpost.com/opinions/mark-zuckerberg-immigrants-are-the-key-to-a-knowledge-economy/2013/04/10/aba05554-a20b-11e2-82bc-511538ae90a4_story.html.

Zweig, David. "Learning to Compete: China's Efforts to Encourage a 'Reverse Brain Drain.'" In *Competing for Global Talent*, edited by Christiane Kuptsch and Eng Fong Pang, 187–214. Geneva: International Labor Office, 2006.

Zweig, David, and Changgui Chen. *China's Brain Drain to the United States: Views of Overseas Chinese Students and Scholars in the 1990s*. Berkeley: Institute of East Asian Studies, University of California, 1995.

Zweig, David, Chung Siu Fung, and Donglin Han. "Redefining the Brain Drain: China's 'Diaspora Option.'" *Science, Technology & Society* 13, no. 1 (2008): 1–33.

Zweig, David, and Huiyao Wang. "Can China Bring Back the Best? The Communist Party Organizes China's Search for Talent." *The China Quarterly* 215 (2013): 590–615.

致　谢

如果这本书讲述的是创新，那么完成本书便是我学术生涯中的创新。我的第一本书以美国为背景，聚焦中国和印度的外交政策。本书的重点恰恰是相反的，本书介绍了许多创新，因此对这些创新进行追根溯源是非常必要的。我在华盛顿郊区长大，这里总是被立法者和游说者包围着，因此，美国政治对我的影响很大。虽然我对亚洲事务的兴趣越来越浓厚，但是当我25岁时在塔夫茨大学弗莱彻外交与法律学院攻读硕士学位时，很自然地就选择了研究美国的外交政策。随后的几年，我在香港、北京和华盛顿担任顾问，认真研究美国与亚洲国家的政治和经济关系。我对美国的外交政策，尤其是美国对亚洲国家的外交政策的热情，驱使我从一开始就想要成为一名外交政策学者。

本书介绍了美国外交政策的一个方面：其应对技术创新全球化的方法。我关注这个问题不仅在于它非常重要，还在于它很难理解。它的重要性显而易见，70多年来，美国在技术方面的优势促使其在国际体系中一直占据经济和军事上的领导地位。与此同时，中国和印度这样崛起的新兴大国也非常羡慕美国所取得的成就，并

致 谢

寻求使本国成为创新强国的方法。但是对于创新的探索并非孤立地进行的。由于高技能人才的跨境流动和史无前例的高科技投资，美国、中国和印度在追求技术领先地位的过程中日益紧密地联系在一起。随着这一过程的展开，全球创新领导者美国的政策日益重要，而且正如我在引言中所阐述的，这些政策也非常令人费解。我认为没有人能够对此进行解释。基于这些原因，本书关注全球创新过程中，美国与中印两国进行合作的背后所蕴含的政治因素。

在本书调研和撰写的过程中，我有幸得到了很多人的帮助。首先，特别感谢众多美国、中国和印度的个人同意接受采访。其中许多人都在各章节的注释部分被提到，也有一些人希望匿名或者仅在背景中被提到。非常感谢所有参与的人。

还要感谢很多人。我很感谢众多学识渊博并且能够慷慨对本书原稿提供反馈的学者，他们是：比约恩·德雷塞尔、大卫·安瓦尔、傅泰林、卢克·格兰维尔、吴翠玲、卢埃林·休斯、戴维什·卡普尔、斯科特·卡斯特勒、艾德里安·凯、艾米·金、李秉勤、林明伦、安德鲁·麦金太尔、安·内维尔、玛格丽特·彼得斯、约翰·拉文维尔、埃泰勒·索林根、海伦·泰勒、乔安妮·沃利斯、菲奥娜·雅普、叶敏和张锋。在我的父亲宾汉·肯尼迪的指导下，本书的逻辑更加清晰易懂。多年来，一些研究助理也热情地支持我，他们是：陈宥桦、管佳、柳楠、潘荣芳、尼米塔·潘迪、阿迪亚·帕罗利亚、齐震、理查德·里德、张海阳、张佳一。与以下这些人的交流也让我受益匪浅，他们是：希罗·阿姆斯特朗、张太铭、丹尼尔·科斯塔、克里斯蒂娜·戴维斯、素密·甘古利、丹·戈尔德、戴维·哈特、罗恩·西拉、斯科德·肯尼迪、罗伯特·基欧汉、阿努帕玛·卡纳、柳卸林、坦维·马丹、帕塔·麦考帕特耶、普拉塔普·巴努·梅赫塔、巴里·诺顿、尼尔·鲁伊斯、迈克尔·泰特尔鲍姆和帕特里克·希伯德。最后，感谢哥伦比亚大学出版社的两位匿名评论员为本书做出了非常有建设性的评论。本书所有的责任均由我本人承担。

非常感谢众多机构的支持。自2010年以来，我一直在澳大利亚国立大学克劳福德公共政策学院从事学术研究，其跨学科和高度学术化的氛围为撰写本书提供了极好的环境。2013—2017年，澳大利亚研究委员会通过早期职业研究员奖计划慷慨资助了本研究。2013年，宾夕法尼亚大学印度高等研究中心和印第安纳大学中国政治与商业北京研究中心两大优秀的组织邀请我作为访问学者。2012年，我有幸参加了在加州大学圣地亚哥分校全球冲突与合作研究所举办的为期两周的中国创新崛起研讨会。

哥伦比亚大学出版社的编辑斯蒂芬·韦斯利是一位模范编辑。他耐心、热情，并且提供了很好的建议。这本书被评选为唐耐心和孔华润关于美国—东亚关系研究的系列书籍，非常感谢丛书编辑马克·布拉德利、柯庆生和罗斯玛丽·福特——他们决定将本书纳入其中。

谨以此书献给我的三位亲人：沙姆米、萨尼亚和贾斯珀。希望有一天萨尼亚和贾斯珀会意识到他们给他们的父亲带来了多大的鼓舞，以及他们的父亲为能够娶到他们的母亲感到多么荣幸。